A CHURCH COLLEGE FOR THE TWENTY-FIRST CENTURY?

For the Students, Staff and Governors
of the College
Past, Present and Future
With Admiration, Thanks and High Expectations

A Church College for the Twenty-first Century?

150 Years
of
Ripon and York St John
1841-1991

A Study of Policy and its Absence
Gordon McGregor

Foreword by the Archbishop of York

William Sessions Limited
York, England
for
University College of Ripon and York St John

ISBN (Hardback) 1 85072 080 0
ISBN (Paperback) 1 85072 079 7

Published 1991

All Royalties from the sale of this book will go to the
COLLEGE OPPORTUNITY FUND
to support cultural, professional, sporting and
recreational opportunities for College students

Printed in 10/11 point Times Typeface
by William Sessions Limited
The Ebor Press, York England

Contents

List of Illustrations

Front Cover: *River of Life,* stained glass window in the South Transept of the York Chapel designed and made by Third Year BA student Catherine Nutkins, 1990, to celebrate the beginning of the College's 150th Year.

Rear Cover: The Lord Mayor's Walk frontage, York, and the main College building at Ripon.

Preface and Acknowledgements

MOST INSTITUTIONS DO NOT LAST 150 YEARS. Those that do have usually been good or lucky – or both. This study is offered in the hope that the balance of good quality and good fortune in the endurance of one institution may be both intrinsically interesting and useful in offering guidance for its future. A number of themes are pursued, best summarised as questions: Can an institution which depends from the outset on government funds have any real 'autonomy'? What was the actual balance – and what might have been the acceptable one – between State and Church influence in higher education in the 19th century and between State and Local Authority influence in the 20th? What has been the college's contribution to breaking down class and sex barriers in education and widening access to it? How has it balanced the conflicting claims of professional training and individual culture in the education of teachers? Has it matched Christian conviction with intellectual openness in its religious education and its community life? Has it been diligent in its support of wise government policies for education and strenuous in its opposition to destructive ones? Is there a distinctive role for the kind of college we aspire to become into the 21st century and can we earn the right to play it?

My written sources will be apparent from the Notes and References. A study of the policies pursued by and for a college over 150 years must inevitably lean heavily on the written records left by governors and principals. Where written evidence has been left by others whose impressions seemed authentic I have tried to use them, believing, with G. M. Young, that 'the real central theme of History is not what happened but what people felt about it while it was happening'. But I am acutely conscious that in quotations and in references any college history that is not largely anecdotal must do less than justice to many hundreds of faithful and influential students, staff and governors.

The book has been written in the spare hours of a fairly active academic year and owes much to the help and encouragement of many colleagues and friends. Two debts are pre-eminent: My colleague Dr John Addy, College Archivist and Senior Research Fellow – who in

viii

his 81st year is still himself publishing distinguished books – has kept me promptly plied with source materials from his excellent college archive, has advised me on many facts and judgements, and has kindly read chapters as I have completed them. My secretary, Diana Wetherell Terry, has somehow found time amidst countless other demands, to transform week by week and with unfailing enthusiasm, my mutilated drafts into impeccable typescript and has saved me from many errors.

Some written sources deserve special mention: Bill Etherington's 1969 MEd thesis on the early history of St John's College has been a valuable source of reference for the early chapters, as my notes reveal; A. M. Wilkinson's little centenary history of the Ripon College to 1962 highlighted key personalities and incidents; my senior colleague Marilynne Davies' 1980 MEd thesis provided a detailed, 'participant-observer' view of the negotiation of the 1975 reunion of the Ripon and York colleges. For the political and educational background to the development of the college I have drawn heavily on the references, and parts of the text, of my own published doctoral study *Bishop Otter College and Policy for Teacher Education 1839-1980* (Pembridge Press, 1981).

Revd Canon Philip Lamb, Christopher Chapman, James Fairbairn, Stanley Barnes and John Barnett commented helpfully on parts of the study. My former secretary, Barbara Peel, knowing that I would get down to it 'one day', stored some valuable papers; colleagues John Greenwood and Trevor Jones advised and assisted with photographs, and Trevor designed the cover. My friend Clive Jones-Davies, Principal of Trinity College Carmarthen, kindly donated a copy of the Carmarthen portrait of Principal William Reed.

I am most grateful to Archbishop John Habgood for reading the complete text and providing such a generous Foreword – the latest of many kindnesses to me and to the College. Colleagues John Axon, Revd Greg Hoyland, Malcolm Jennings, John Maw, Frances Walder and Ralph Wilkinson also read the complete text and, to a tight deadline, provided many valuable corrections and improvements. Bob Sissons and his colleagues at the Ebor Press have made the production process a great pleasure; their courtesy, speed and skill have been exemplary. Finally I thank my wife, Jean, for many hours of quiet encouragement.

Without such generous help the book could not have been ready for our 150th Anniversary celebrations. In recording my appreciation I must add that for the faults that remain, for the choice of themes and incidents and for the judgements and opinions expressed, I am entirely responsible.

GORDON McGREGOR
New Years Day, 1991

ix

Foreword
by Dr John Habgood, Archbishop of York

THE PRINCIPAL OF RIPON AND YORK St John has written more than a College history. He tells the story of the growth, development and transformation of Teacher Training Colleges from their humble beginnings in the last century to their incorporation into the new structures of Higher Education. Though centring on a particular Church College, now the biggest of those surviving, the story embraces much wider themes and should provide valuable insights for all those concerned with educational policy, or the lack of it.

The subtitle says it all. Dr McGregor is unsparing in his criticism of the muddle, manipulation and vagaries which, from the receiving end, seem to have characterised government policy toward the Colleges. But the early years, under direct Church control, were not particularly brilliant either. The Churches seem rarely to have given their Colleges the support they felt they needed, and the Colleges themselves have only with great difficulty found a proper relationship between their Christian commitment and educational integrity.

The latter problem is still high on the agenda and all those who wonder what is, or ought to be, distinctive about a Church College, will find much food for thought in the story told here. The book appears at a good moment. The future of the Church Colleges is still by no means assured, and they need vigorous self-analysis if they are to survive and flourish in today's highly competitive environment.

Yet in the end the story is a cheering one. It tells how a College which has not been afraid to fight for its beliefs can win through and not merely survive, but become the impressive and lively institution which it is today.

I am confident readers will enjoy and profit from this book with its mixture of humour, anger, scholarship and dedicated commonsense.

DR JOHN HABGOOD
Archbishop of York

CHAPTER I

Monkgate 1841-46

THE COLLEGE MADE A MODEST START. It did not in fact open on 10 May 1841 as advertised (see overleaf) because no students turned up. It opened a week later on 17 May. There was one student, Edward Preston Cordukes, a York boy, aged 16. He remained the sole student resident until July, when another arrived; two more joined in September. Recruitment problems are not new in Teacher Education.

Economic recessions are not new either, and in its first Annual Report, in 1843, the Ripon Diocesan Board of Education, having noted that one of its first objects had been

> to establish, in conjunction with the Diocese of York, if thought desirable, an efficient training school, with the view of obtaining religiously and competently trained Masters and Mistresses for the Schools of the Dioceses,

recorded both success and apprehension:

> The Board, while lamenting as it has done, the inadequacy of the funds at its disposal to carry out the several other great objects for which it was instituted, cannot but congratulate the members and subscribers generally on the formation of the Training Institution at York, as one of the most essential features in a sound system of Religious Education, to which alone we must now look, under Divine Providence, as the surest foundation of public and social happiness and prosperity, and as the means of averting those evils which are the inevitable result of an overgrown and irreligious population.

> The universal depression which has for some time prevailed in every branch of industry, pressing with severity upon the resources of individuals in almost every rank of life has induced the Board to suspend a more active canvass for pecuniary assistance until a returning season of prosperity shall render such

1

YORK
DIOCESAN TRAINING AND MIDDLE SCHOOL

This School will be opened for the reception of Pupils, on Monday the 10th of May.

DAY SCHOOL.

THE SUBJECTS OF INSTRUCTION WILL BE:

HOLY SCRIPTURE, CHURCH CATECHISM, LITURGY, AND CHURCH HISTORY.

READING, WRITING, ARITHMETIC, ENGLISH GRAMMAR, HISTORY, AND GEOGRAPHY.

BOOK-KEEPING, MENSURATION, ELEMENTS OF ALGEBRA, GEOMETRY, AND PRACTICAL MECHANICS.

MUSIC, LINEAR DRAWING, THE RUDIMENTS OF LATIN.

LECTURES will be occasionally given on the Elements of BOTANY, NATURAL HISTORY, and NATURAL PHILOSOPHY.

The Hours of Teaching to be from Nine to Twelve, and from Two to Five.

THE TERMS:—One Guinea per Quarter, payable in advance. Boys who are admitted during any part of a Quarter, shall pay for the whole Quarter, but from the opening of the School till the Vacation in July only 1s. will be charged.

Modern Languages to be paid for as extras.

TRAINING SCHOOL.

Candidates for the Training School will be required to bring a Certificate, from the Diocesan or a District Board, as to moral character, docility and general aptitude for the way of life on which they are to enter. They will have to pass an examination, before they are received; and, after remaining in the Institution three months, if their conduct and character shall be approved, and they be found to possess the requisite ability, they will be put upon the list of Training Pupils in the Institution, until they are considered fit to receive a Certificate of Competency.

TERMS:—Pupils will be received into the Institution, and boarded by the Society, for the sum of £20. per annum, paid quarterly by advance; the £20. to include Bed-Linen, but not Washing.

Except in cases where it may be otherwise determined by a Committee of the Society, no Pupil shall be admitted into the Boarding House, for training as a Schoolmaster, before the age of fifteen, nor be eligible for recommendation to a School before the age of eighteen; and no such Pupil shall receive a Certificate from the Society, unless he has resided a full year in the Institution.

National Schoolmasters, or persons above the age of eighteen, desirous of qualifying themselves for that office, but unable to pass through the regular course of the Society, shall be allowed to attend the Training School, during shorter periods, on the recommendation of the District Boards.

₊ Any further Information may be obtained on Application to the Principal, THE REV. W. REED, at the Diocesan School, Monkgate.

J. BROWNE,
J. DOBSON,   *Hon. Secretaries.*
W. WHYTEHEAD,

The Advertisement of the Opening of the College, April 1841

2

a step less likely to be attended with inconvenience to the benevolent and well-disposed. When this period shall arrive, the Board will be prepared to prosecute their canvass with vigour, and they doubt not but that an appeal then made will be cheerfully responded to . . .

So it was a difficult and hesitant opening. Only two years before in 1839 government had offered its first grant to assist the training of teachers, and six years before that, its first contributions towards the building and maintenance of Church schools. To understand why the two dioceses launched a new college at this troubled time we need to take a brief account of events and changing attitudes to education in the previous 40 years.

Historians of teacher education in 19th century Britain agree that, at the beginning of the century England lagged behind the best developments in Europe, particularly Germany where there were already three-year courses of training.[1] Individual Anglican and Non-conformist clergy opened many small schools in the 1780s and 90s, but it was the work and influence of Andrew Bell, for the Anglicans, and Joseph Lancaster, for the Non-conformists, which created a new growth of schools on such a scale that a system for training teachers had to be considered. In 1808 the Dissenters founded the Royal Lancastrian Society which became, in 1814 the British and Foreign School Society. The rival Church of England initiative was inspired by Bell's 1808 *Sketch of a National Institution for Training up the Children of the Poor*. This led to the founding in 1811, of the *National Society for Promoting the Education of the Poor in the Principles of the Established Church*, still at work 180 years later.

The work of the Society will be a point of reference throughout the first part of this study, not only because of its obvious relation to a Church of England College for teachers, but because it formulated in its early years policies which the State later imitated, especially in making grants to schools and colleges. The Society was determined to stimulate local effort, not supersede it. Its grants for buildings therefore depended on the tenure of a proposed site being secure, the school opening free of debt, and on the sum requested being less than that raised by local subscription. An important difference between early Society and State efforts was that the Society offered no assistance towards recurrent costs. It received many applications for contributions to teachers salaries, for example, but refused them.

The Society could not afford to pay teachers but at once set itself to train them. Lancaster had urged this on the first members of his Society. His school at Borough Road was rapidly established as a training ground, later to become the Borough Road College. This was the first recognisable teachers' college in England – if we discount Byngham's brief Cambridge experiment in the 15th century, refounded as Christ's College. Bell knew of the progress at Borough Road, and in 1811 he warned the founder members of the National Society

> We shall never thrive as we ought till we have one school in perfect order in the metropolis, where masters may be trained and to which they may be referred.

The Society responded promptly and its Central School at Baldwin's Gardens was the focus of its teacher training activities from 1812 until the foundation of the first Church Training Colleges in 1839.

This London example was followed elsewhere, on a smaller scale. In 1813 the Society reported that the Central School at Winchester had already 'trained' 20 masters and 5 mistresses, and the one at Norwich 12 masters. Both religious Societies soon acknowledged the shortcomings of the monitorial method however and in 1821 the National Society appointed General Visitors to inspect each 'National' school in a county at least once a year. Inspection could not, however, remedy the fundamental weakness of the system which was the very low level of education achieved by even the brightest 'monitor'.

> . . . the method failed very largely because that higher culture which was provided to some extent by the normal schools on the Continent was lacking in England . . . The great hindrance to progress all along was the lack of secondary education for the lower and middle classes, and until that deficiency has been supplied, the training college was bound to be a somewhat anomolous institution, being turned aside from its main business to do the work that properly belonged to an institution of another type.[2]

Quality might be lacking but there was no doubt that the method produced quantity. Within 20 years the National Society had sponsored the establishment of more than 3,000 new schools with about 350,000 pupils; Diocesan Societies were active all over the country. York's was one of the first, established in 1812. Its achievements have been well documented in a research study by the archivist of Ripon and York St John, Dr John Addy. He records that its inauguration was greeted whimsically by Revd Sidney Smith, at that time vicar of Foston on Clay:

> We are about to have a meeting at York respecting the Education of the Poor in the principles of tithe paying etc. . . . I am sorry I shall be absent or I should certainly make a speech; at all events I will subscribe my money – but it will never do. That the Church should make itself useful and bestir itself to diffuse secular

4

knowledge among the poor and continue to do so for any length of time, is scarcely credible. I believe it is only a plan to prevent little boys from learning at Lancaster's . . .[3]

Other well-disposed clergy and church members were uneasily aware, in spite of bombastic advertising by Diocesan Societies, that the provision of anything like a national system of education, was beyond the resources of the Voluntary Societies. Government 'interference' might be feared in Church circles, but it was as well for the country that the energetic efforts of the Societies were accompanied by the first stirrings of Parliamentary interest in the possibility of national education.

Whitbread's Bill of 1807 and Brougham's of 1818 proposing government-sponsored expansion of school provision, were both defeated. Brougham's further proposals of 1820 for control of schools and safeguarding of religious instruction now read like a reasonable compromise between Church and Non-conformists. At the time they were therefore rejected by both parties and his Bill was again defeated. Brougham continued to press the cause of popular education by his support of the Mechanics Institutes and through popular pamphlets promoting discussion of the issues raised by a Select Committee of 1818 – issues which would have to be confronted throughout the 19th century and well into the 20th: What was the right educational provision for an advanced industrial nation? What obligations had the State in this? Should it co-operate with the Church? What was the place of religion in education? Should the State underwrite the dogmas of its Established Church in any scheme of education which it fostered? Could it also meet the claims of Dissenting and Catholic families and of a growing urban population many of whose lives – as clergymen themselves assured the Select Committee – were untouched by any Church allegiance? Where was an adequate teaching force to be recruited for the schools? Who should train it? Who should pay for it? Most disturbing question of all, how was the money to be raised to provide the massive development of schools which so many men and women of social conscience – Christian, agnostic and atheist – now agreed was right for the people and essential for the progress of the State?[4]

There were at the time, enthusiasts on both sides who believed they were engaged in a straight fight between Church and State for control of whatever education system might emerge. The evidence is of a more complex conflict in which wiser participants recognised that neither side could succeed without the other. Anxieties about indoctrination were probably excessive, particularly among Churchmen.

In the early part of the century indeed, fears of the political theorists that the state might use the schools for its own ends

5

appeared a little unreal in the face of its very moderate interest in elementary education and its reluctance to assume greater responsibility.[5]

The Factory Acts of 1802, 1819 and 1833 and the First Reform Bill of 1832 all helped to create conditions in which more schools could be opened and more children freed to attend them. By 1833 Roebuck had succeeded Brougham as the chief advocate of State intervention in education. In August he introduced to the Commons a Bill which foreshadowed the main provisions of the 1870 breakthrough. It proposed that all children aged 6 to 12 should be required by law to attend school and that government should organise a system of infant, industrial, normal (i.e. teacher training), and evening schools. This was to be financed through new taxation, and redistribution of existing endowments for education, and the payment of fees by parents who could afford them. It would have ended the Voluntary provision of schools, which the religious Societies regarded as firmly entrenched. The Bill was rejected, but a barely quorate House then carried, by 50 votes to 26, a motion by Lord Althorp for the government, that £20,000 be at once provided 'to assist private subscriptions for the erection of school houses for the education of children of the poorer classes'. It was a compromise decision and possibly unrepresentative, but upon it has gradually been erected the massive modern responsibility of the State for the education of its people.

The Parliamentary grant was to be reviewed annually and divided equally between the National Society and the British and Foreign Society. The only stipulation was the established National Society one that, for every school, local contributions must at least equal the grant centrally provided. Anglican suspicion of imminent government intervention was lulled:

> . . . the Church could feel that, so far, State aid had no strings attached and therefore raised no issue. The result was a short period of peaceful and gradual expansion such as might have followed from a similar augmentation of funds from private sources.[6]

One theme of this study will be that this first acceptance of a government grant which, once awarded, was to increase steadily, sacrificed that very autonomy which the 'Voluntary' Colleges have been so anxious to 'protect' ever since.

In 1834 a Parliamentary Committee again took evidence on the State of Education. Brougham was now Lord Chancellor and had changed his view. In 1828 he had been one of the prime movers in the founding of University College London, the first secular university institution in England. It was largely in protest against the religious requirements for admission to Oxford and Cambridge and promptly countered by the Anglican foundation of Kings College, London in 1830. Brougham now seemed better disposed towards religious initiatives in education, at least at school level. He noted that, since the 1818 Committee Report the voluntary societies had doubled the number of school places to more than a million and a quarter.

> I am of the opinion that much good may be done by judicious assistance, but legislative interference is in many respects to be altogether avoided or very cautiously employed because it may produce mischievous effects . . . Suppose the funds were easily to be had, and no diminution to be apprehended from the interference of the Government, I do not see how such a system can be established without placing in the hands of the Government, that is of the ministers of the day, the means of dictating opinions and principles to the people.[7]

Yet he was adamant that Government *should* control the training of teachers:

> I am of the opinion that it is expedient to establish schools for the instruction of teachers . . . The expense thus bestowed is perfectly free from the objections which I have stated against a general national school system; and the government has . . . no more imperative duty cast upon it than to make this provision for teaching masters. The beginning might be made in London . . .

The National Society, however, made its own imaginative proposal to the Select Committee for a Normal College under its auspices in London. The Government grants of 1833 encouraged the work of both Societies and also the foundation, in 1836, of a third. In the Home and Colonial Schools Society Evangelical Churchmen and Dissenters worked together to establish a training college for infant teachers, much influenced by Pestalozzi. This met a need for younger children which the National Society had been slow to recognise.

By 1838 a group of influential High Churchmen, including Gladstone, S. F. Wood and a Sussex rector H. E. Manning – the future Roman Cardinal – roused the Dioceses to form Boards of Education. Wood wrote to Manning:

> Diocesan seminaries and a central college are our keynotes; the former to be closely connected with the cathedral and its officers and to be the sole academy for ordinary masters. But a few of the ablest and most deserving should come to the central college to complete their education and fit them for the higher situations: the cathedrals and others to found exhibitions to maintain them . . . The college to be, if possible a branch of Kings College . . .[8]

They invited leading members of the National Society to join them in a Committee of Enquiry and Correspondence with a wide brief for all the educational work of the Church. They developed Wood's proposal for the London teachers college, referred to in their minutes as 'The Queen's Hall', with the Master to be Professor of Education at King's College. This seemed unduly adventurous to the Society, still devoted to the monitorial enterprise at Baldwin's Gardens. In May 1839 it braced itself for action; but Government had already moved.

In February, Lord John Russell, Secretary of State for the Home Department, had asked Lord Landsdowne, Lord President of the Council, to form a Committee of the Privy Council 'for the Consideration of all matters affecting the Education of the People'. It was to allocate all funds voted by Parliament, and give immediate attention to the founding of a Normal School. The Committee was announced on 10 April. Its Secretary was to be Dr James Kay, later Sir James Kay-Shuttleworth, known for his work as an assistant Poor Law commissioner. His educational ideas had been influenced by Pestalozzi, Vehrli in Switzerland and Stow in Glasgow and he had started an experimental school at Norwood. Russell had touched blandly on the religious issue in his letter to Landsdowne:

> Much therefore may be effected by temperate attention to the fair claims of the Established Church and the religious freedom sanctioned by the Law. On this subject I need only say that it is Her Majesty's wish that the youth of the kingdom should be religiously brought up and that the right of conscience should be respected.

But neither Landsdowne nor Kay-Shuttleworth had many illusions about the hazards of the proffered secretaryship:

> He told me that the Government had some doubt as to the propriety of asking me to take what might prove a precarious and would certainly be a very obnoxious position – subjecting me to much opposition. . . . I at once replied that I thought the object to be attained so great that I was quite ready to take any risk.[9]

A plan for a government college in London was announced three days after Kay-Shuttleworth's appointment. The proposals for religious education divided 'general' periods from 'special' periods for 'such peculiar doctrinal instruction as may be required'. It was implied that government officials would decide what was 'special' and what 'general' in religious instruction.

The proposals created sudden consensus among clergy and laymen of widely differing views on education, united against the common threat. In little more than a month a minute of the Committee of Council of

3 June reflected the insistence of the Bishops in the Lords, and of Peel and others in the Commons, that the storm could not be ridden:

> The Committee are of the opinion that the most useful application of any sums voted by Parliament, would consist in the employment of those monies in the establishment of a Normal School, under the direction of the State, and not placed under the management of a Voluntary Society. The Committee however experience so much difficulty in reconciling conflicting views respecting the provisions they are desirous to make in furthering your Majesty's wish . . . that it is not in the power of the Committee to mature a plan for the accomplishment of this design without further consideration and they therefore postpone taking any steps for this purpose until greater concurrence of opinion is found to prevail.

The immediate result for teacher education was that the Committee, frustrated in its plan for a Government college, agreed to divide £10,000, which had been voted in 1835 for the erection of Normal Schools but had not yet been allocated, between the National Society and the British and Foreign Society.

The Anglican party, not content with forestalling the Committee's prime object, now tried to destroy the Committee itself. Government moved a motion to increase the annual grant to the Committee to £30,000, whereupon Lord Stanley moved an amendment requesting the Queen to rescind the order constituting the Committee. This was defeated by only 280 votes to 275 and the substantive motion was eventually carried by two votes. Gladstone and Disraeli both voted against it. Meanwhile, in the House of Lords, the Archbishop of Canterbury had won a large majority for his address to the Queen, requesting that any future plan for the general education of the people be fully discussed in the Lords, where the Church party had a powerful voice. Ten days later, yet another non-Sectarian Education Bill, moved in the Lords by Brougham, was strenuously opposed, and withdrawn.

The protagonists of State education felt routed, and Brougham himself wrote:

> A controversy of thirty years, with all the reason and almost all the skill, and until very lately all the zeal, on our side, has ended in an overthrow somewhat more complete than we should in all probability have sustained at the commencement of our long and well thought out campaign.[10]

We need to take note of these bruised feelings, and of the considerable suspicion of the motives of the clergy in establishing the first colleges, if we are to understand subsequent difficulties, from the establishment of the rival Local Authority colleges 60 years later to the residual hostility which Church Colleges and schools still encounter in some quarters today. In 1839, some who championed the colleges' cause did so from Christian love of the poor. Others seemed more concerned to extend the secular power and influence of the Church and diminish that of the State.

With hindsight Brougham's gloom seems unwarranted. The crucial outcomes were that the government had survived a scathing attack and so had its Committee of Council for Education. The Church had, for the present, defeated the project for a State Normal College, but, as the historian of the National Society conceded, it had

> failed to prevent the establishment of a rival authority within what had hitherto been acknowledged as its own preserve.[11]

Moreover the Committee of Council now prescribed conditions of inspection for all schools which were to receive government grants, so the spectre of State interference was not laid. Even staunch churchmen soon realised that the transfer to the two main religious societies of the grant originally intended for the government college was a muted triumph for the Church. It now had an urgent and costly obligation to provide that expansion of teacher education for which it had frustrated the government's initiatives. It did so.

The National Society Report for 1839 records that during the year 15 Diocesan Education Boards were established. Enthusiastic meetings in London, Lichfield and Warrington urged the speedy foundation of training colleges, and in January, February and April of 1840, the first students were admitted to the first three Church of England Colleges at, respectively, Exeter, Chester and Chichester. York was not far behind.

The Foundation meeting for the college was held on 11 December 1839 and its resolutions announced publicly on 21 December (see opposite). The aged Archbishop, Vernon Harcourt chaired the meeting, but it was his son Archdeacon William Vernon Harcourt who vigorously pursued the main decision:

> It was resolved upon, as the most powerful means of remedying the existing defects in the Education both of the Poor and Middle Classes of Society to establish a School for the purpose of Training Masters in the Art and Practice of Teaching; and it was determined to found such a School at York as soon as sufficient funds should be raised in the Diocese to maintain it.

Harcourt had already been a founder and promoter of the Yorkshire Museum (1827), the British Association (1831), and the Yorkshire School for the Blind (1834). He wrote letters to influential patrons, sent committee members on tour to advertise the College and by April 1840 felt confident that the committee could advertise the Principalship.

YO,K
CENTRAL DIOC;SAN SOCIETY,

FOR TE

EDUCATION OF THE POOR.

At a General Meeting of this Society held in the Minster Library, on the 11th of Dember inst.

HIS GRACE THE ARCJBISHOP IN THE CHAIR,

It was resolved upon, as the most poweril means of remedying the existing defects in the Education both of the Poor and Middle Clases of Society, to establish a School for the purpose of training Masters in the art and ractice of Teaching ; and it was determined to found such a School at York, as soon as suicient Funds should be raised in the Diocese to maintain it.

In the hope that the Inhabitants of York vill be amongst the most forward to support the new and much wanted Institution which it is ths proposed to found in this City, the Central Committee have requested a Deputation of Gentemen to solicit Contributions in the different Wards, during the ensuing week, and to offer anj further explanations which may be wished for of the objects and intentions of the Society.

JOHN BROWNE,   ⎫
                   ⎬ *Secretaries.*
WILLIAM WHYTEHEAD, ⎭

YORK, *December 21st,* 1839.

11

First attempts were not fruitful and in August the committee agreed to open the post to laymen. Ripon Diocese was now offering assistance and advice however, and its Bishop objected. In a revised advertisement the salary was raised from £200 per annum to £250 but only graduates 'in orders' were invited to apply. Not until November was the committee able to offer the appointment, to Revd Edward Smith of Bocking, requesting him to visit the training schools at Lichfield and Chester on his way to taking up the post at York. This advice appears not to have had the desired effect. Smith duly reported on his visits at the end of December and at the same time tendered his resignation! On 23 February 1841 Revd William Reed was appointed. He was aged 33 and his preparation for the post had been exotic. Born in Jamaica, he entered Queen's College Oxford in 1827 aged 19 and having graduated returned home to become first a military chaplain and then, from 1836 till his translation to York, chaplain to the Bishop of Jamaica.

Meanwhile the college had acquired its first premises. In August 1840 the committee investigated the buildings of the former Dissenting Academy, Manchester College in Monkgate, the Academy having decided to return to Manchester. They were not ideal, but offered more than the clergy houses in which colleges had already been launched at Chester, Chichester and Durham for example. The site, with a 25 yard frontage and depth of about 100 yards, was opposite the County Hospital. Its rambling buildings, scattered gardens and small play area allowed no scope for expansion except through possible future purchase of adjacent buildings. But the Committee first leased it for £130 a year and then, after 18 months use, bought it in November 1842 for £1,960. In April and May 1841 £400 was spent on repairs, decorations and alterations including the adaptation of stables into a schoolroom and the installation of gas. Further additions and improvements in 1842 cost almost £600.

Regulations for the first entry of students were approved by the committee in March 1841 and published in April (see page 2). Students could enter at the age of 15 – raised to 17 in 1844 – but would not be recommended to take charge of a school until 18. Evidence was required of 'moral character, docility and general aptitude for the way of life on which they are to enter'. There was an entrance examination, a three month probation period and the prospect of a Certificate to be awarded after at least a year's attendance. As in most colleges founded in the 1840s, the curriculum appeared formidable and slightly pretentious; the daily routine was tough. The subjects listed were those of a typical Middle School, with the Latin added perhaps in deference to the high church Committee of Enquiry and Correspondence, or simply to the 'public' school tradition.

Holy Scripture, Church Catechism, Liturgy and Church History; Reading, Writing, Arithmetic, English Grammar, History and Geography.
Book-keeping, Mensuration, Elements of Algebra, Geometry and Practical Mechanics.

Music, Linear Drawing, Rudiments of Latin.
Lectures will occasionally be given in the Elements of Botany, Natural History and Philosophy.
Modern Languages to be paid for as extras.

This, with whatever training in the skills and practice of teaching could be provided, was the kind of programme by which several Dioceses hoped to meet two recognised needs: one for a cadre of teachers educated beyond the top level of the National Schools; the other for an organised system of schools for the lower-middle classes, not modelled on the classics-dominated curriculum of the 'public' schools.

The combination of Middle School and Training Institution was soon under heavy criticism from HMI, but in these first years there were two unanswerable arguments for it: without the fees of large numbers of pupils the whole institution could not be afforded; without a large number of school pupils the staff could not be adequately employed with the few student-teacher entrants in the early years. The Middle School also provided immediate and accessible 'practice' opportunities for the teachers in training and by 1845 was already being referred to at York as 'The Middle or Practising School'.

The original advertisement had announced 'The hours of teaching to be from Nine to Twelve and from Two till Five'. The demanding curriculum soon extended this timetable. Inspections of the mid-forties recorded a rising bell at 5.30 am, the first study period from 6.00 to 6.45 followed by breakfast and prayers. Between 5.00 pm and 6.30 there was work in the gardens or military drill and after supper more study from 7.00 pm to 9.40, followed by prayers and 'Gas Turned Off' at 10.00. The routine was probably well-intentioned rather than repressive. The pupils were poorly educated when they arrived; their needs were great and so was the country's need for teachers. Time and money were short. Early York students did at least go to bed an hour later than Chester's and were spared a discipline imposed on those at Chichester, who had each to put in 100 strokes a day at the pump to maintain the water supply.

Once Cordukes' solitary sojourn had been relieved numbers rose steadily, by comparison with some of the other new foundations. Of the four students in residence in December 1841 three, it was later alleged by a contemporary, were seriously handicapped, one with a wooden leg and two with physical deformities.[12] They were joined by seven more in 1842.

13

One of the original four withdrew, but in 1843 27 new students were admitted and the College was full. The Middle School began with seven pupils in the first term and by June 1843 had 35.

The ages and social range of the early College students remind the present generation that we did not invent 'mature' students or 'wider access'. The 1842 entry were aged from 15 to 24 years; the 1843 entry from 14 to 28. For both years the average age was 19. The 1844 entry ranged from 16 to 30 and averaged 21. For 1845 the average was 22 and this was maintained for the rest of the decade, though in 1846 the range was 17 to 40. Patterns of entry were similar elsewhere, though York seems to have decided early against young admissions, whereas Culham, Oxford in its first 10 years admitted 34 students under 16, and at Chester the average age was lower than at York.

The register of York students from 1841 to 49 records 175 parental occupations. These included 44 textile workers, 18 farmers, 18 labourers, 13 schoolmasters, 4 miners, a solicitor, an architect, a curate, an engineer, an excise officer, 3 inn-keepers and a range of skilled occupations such as teazel-grower, coachman, warehouseman, sexton, basket-maker and saw-grinder. Three fathers appeared to be men of independent means. Again the selection is not strikingly different from those in other colleges – Durham and Chichester for example.

Reed had no previous experience of formal teaching and for his first three years he had only one assistant. William Start was described in the first prospectus as having been 'lately employed in the Commercial School in London in connexion with the National Society'. He left in 1844, before the College had been subjected to full inspection so we have no detailed evidence of his skills, though he was given a warm testimonial. Reed himself is referred to in a National Society publication of 1844 which praised 'the successful management of the Training Institution at York . . . under its excellent Principal'. The first HMI report of 1847 was less enthusiastic, noting that Reed relied on the 'catechetical' method rather than the formal lecture which was much used at Battersea and Cheltenham, and praised by HMI. Fashions change. Whatever the merits of his teaching methods Reed seems to have liked and admired his students. In his 1844 report he described them as

> docile, dutiful, patient, industrious, and good-tempered, affectionate to their teachers and to one another.

'Docile' at that time meant simply 'amenable to teaching' and had not yet acquired the nuance 'lacking in spirit'. There seems to have been plenty of that and Reed had to expel students in 1843, 1846 and 1847. But he insisted that the students were 'rich in moral qualification' though he acknowledged that educationally they were 'miserably deficient'. The first HMI reports endorsed this estimate:

> A considerable number of the pupils in their first year, and those lately come, were extremely illiterate and sadly deficient in qualifications of any kind. It was clear that not a few were entering the profession of a schoolmaster merely on account of their unfitness for anything else. It seems that those who conduct the college are not unaware of this; but that they feel themselves obliged to admit such as they can get, and would gladly get better material to work upon if they could.

HMI Watkins, visiting a year later in 1847 embellished this depressing picture:

> The young men who enter the institution are not in general such as are either naturally, or from the condition and habits of their previous lives, well qualified for the office of a schoolmaster . . . some, and they are not the least promising, are inexperienced boys who, without any peculiar fitness for the duties of a schoolmaster, or much desire for his office have passed creditably through their respective schools . . . to the Training College. There are others who have already been at work in the world – tailors, gardeners, shoemakers, some from the loom, others from the plough, from the mine, from service in gentlemen's families, and from various other occupations. Many of these have a desire for the office of schoolmaster – not a few, I believe a strong liking for its labours; but it may fairly be questioned whether they are likely to succeed in it; whether in the short time which the demand for schoolmasters on the one hand and their own exigencies on the other, allow them for instruction at the Training College, they will become qualified to go forth as intelligent and skilled teachers of ignorant and undisciplined children.

This seems to have been a fair assessment of national recruitment. Kay-Shuttleworth wrote similarly of the early students at St John's Battersea, and HMI Moseley of those at Chester. Yet in all the colleges tutors were soon having to be drawn from the best of these unpromising recruits. The first at York was John Field, who became the third appointment to the staff when Start left in 1844. Reed thought well of his work and by 1847 Field was Master of the Middle School. During 1844 however, the two of them provided all the 'qualified' tutoring for 42 college students and 42 Middle School pupils at varied stages of their educational development. A further appointment was made in January 1845 when John Young became Master of Music. In spite of HMI criticism that the staff was too small no further appointment was made until 1847.

Staff responsibilities were not limited to full-time students and pupils. From the outset Reed seems to have been expected to help organise York National Schools and to act as Inspector for them. In 1841 this must have taken much of his time. He reported that he had 'remodelled' the school at Micklegate and proposed to do the same for the Manor School. He made wide-ranging criticisms of schools from Bridlington to Doncaster, but took a realistic view of the monitorial method, which he, Start and Field must have had to use heavily.

> Whatever faults may be attributed to the monitorial system it is useless to allow ourselves to dwell on them till we are ready to supersede it by something more effective . . . In this matter Time and the Training School are our chief remedies. A new order of Masters will produce a corresponding change in monitors.

In-service training was also provided for practising schoolmasters. Ten attended a four week course during the 'Harvest Holiday' of 1843, and groups as large as 70 followed, severely reducing vacation time for the college staff. In spite of these pressures, recreational facilities for the resident students were not neglected. Football and cricket seem to have been quickly established, a fives court was improvised in 1843, and the committee made arrangements for regular swimming.

With such under-educated students and an overworked staff it must have been impossible to find enough time for the theory and practice of class-room methods, even if the staff had been qualified to teach them. The elusive balance between the education of the student and the training of the teacher is likely to remain the perennial challenge for teacher education into the 21st century and beyond. It was well understood in these pioneer years, especially by HMI Moseley, whose work and influence deserve note in even a brief account of the 1840s and 50s. He travelled the whole country and recorded his opinions on the developing characteristics of individual colleges. The daily timetables at Battersea, St Mark's Chelsea and Chester, for example, were little different from that at York in Reed's time. Yet after visits in the mid 1840s Moseley considered Chester inclined to over-emphasise industrial pursuits for students at the expense of the literary and recreational. Battersea he thought gave more prominence to teaching method than any other college but in the process tended to deprive the students of initiative and the taste for self-instruction. At St Marks, where Derwent Coleridge had been accused of giving students ideas above their likely stations, Moseley felt that literary, abstract and passive inclinations were fostered to the detriment of classroom practice and crucial skills of exposition and simplification. He posed the challenge in terms which present-day HMI or National Curriculum Council could surely endorse:

> I am not urging the claims of any of the particular schemes or methods of instruction . . . I am simply insisting on the necessity of making teaching as an art the subject of study in a training college in respect of each subject taught; of viewing each subject under a double aspect, as that which is to become an element of the student's own knowledge and as that which he is to be made capable of presenting under so simple a form, that it may become an element in the knowledge of a child . . . It is not the fact that the teacher knows too much, which makes him unintelligible to the child, but that he knows nothing which the child can comprehend, or that he has never studied what he has to teach in the light in which a child can be made to comprehend it.[13]

Progress towards such a synthesis was halting at York, as elsewhere.

The college also shared with all others, problems of finance and accommodation. Throughout 1841 the college management remained in the hands of a small committee, chaired by Vernon Harcourt and joined, as soon as he was appointed, by Reed. Most of the running costs had to come from donations and subscriptions to the District Boards of the Diocesan Society. Two years after the opening, as we saw from the Ripon Diocesan Board report, much more support was needed. But the original committee had anticpated this. The Archbishop had launched their appeal early in 1840 with a donation of £200, circulars had been sent 'to the principal nobility and gentry throughout the Diocese, soliciting their subscriptions', and in York, door to door collections had been organised using printed handbills.

As suggested above, the political motives of the Church in founding its colleges were mixed and dubious, yet there can be no doubting the sincere support of many individual clergy for these projects, which had little popular appeal. As the Newcastle Commissioners were later to remark:

> An institution which produces good teachers may be the most efficient of all aids to education, but it appeals to no sympathy, it relieves no immediate distress, and it accordingly obtains subscriptions with difficulty.

The commissioners also expressed the view that rural landowners 'as a class do not do their duty in the support of rural eduction'. With the formation of the Ripon Diocese in 1836, the woollen districts were lost by the York Diocese which became heavily influenced by the clergy, by a group of York professional men mostly lawyers, and by a few landed families. It was these who bore most of the cost of developing the college, with the clergy especially generous. Of the 366 subscribers listed in the York Diocesan Society report for 1844, more than half were clergy or members of clergy families; in five of the district boards 35 subscribers out of a total of 42 were clergymen. The Committee had calculated in 1840 that running costs would necessitate subscriptions of at least £500 a year. Comparable budgets at Battersea and Chester suggest that this was probably a serious under-estimate, but even this was not achieved. A target subscription of £1 per parish was still proving wildly over-optimistic in 1847.

The involvement and financial assistance of the Ripon Diocese was therefore a welcome relief. The first Bishop, Longley, was active on the National Society's central committees and had seen the wisdom from the outset, of a joint training project with York. So in September 1842 a 'Committee of the Two Dioceses' was formed, and took over responsibility for the management of the college, with Bishop Longley in the chair for all important meetings.

Even before the exceptional entry of 1843 had filled the Monkgate building, Longley aspired to bigger and better facilities on a new site. Land was available, on Lord Mayor's Walk which leads off Monkgate along the North Wall of the city. In March 1843 the new joint Committee invited G. T. Andrews, the chief architect of the railway magnate Hudson to prepare plans for a new building. After their difficulties with recurrent costs the Committee members realised that it might take some time to raise the money but briskly launched Diocesan appeals and a petition for a grant from government. Chester College had obtained £2,500 from the Committee of Council in 1842 to build on a site given free to the college by its diocese. The conflicts about the State Normal College and government inspection of Church schools or colleges had made the Committee of Council wary of further contributions however and it took the York and Ripon committee until August 1844 to negotiate a grant of £3,500 towards their planned new building for 52 students at a cost of about £8,000. Within a year appeals from the Archbishop and the Bishop of Ripon to the two dioceses had been so successful in raising a further £5,000 that the new building was a realistic project. In February 1845 the committee bought a three acre plot on Lord Mayor's Walk for £1,300, a high price at that time. In later years the Lord Mayor's Walk site – now one of five college campuses in York – has been criticised as too cramped and a 'bad buy'. But the location right in the heart of the city, under the North Wall has been invaluable in community terms, the rapid and limiting development of the city in the area could not easily have been foreseen, and the committee bought as much at the time as they could afford. Longley passed Andrews' plans for comment to William Railton, architect to the Church Commissioners who had designed the Bishop's

Palace at Ripon. With a few amendments they were then approved by the committee in August 1845; the contract for building was placed with Bellerby's of York.

The Committee's Annual Report for 1845 hinted that subscribers should not expect too much. The buildings, it declared

> promised to be admirably adapted to the purpose contemplated in their erection. It was the wish of the committee to give them a character suitable to the objects of the Institution, to waste nothing in superfluous ornament, but to unite with the more solid requisites, something of that regularity of plan, and harmony of details, which would stamp it as a place devoted to the interests of Religious learning.

Enforced economies seriously affected the furnishings and equipping of the new building for years after its opening in 1846 but having to stint on the building itself was unfortunate and was thought so at the time. The number and size of the windows was limited to save tax and HMI Thurtell referred in the first inspection report to

> A spacious building of Elizabethan architecture whose design might, with no very great additional expense, have been made to present a very considerable degree of beauty . . . Unhappily however the necessity for consulting economy in the outlay has greatly diminished the architectural effect.

The Committee of Council had been persuaded to approve a grant for the Lord Mayor's Walk building partly on the grounds that it would also enable the two Dioceses to provide proper training for mistresses. To fulfil this promise the men began the move to the new site in May 1846, before it had been adequately serviced, equipped or landscaped. In spite of all the difficulties the York and Ripon College was already regarded nationally as a success. The Committee of Council Minutes listed 20 Church Colleges which had admitted at least their first students by the end of 1845. Recruitment was strong at Battersea with 71 students, Whitelands (54 women), St Mark's, Chelsea (53) and Chester (41). York and Ripon had 36 – which rose to 48 the following year – Lichfield and Salisbury each had 26, and Warrington 20. Four colleges had fewer than 10 students and the wide disparities in numbers and resources to educate them showed that it was one thing for churchmen to conceive a national system but quite another to finance it. It was already crucial that more central support be provided on a permanent basis through the Committee of Council if the work was to prosper.

Like all the others the York and Ripon College was officially a Church foundation. To what extent its work in these early years was imbued with Christian spirit and motivation is hard to gauge from this distance – if

19

indeed such an assessment of any institution is possible at any time. There was certainly a great deal of church-going in the 1840s but probably only because the compulsory attendance which most Christians now deplore was still largely taken for granted in early Victorian times. Reed's comments suggest that he thought many of his students strong on Christian motivation and willing to act it out. He gave a notable illustration: in one of the Committee's first responses to the criticisms of an HMI report he had urged on the students' behalf

> The great impediment with which we have hitherto had to contend is Poverty.

Yet after the examinations at the end of that year, some of the men had been so impressed with their own deficiencies, that in spite of their dire need of a regular income they declined offers of teaching posts in order to stay on at College for further training. Reed was quietly proud of that:

> Conduct of this kind in men steeped in poverty, tells no unpleasant tale. They have learnt better to estimate the requirements of a schoolmaster, and the community will eventually learn to do the same.

From the records there is little doubt of Reed's own enthusiasm – for the students, for the development of the college, and for its Christian witness and worship. He was shortly to pay a price for it.

CHAPTER II

Lord Mayor's Walk and the College for Mistresses 1843-1854

FROM THEIR EARLIEST MEETINGS IN 1839 the founders of the college had expressed interest in training schoolmistresses. In October 1842 the 'Committee of the Two Dioceses', having at its previous meeting confirmed expenditure of more than £3,000 on the purchase, renovation and equipment of the Monkgate premises for men, resolved

> That for the purpose of making temporary provision for a Training Establishment for young women as schoolmistresses, a sum of money not exceeding £100 be placed at the disposal of the Monthly Committee, for the purpose of carrying out such measures as may to them seem advisable: such sum of £100 to include all charges for the requisite furniture.

In January 1843 the Committee considered the offer of the mistress of the Model National School for Girls in York, Mrs Fearnley, to undertake temporary supervision of young women wishing to become schoolmistresses. She was willing to make boarding arrangements for them, if the Committee would provide premises, household supplies and furniture. The predicted cost had now rocketed to £120 but the Committee braced itself. The Ripon Diocesan Report for 1843 recorded that

> A house capable of accommodating twenty pupils was hired . . . The terms of admission are eight shillings per week which sum covers every expense except washing. During the year ten pupils have been received into the Institution, of whom eight are still in it, one has taken charge of an infant school at Ripon, and one, who being already in charge of a school, came for improvement during the harvest, has returned to her own school . . . This Infant Establishment is effectually performing the object for

which it was formed, and preparing the way for that larger scene of operation which will supersede it when the plans of the Board are more matured.

It was to take the Board more than 20 years to 'prepare the way' for a 'scene of operation' comparable to that provided for the men within three years. The York Diocesan Report for 1844 informed subscribers that the instruction of schoolmistresses remained in the hands of Mrs Fearnley. Fifteen young women had been in attendance at 14 Monkgate and six of them had been appointed to take charge of schools. A third National Society School for girls had now been opened in York at the Manor House; the number of boys and girls in the York National schools was over 1,000. The report included the text of the Board's memorandum to the Committee of Council requesting grant for 'new buildings' for the 'Normal Training Schools for Masters and Mistresses'. It also regretted the death of a male student during an epidemic of scarlet fever 'in spite of every precaution being taken which the premises admitted of', and stressed the unsuitability of the Monkgate site:

> This first case of infectious sickness . . . sufficiently testified how inadequate the existing premises must be considered for the proper accommodation of the number of pupils resident therein. With overcrowded rooms, without a hospital or the power when full of isolating an invalid, the Board have much cause for thankfulness that, with this exception, the health of the pupils in the school has been almost uninterrupted. With no less satisfaction do they look forward to the time as speedily approaching, when on a site well suited to its object . . . with ample accommodation for the requirements of sickness or of health, the York School for Masters will assume a character and appearance more consonant with the dignity of its office.

The same Report reprinted the Pastoral Letter from the Archbishop, appealing for support for the Lord Mayor's Walk project. It revealed the economic use to which the 'inadequate existing premises' were to be put:

> There is not, as yet any permanent establishment for the training of School Mistresses, an object of scarcely less importance than the training of Masters. On these accounts it is proposed to appropriate the present building to the former purpose and to erect a new one for the latter.

The women students continued at 14 Monkgate until July 1846 when the Committee recommended the appointment of Miss Winifred Cruse to be Mistress of the Female Training School at the now vacated buildings of 33 Monkgate. She was to recieve a salary of £80 and her sister Miss Catherine Cruse was to be Assistant Mistress at £35. A third sister,

Mary, was admitted into residence to assist with household managment but was unpaid for the first few years. The College archives offer no information on the early life of the Cruse sisters, or their previous experience, but Committee minutes soon began to record satisfaction with their work. Overall responsibility for both Training Schools rested with Reed, but he seems to have given Winifred Cruse wide authority over the 'Female School' and she made prompt use of it.

She drew up a timetable as strenuous as the men's, running from 6 am to 9.45 pm and including domestic chores from which the men seem to have been exempt; the women had to clean their own rooms, and prepare their own meals communally. Their family backgrounds and parental occupations were similar to those of the men; only three of the first 40 women students had 'professional' fathers – a lawyer, a clergyman and a schoolmaster. Their curriculum closely followed the mens' but with less mathematics, no Latin and some additional domestic training. The women were more closely supervised. Dress had to be plain, with 'ringlets, flowers, veils, flounces and ornaments' forbidden. Permission had to be asked to go into York or to write a letter and all envelopes had to be signed by the Mistress or assistant. There were severe requirements for cleanliness and tidiness and Miss Cruse insisted that

> Strict adherence to the rules of the house is required by everyone, as the only means of ensuring comfort and regularity.

There was plenty of regularity but not much comfort. The Committee did vote £500 for renovations in 1847, but Miss Cruse was continually pressing for small, inexpensive improvements. Throughout her 16 years as Superintendent the premises were heavily criticised by successive HMI and never considered adequate in scale or quality. Compared with the provision for the men the training of schoolmistresses at York was done as cheaply as possible and there was little attempt to conceal this.

York and Ripon attitudes were not especially reactionary. All over the country Dioceses tended to give priority to opportunities for men. In Sussex, in 1848, the attempt to merge Bishop Otter's College for men at Chichester with the Diocesan College for women at Brighton was berated in a widely circulated pamphet which particularly deplored female 'wastage' through marriage:

> I do not hesitate to say, supported as the assertion is by the views of influential persons among ourselves and by the dictates of common sense, that the training of Schoolmistresses is decidedly of inferior moment to the training of Schoolmasters. The former, no doubt, have their peculiar use, and in many respects their services cannot be replaced by those of men; but the staple of teaching in any school must after all come from the Master; and

his lore is of a kind more capable of being imparted by direct training, so that of the two, if circumstances allow of one kind only being trained, the Masters should by all means have the preference . . . In fact it is a moral certainty that a large proportion, perhaps not less than half of the money expended in training schoolmistresses will ultimately be found to have been thrown away.[1]

The move to 33 Monkgate coincided, however, with a dramatic improvement in central government support which helped the Female Training School to stay solvent and grow. As at the men's college a limited number of exhibitions had been made available in 1845 through the generosity of individual members of the Diocesan Committee. The Committee of Council's Minutes for 1846 launched the 'Pupil Teacher' scheme nationally and established scholarships for Training Colleges. Selected schools which had been favourably reported on by HMI – including some of the National Society's schools in York – were to be approved for the training of pupil-teachers. Candidates were to begin a five year apprenticeship at the age of not less than 13 and be paid £10 a year, rising over four years to £20. Schools were to be allowed one pupil-teacher for every 25 pupils, and headteachers were to receive additional salary at the rate of £5 for one pupil-teacher, £9 for two and £3 for each subsequent recruit, in return for the obligation to provide one and a half hours instruction for each pupil-teacher every day. Having completed this apprenticeship the pupil-teachers could sit an examination for Queen's Scholarships to the value of £20 to £25 a year at a recognised training college, which would receive additional grant for each year of a Queen's Scholar's training to a maximum of three years.

There was good news for qualified teachers as well as for the colleges. Trained teachers were to receive proficiency grants from government and pensions were introduced for those retiring with 15 or more years service. Further grants were to be offered to schools for books, workshops and gardens. Kay-Shuttleworth's new regulations were bold, far-sighted and expensive; in 1847 government expenditure on education topped £100,000. Teaching became a more attractive profession with enhanced status, salary and security. To the colleges the new regime held out prospects of stability, expansion, co-operative working relationships with neighbourhood schools and a steady supply of able, well-motivated, experienced students. These were similar objectives to those which our government of the 1980s espoused, but Ministers in the 1840s set about achieving them in more sensitive and generous ways and deservedly made good progress.

The York and Ripon Committee welcomed the 1846 Minutes in an ecumenical spirit, remarkable for the time:

> It is clear that no schools will obtain the assistance offered by government, except those that are well and efficiently conducted . . . and that it is the intention of the Privy Council to encourage young persons to go through the full three year training in Normal Schools, in order that they may be duly qualified for their future work . . . It surely will be a matter of congratulation to the promoters of Church Education that this Board has laid the foundation for obtaining for this Diocese a due share of the parliamentary grant. The assistance offered in the Minutes is intended for those who will do most for themselves, and certainly if the principle be conceded that not only full toleration, but actual support is to be given by the State to all religious denominations, no fairer principle of adjustment could be laid down that that those who exert themselves most, and qualify themselves best, shall have the largest share of assistance.

Such support for the efforts of denominations outside the Established Church was the more surprising in the light of the Board's treatment of its own college Principal inside it.

Reed's responsibilities had grown fast. He was now not only in overall charge of two training schools and the growing middle schools which served them. In April 1845, Lord Morpeth, the former Whig minister, proposed to the York and Ripon Committee that 'a group of noblemen and gentlemen' he had enthused should be permitted to build a boarding establishment alongside the new Men's Training School. The 'Yeoman School' was to be for the sons of clergymen, farmers, manufacturers, tradesmen and others who could not afford the fees of established public schools. The school was to be owned and financed by a separate board of trustees, but managed by the Training Schools Committee. The boys were to attend the middle school in the new college buildings, alongside the day boys and the student teachers in training. The scheme was rapidly approved and the building, designed by Andrews, was completed and occupied by the end of 1846. It was later to be taken over by the Archbishop Holgate's Grammar School, and in 1958 to be incorporated into the College, forming a handsome extension of the Lord Mayor's Walk frontage. Early in 1847 there were already 20 pupils in residence in the Yeoman School and in 1848, 77.

While this extension of his responsibilities was being planned and built, Reed was enduring public criticism of his alleged religious convictions and practices. 1845 was a tense year for the Anglican Church, as the Tractarian controversy came to a head. Newman defected to Rome and the Wilberforces and Henry Manning – a powerful influence in the founding of the Church colleges – agonised over their doctrinal positions.[2] After some unsatisfactory arrangements for students and staff to worship in other local churches, the Diocesan Committee reached agreement with St Michael-le-Belfrey Church in 1845, for services to be conducted, by Reed and others, at times when the parish was not holding its own services. Some parishioners chose to attend the college occasions and in August several of them walked out of a service in protest against what they described as Reed's 'Tractarian practices'. The local press relished the incident. One headline denounced 'Puseyism is York' while another paper's editorial described Reed's alleged abuses and referred to W. G. Ward's conversion to Rome in the same week.

Reed's liturgical abberations seem trivial today. He had left out the usual prayer before the sermon, preached in his surplice, read prayers and pronounced absolution from the communion rail, and failed to use metrical psalms. In September the *Yorkshire Gazette* expressed a widely held view:

> There are doubtless degrees of departure from Protestant principles. The laity however do not draw fine distinctions – they cannot split hairs – but view all who entertain Tractarian sentiments to be upon a sloping roof and verging in various degrees from the Reformation until too many drop into the gulph of popery.

There had been riots at Exeter in the previous January over the use of the surplice from the pulpit, so Reed would have been aware that, as Chadwick later put it

> The inarticulate laity learnt from the press to identify the surplice, when used in a pulpit, with the badge of a party which declared war on the Protestant Reformation.[3]

The Committee of the two dioceses summoned Reed before a special meeting in September 1845, chaired, ironically, by Archdeacon Robert Wilberforce, a Tractarian who himself was to convert to Rome in 1854. Reed was required to write a letter to the Committee denying any Tractarian intentions, to adhere in future to the usual practices of the parish churches of the York Diocese and to see that the Training School students continued to receive practice in the metrical psalms. He did so without any recorded protest and, apart from a complaint from a local vicar in 1847 about the students intoning responses, there were no further liturgical altercations in Reed's time. After the 'tribunal' he transferred the Training School services from St Michael's to Holy Trinity and St Maurices where there was less likelihood of complaints. But he was soon in difficulties over other matters.

Although Diocesan and HMI reports from 1842 to 1847 include various tributes to his skills as academic leader, and domestic manager, of the Training Schools, there were dissensions beneath the surface. As early as 1843, when the Female School made its tentative start, Reed had applied for his salary to be doubled to £500 and had complained of an unsatisfactory confusion of the accounts for his personal domestic costs and those of the Training Schools. The committee offered an additional £50 per annum and agreed to pay him £300 for the furniture which he had provided for the Principal's quarters. Three years later, when it emerged that a number of payments against the college's accounts had been long delayed, Reed was criticised for not settling his own domestic bills promptly. He again complained that these were often confused with those for the college. His proposal to the committee that a separate kitchen should be built within the new Principal's house in the Lord Mayor's Walk building was rejected. Tensions continued into 1848, when the Committee finally agreed to offer Reed the desired salary of £500 'Without perquisites or additional allowance of any kind'. It was also proposed however that he should cease to control the domestic arrangements of the college, which would be under the direction of a Matron, to be appointed. The combined additional expenses of such a new regime would have been at least £250 a year. Yet only a few weeks earlier the Committee had considered a request from Catherine Cruse for a £5 addition to her annual salary of £35 and had resolved 'That the present state of the finances will not admit of the augmentation of Miss C. Cruse's salary'.

In April 1848, Reed indicated his dissatisfaction with the proposed arrangement and the Committee conceded that he might continue to appoint and have general control over domestic staff. Reed then formally resigned the Principalship on the grounds that even under the revised proposals he would not have full control over the daily running of the college.

The parting seems to have been amicable in the end. The Committee expressed a warm vote of thanks for Reed's services and he announced his acceptance of the Principalship of the Diocesan College about to be launched at Carmarthen, which had no doubt been in the offing for at least the final few weeks of his dispute with the Committee. There was little in the episode for the York and Ripon Dioceses to congratulate themselves on in future years. Only three months earlier, the Annual Report for 1847 had commended Reed's stewardship

> It is but just to the Principal to say, that it is owing to his unceasing vigilance and careful superintendence of the household arrangements that the cost of maintenance has, during the past

year – one of scarcity and high prices – been kept so low, averaging tenpence half-penny a day per head. Indeed his indefatigable exertions and the lively interest which he takes in all the details of the institution under his charge, are deserving of the highest praise.

He served Carmarthen with notable success for 20 years and has the posthumous distinction of having been the founder principal of two of the earliest Church Colleges which were eventually to be among only eight of the 1840s foundations to survive the drastic closures of the 1970s, and seem likely to endure from the 19th century into the 21st. Student magazines were not launched at York till the 1890s and we have no impression of Reed as a personality except from Minute books and annual reports. But an early magazine from Carmarthen offers this endearing insight

> Our Principal was a good type of the 'Fine Old English' gentleman. Tall, well set up, genial, fond of good things, especially Yorkshire, and anxious to make men of those under his care. He had his peculiarities of course. One was that when ruffled his lips would protrude, and he would emit a sort of grunt, which was sometimes infectious. His dog caught the habit from his and would often put in a grunt of his own.

The habit may well have been developed in York, where Reed had quite a lot to grunt about.

The new Principal was Revd George Hodgkinson who came from the Principalship of the Royal Agricultural College at Cirencester. He was 32, had taken first class honours in Mathematics at Trinity, Cambridge in 1837 and been second master at Bury St Edmunds Grammar School for three years. He was an Alpine climber, meteorologist and astronomer of some distinction and later in his career was to receive several grants from the Royal Society for the construction of instruments he had invented.

He made an energetic start at York, resolving the domestic problems which had thwarted Reed, by separating the accounts for the college and his own house, and by paying the boarding charges for his own domestic staff. He persuaded the committee to grant £100 in the autumn of 1848 to furnish rooms in the Lord Mayor's Walk building which were still unused, and to provide some water-closets, washing facilities, ventilators, and gas burners in the classrooms to allow study beyond daylight hours. He also persuaded the committee to respond to the continual demands of the HMI and the Committee of Council for better practice facilities for teaching. HMI had always deprecated the arrangement with which many colleges had begun, of student teachers 'practising' in the middle schools housed in the same buildings and frequently taught by the college tutors.

Hodgkinson transferred all practice for the men to York National Schools but pressed for a separate practice school on the Lord Mayor's Walk site. He blamed poor examination results in 1849 on the lack of such a facility and the Diocesan Societies then agreed to help finance one. Andrews produced plans for an 'ornamental building' with two large rooms fronting Lord Mayor's Walk and a tender was accepted for £659. The history of the main building was quickly repeated however and the Committee eventually sanctioned only a 'plain room' at a cost of £370. The two dioceses did not manage to raise even this amount, £100 being contributed by the Committee of Council and £40 by the National Society. Even these modest levels of expenditure were not easily approved as college finances remained shaky. The beneficial 1846 regulations took effect slowly, partly because Queen's Scholars were till 1853 limited to a quarter of the total students in a college and partly because at York the success rate in the qualifying examinations was moderate. At the end of 1848 the college was £1,125 in debt, though during 1849 the Ripon Diocese contributed £725 and York £550 to help redeem this. Several titled supporters of the college also made large donations, but in 1851 the overdraft was still £550.

All this seems not to have daunted Hodgkinson and in his first year he revived a proposal, which Archbishop Harcourt had earlier discouraged, for the building of a College chapel. By May 1850 he had enough money subscribed or promised to start planning the building and told the Committee. It responded tartly, agreeing to appoint

> a Sub-committee with power to adopt plans, subject to the approval of the Diocesans, to determine the site and to carry the building into execution, with the distinct understanding that this Committee is not to undertake to collect funds.

Hodgkinson could have the kind of chapel the Committee approved as long as the Committee did not have to contribute to it. Andrews designed the building, fronting Lord Mayor's Walk and it was completed before the end of 1851 for a total cost of £1,050 which was paid in full from Hodgkinson's Fund. It was to be the centre of college worship for more than a century, and now houses the Drama Department's excellent modern studio Theatre and Workshop.

Meanwhile the Female part of the college was also making progress. Miss Cruse had admitted 24 students at 33 Monkgate in 1846-47, and at the end of the year provided in-service training for 20 local school-mistresses. Many of the women students were too poor to stay long enough to qualify as Queen's Scholars, and went out to school posts after less than a year, though bursaries provided by supporters of the college increased recruitment in 1848.

The HMI inspection and government examinations at the end of 1849 caused a stir. It may have been a preoccupation with drafting its protest to the Committee of Council that caused the May 1850 meeting of the Committee to give short shrift to Hodgkinson's chapel project. The minutes include the text of a long letter, appreciating that the Inspection of colleges was still a new field of work in which there was much to learn, but assuming that their Lordships were open to suggestion: the Committee was convinced

that the examination of the female pupils was both too long and too difficult. They find that the protracted excitement occasioned by such an examination is too severe a trial for the nervous system of young women and it is with some difficulty that those who have once undergone the ordeal can be persuaded to remain in the Institution to submit to the repetition of the same . . . It hardly appears necessary to raise to so high a standard the instruction of Females who are intended to educate those who for the most part will be domestic servants, or will occupy some subordinate situation in life.

The elegancies of science and grammar and general literature might well be dispensed with in their case, nor will they be the less efficient schoolmistress if they are ignorant of such points as several of those contained in the papers on Geography, Grammar and Literature, History and Biographical memoirs. If they are well versed in Holy Scripture and possess some knowledge of History and Geography, if their information, though it may not go far, is accurate, if they can teach their pupils to read and write and spell correctly, and for this purpose are able to instruct them in the elements of Grammar – if they are good needlewomen and capable of imparting some notions of domestic economy, with a view of making their pupils good servants and mothers, they would seem to possess nearly all the qualifications requisite for teachers in the class of schools over which they are likely to be placed.

The Committee of the York and Ripon Training Schools are persuaded that the standard of the last Government Examination is not within the compass of the capabilities of those young women who ordinarily enter training schools . . . The Committee would therefore pray that the period of examination be shortened and its character reduced to such that may be fairly expected of young women in a humble class of life, and which, without attempting display is calculated to encourage a sound practical system of education for those whose object is to qualify themselves for becoming teachers of the *poor*.

The letter assured their Lordships that the College Committee sought to 'employ the language of suggestion rather than complaint'. The Committee of Council's reply, on 4 June, was lengthy, courteous, and firm. The Secretary to the Council claimed that the issues raised had 'for some time been receiving their Lordships earnest considertion', and carefully rebutted the detailed criticisms of the examination papers, emphasising the range of choice offered. On the fundamental issue of the education of women their Lordships took a longer view than the College Committee:

> The girls attending elementary schools have to be regarded as the future Mothers of English families. It is from this side probably that the most sensible impression could be made upon the education of the next generation. At present the mother in the labouring classes parts with her children to the infant school (if she wishes to educate them) at an age which nature appears hardly to have intended for such a separation. At a later stage she can neither talk to her children about their lessons in school with intelligence, nor help them in preparing those lessons. The instruction of home is at present little, if at all, subsidiary to the instruction of school. All the information which the child of affluent parents receives from the daily conversation of the family circle is lost to the child of the poor.
>
> The Mothers who could supply this void must have passed through the hands of well educated teachers.

Conceding that some examinations might be reduced in number and simplified, they stressed the importance of the continuing inspection of the Female Training Schools, which might 'with advantage be made a more special and separate duty than it is at present'. Their Lordships appeared to regard their reply as a manifesto of national significance, and were not prepared to have it selectively quoted.

> Should you deem it necessary to communicate this letter to the National Society for insertion in the Society's monthly paper, I am to request that you will endeavour to procure its insertion, if at all, without modification or omission.

Although the complaints which Miss Cruse had presumably supported were not accepted by the Committee of Council, she should have been heartened by the importance the Committee attached to the work of Female Training Schools.

In October 1850, HMIs Watkins and Cooke attended the meeting of the Female School Committee and explained in detail the principles on which inspections and examinations were based. The Committee expressed itself satisfied and the subsequent visitations were constructive and fruitful. But the inspectors continued to be forthright. In 1852 HMI Cooke again drew attention to the inadequate number of staff, the excessive demands of the Middle School in the same unsatisfactory building, the grave defects of the Practising School which he thought 'quite unfit at present for all purposes of training' and the miserly scale of financing compared with similar institutions elsewhere. At the end of the year he visited again to check that some improvements had been made to the Practising School and repeated his admiration for the achievements of Miss Cruse and his censure of the excessive demands made on her. She was still responsible for all the administration and virtually all the teaching of the students in training, since the Middle School fully occupied her sister Catherine. There were now 20 students and results had improved, but

> Mr Watkins concurs with me in the opinion that whilst very great credit is due to this lady, whose moral influence in fact pervades the institution and whose exertions have achieved results beyond all reasonable anticipation, yet that it is scarcely possible for all persons to discharge permanently such multifarious and to some extent incompatible duties. All other institutions have found by experience that even a small number of students require a *staff* of teachers, some of whom have to devote their time and attentions exclusively to the work of instruction. It does not seem that sufficient provision can be made for the instruction of Queen's Scholars without some considerable addition to the present organisation.

In 1853 little had changed. The Practising School was slightly improved but was 'not organised upon such a footing as to secure fair advantage to the students' of the Training School. In a report sent to the Committee of Council Cooke again deplored the load on Miss Cruse, but saw

> little probability that these deficiencies will be supplied in the course of this or of next year, and indeed within any reasonable time, unless a vigorous effort be made by the Management Committee. . . . The annual expenditure falls very far short of what other institutions find requisite to maintain themselves in an efficient state . . . We feel ourselves bound once more to submit to your Lordships our opinion that this institution requires considerable changes and additions in order to supply a complete professional training to schoolmistresses, especially to Queen's Scholars.

The chronic neglect of the women students and their Superintendent contrasts starkly with staffing developments at the Men's college in

Hodgkinson's early years. The formidable HMI Moseley had been given overall responsibility for the inspection of training colleges in 1850 and soon made his mark at York. His insistence that more attention be given to the skills of classroom teaching was reflected in a wholesale change in Hodgkinson's staff within a six-month period of 1850. Field who had been the outstanding tutor in method, had gone with Reed to Carmarthen and Moseley complained that training colleges tended to appoint too many university men who could not cope with the elementary school curriculum and so gave students snippets of a university curriculum, notably in mathematics and science, which they would never be called upon to teach. In 1851-2 three university men on the staff were replaced by certificated teachers, one of whom, Robert Charlton, had taken a First Class Certificate at York. Another was J. T. Fowler from St Mark's Chelsea. Revd J. Pix, an Oxford man replaced Ford as Vice Principal, but was himself replaced in 1853 by Revd G. Rowe, also MA Oxon who was to have a chequered career. Moseley's persistence had steered the Men's college to a competent teaching staff of five for a student body which in Hodgkinson's tenure did not exceed 50. Meanwhile Miss Cruse was left to provide for between 24 and 32 students virtually alone.

As the 1846 regulations took effect in the early 1850s the calibre of applicants to the Men's college improved. So did their prospects. Throughout the 1840s most of the men trained at the college had gone on to small rural schools. Improvement in the National system was small and slow in spite of the efforts of the colleges. In 1851, out of 273 schools in the East Riding only 53 qualified for grant and even by 1864 the Diocesan Society estimated that of more than 1,600 parishes in Yorkshire, only 400 had grant-aided schools with a certified teacher. Until 1853 there was still room in the Men's college for the in-service training of what were called 'extraordinary students' – serving teachers following short courses to improve their skills and prospects. Between 1849 and 1853, 75 men whose ages ranged from 20 to 48 attended the college for periods from one week to ten. After 1853 the number of Queen's Scholars at the college increased greatly. There was no longer time and resources for the 'extraordinary students' and valuable links with schools in the area were lost.

By 1853 with the relaxation of the regulations for Queen's Scholars, most students were staying on longer at York and the entry age was dropping. In 1848-9 the average entry age had been 23 and the length of stay 15 months; by 1853 entry age was down to 21 and the period in residence up to an average of two years and two months, which was well above the national norm. Only St Mark's Chelsea, with an average stay of two years eight months was close to German achievements more than 50 years before. In the 1990s economic analysts continue to press the charge that we 'fail to compete educationally with our main industrial rivals in Europe' as if it were a recent revelation; it is in fact an old story.

Students who performed adequately at college were assured of employment, and from York they could look increasingly far afield. In 1849 there were 75 posts on offer in the Yorkshire area for the 21 men leaving college. They were therefore less likely than their predecessors to remain long in small village schools where salaries and government grants were meagre. Recently qualified teachers became much more mobile and in 1851 HMI Watkins reported that of the 235 schools in his northern district, 90 were losing their teacher to a more attractive post. Government introduced new penalties in 1853 for teachers who moved school too frequently and in that year four out of York's 18 successful trainees obtained posts outside Yorkshire. The Church of England's attempt to establish a national system was having some effect at least on the attitudes of students who were beginning to feel confident to compete for the better-paid school posts anywhere in the country.

York students under Hodgkinson also benefited from some liberalising of the curriculum. Moseley's 1854 protest at the absence in most schools and colleges of any serious effort to teach the 'science of common things' was probably sharpened by his visits to York, where Hodgkinson had already added Natural Science to the curriculum and managed to buy a good deal of basic apparatus. In the 1853 national examinations the York results in Physical Science were reported by HMI to be the best in the country.

None of these achievements saved Hodgkinson in his turn from a theological and liturgical mauling more protracted and severe than Reed had endured; this time even Miss Cruse was embroiled. The whole petty and destructive episode has been well summarised by Etherington,[4] was reported zestfully over a four year period by the local press, particularly the *Yorkshire Gazette* and was described in detail by Hodgkinson himself in a privately printed pamphlet entitled *The Doctrine of the Church not to be proscribed in her Normal Schools* described by the Dictionary of National Biography as 'a defence of the curriculum at the Ripon and York Diocesan College'.[5]

It was sparked by the notorious Gorham Judgement of 1850 by which the Privy Council over-ruled a decision of the Ecclesiastical Court in favour of a pronouncement by Bishop Philpotts of Exeter, that Gorham, one of his evangelical clergy, was heretical in refusing to accept the doctrine of infant regeneration by baptism. This precipitated a crisis among Anglican clergy, particularly the High Church party, not only on the doctrinal issue, but on the political position of the Established Church. A group of Tractarians including Manning, Pusey, Keble and

Robert Wilberforce defended the efficacy of the sacrament of baptism and also protested against the act of a lay body presuming, in effect, to make a doctrinal ruling. Secessions to Rome followed and three months after the judgement, in June 1850 Hodgkinson preached, at a college service, a sermon asserting the Anglican doctrine of baptisimal regeneration.

This may have been courageous but was certainly not wise. He knew the strength of feeling among the evangelical group on the College and Diocesan Committees and it was quickly provoked. The following week Whytehead, a generous former treasurer who had frequently put his hand into his own pocket for the college and for student bursaries, wrote accusingly to Hodgkinson and reported the sermon to the Archbishop, as College chairman. A few weeks later, national demonstrations were widespread against the Papal Brief, re-establishing the Roman Catholic hierarchy in England after a 'lapse' of 300 years. On November 5th anti-papal agitation was particularly vicious in York, the birthplace of Guy Fawkes. In the same month a meeting of the clergy of the York Archdeaconry which Hodgkinson, perhaps unwisely, did not attend, condemned the Papal Brief and all things Roman.

A meeting of subscribers to the College then signed a memorial to the Diocesan Board claiming that Hodgkinson had publicly condemned the Gorham judgement – which plenty of other clergy of many shades of churchmanship had done – and advising the Archbishop that he could not know what kind of theological teaching the Principal was inflicting on the students. Hodgkinson was summoned to Bishopthorpe and the Archbishop read the full text of the sermon, now six months old. Nothing more was heard publicly for more than a year, but the flames were quietly fanned. When, in 1852 the Diocesan Board finally published a mild letter of comment from the Archbishop, the Doncaster Board responded with a protest, regretting

> to find so much prejudice against the York Training School as seriously to affect the support given to it, and that the public impression of the views of the Principal increase such prejudice.

When it was clear that the Archbishop intended to take no further action, Whytehead resigned from the College Committee and was followed by several other members including Baxter who had been a generous provider of bursaries.

In January 1853, Baxter wrote to Hodgkinson, challenging him to make a public declaration of his disapproval of Tractarian views. This was precisely what the Diocesan Committee had pressed upon Reed eight years before, but Hodgkinson refused. He offered to answer any charge Baxter cared to put about any particular example of his teaching, but realised that what the evangelical party meant by 'Tractarianism' by this stage in the long dispute was any theological view they did not share. Divisions deepened when, at the inaugural meeting of the York branch of the Church of England Education Society – an organisation set up in 1851 to counter the High Church tendencies of the National Society – Baxter publicly attacked not only Hodgkinson but also Miss Cruse for Tractarian leanings. Hodgkinson took to the press and launched a vigorous correspondence in the *Yorkshire Gazette*, acknowledging that his views on baptism were unlikely to appeal to the Evangelicals since they were as intent upon evading the plain meaning of the prayer book service as some Tractarians seemed to be in evading the Thirty-Nine Articles. The December 1853 meeting of the Dioceses Committee was rancorous and fully reported in the press. The Board asked the Archbishop and the Bishop of Ripon to hold a full enquiry and to report the result, and their 'deliberate opinion as to the general character of the doctrines taught in this institution'. In effect, Hodgkinson and Miss Cruse were on trial for heresy.

They emerged with credit at the end of January 1854. Hodgkinson faced five charges dating back to the 1850 sermon and including accusations made by ex-students about his course on the Thirty-Nine Articles. He defended himself as sturdily as ever against any Roman tendencies and admitted that in the June 1850 sermon he should have used more guarded language. The charges against Miss Cruse were derisory. One was based on hearsay that she supported a Tractarian clergyman who had been deposed from his London living as a Romaniser; she made clear that she had praised his pastoral care for a college student. The other was that she had used a Tractarian pamphlet and passed it to a student; it emerged that the Diocesans thought the pamphlet unobjectionable and that it had been her sister Catherine, not herself, who had used it. To the general accusation that the York and Ripon Diocesan Training Schools were 'distrusted' Hodgkinson and Miss Cruse had only to quote the pressure for places in both. They were exonerated and a full statement of the findings of the enquiry was printed and tabled at the August meeting of the College Committee. Hodgkinson then published his own pamphlet and announced that he would be resigning the Principalship having accepted the Headmastership of Louth Grammar School, where he had been a pupil. He insisted that he had not sought the post, that it had been offered just as he had brought to a successful conclusion a four year defence of his work at York. A main thrust of his pamphlet was that the Training Schools should have a 'Diocesan Character' and not reflect the views of a particular party. He claimed, with some force, that in spite of defections from the Committee the College 'had never been in so prosperous a condition'.

Hodgkinson held the Headship at Louth for 22 years and enhanced his reputation as a scientist and Alpinist, publishing papers for the Alpine Society and inventing scientific equipment for schools. Within its first 12 years the York and Ripon Training School for Men had harassed and disillusioned two able Principals who took their talents elsewhere with conspicuous success. Miss Cruse persevered, apparently undaunted.

CHAPTER III

Expansion – and Migration 1854-1863

THE NEW PRINCIPAL WAS the Revd Hugh Robinson MA who was 34. He had graduated from Cambridge in 1842, read law at the Middle Temple and been called to the Bar in 1846. He was then ordained and became successively Curate at Wallasey, Vicar of Holy Trinity, Preston, and Vicar of Burley in Wharfedale, where he had taken a keen interest in the local schools. He appeared to the appointing committee to have no Tractarian inclinations and shortly after his appointment, Baxter, Whytehead and other evangelical defectors from Hodgkinson's time, returned to the Management Committee. Throughout his principalship the Ripon and York College flourished, as did most of the Church Training Colleges. Yet when he took over two fundamental and related dilemmas for the colleges were apparent. They remain into the 1990s and can probably no longer be resolved.

The first was that, with the rapid development of sprawling areas of English industry and manufacture, many of the early Church schools and most of the colleges were already considered by powerful advocates to be in the wrong places. W. F. Hook had put the matter bluntly in 1846 in an open letter to the Bishop of St David's 'On the Means of Rendering more efficient the Education of the People'. The Ripon and York Committees might have taken particular note of his views since he wrote as Vicar of Leeds, in the Ripon Diocese, from the heart of their nearest industrial centre. Acknowledging both the inadequacy of the Voluntary System and the heroic efforts of many clergy, he questioned the location of the majority of National Society Schools:

> . . . But where are these schools to be found? In localities inhabited by the wealthy: in districts where the clergy are not only active but numerous and influential, and where a laity possessing leisure are willing to discharge gratuitously the office of teachers and inspectors. But go to our poorer districts, not to our towns but to our manufacturing villages, and there you

perceive how great our educational destitution is. I am myself surrounded by a district containing 250,000 souls, exclusive of the large towns, in which there are thousands uneducated, or receiving an education worse than none.

His conviction that the Church should co-operate with the State in bringing education rapidly to the neglected manufacturing heartlands also addressed the second key issue and was roundly rejected by G. A. Denison, Archdeacon of Taunton in an open letter to Gladstone, as member for the University of Oxford. It was headed unequivocally: 'Church Schools and State Interference' and followed by 'Seventeen Reasons Why the Church of England May have Nothing to do with a Conscience Clause'. His titles make comment or quotation superfluous but he was answered in measured terms by Revd Richard Dawes in 'Remarks occasioned by the Present Crusade against the Educational Plans of the Committee of Council 1850'. Dawes declared that many church schools served the nation badly because too many clergy wished to limit their pupils to an acquaintance with the Bible, the Catechism and a few manual skills 'as a means to preserve the rural status quo'. He was convinced that co-operation with Government was the Christian way forward and he arraigned the National Society for having

> . . . in some measure been a national deception, retarding the cause of education rather than advancing it, by taking the place of a better system.

The details of the protracted argument of the 'Management Clauses' of the 1846 Committee of Council Minutes, need not detain us but the core issue is central to the history of all the Church Colleges and their position in the 1990s.

As we have seen, the Minutes of the Committee of Council for 1846 introduced more favourable conditions for the Colleges, and enabled the most enterprising of them to flourish through the 1850s. But there was a price to pay. Government had not forgotten its defeats at the hands of the High Church party and Kay-Shuttleworth was determined that schools receiving grant aid should not be dominated by the local clergy. He therefore insisted that, whichever of four patterns of management was chosen by a school there must be lay members involved, and that the rights of conscience on behalf of pupils who were not from Church of England families must be respected. He had not budged from this conviction since accepting office with the government and had written in 1843 to Lord John Russell:

> When your Lordship and Lord Lansdowne in 1839 appointed me Secretary of the Committee of Council on Education, I understood the design of your Government to be to prevent the

successful assertion on behalf of the Church then put forth, for a purely ecclesiastical system of education . . . I understood your Lordship's government to determine in 1839 to assert the claim of the civil power to the control of the education of the country.[1]

He had openly avowed this policy for seven years, and even the historian of the National Society, H. J. Burgess, was later to assert in respect of the 1846 Management Clauses,

The attitude of the Committee of Council, influenced as it was by its Secretary's opinions, was therefore logical, straightforward and firm.[2]

It is ironic that a key influence on the decisive vote by the National Society, and so on the future of Anglican Training Colleges, was Henry Manning who would shortly leave the Church of England for Rome. He had written in exasperation to Sidney Herbert in October 1848:

What a mess Kay Shuttleworth is making. You see that the Committee of the Privy Council have refused the terms of the National Society and I must declare my hope that the Church will set to work again as in 1839 to do its own duty and refuse with an absolute firmness all share and entanglement in Government education. This has been my one unchanging conviction for ten years.[3]

He complained that the Church was divided – which it was – and powerless – which at that time, it certainly was not – and that it was allowing 'its education' to fall under the dominance of the State 'by force of petty bribes and low cunning' – a description of government support which is no longer fashionable. Manning shared with the Wilberforces a lofty view of the Church's obligations and rights in education, especially during Sir James Graham's unsuccessful attempts, in the 1840s, to obtain parliamentary approval for undenominational religious education.[4] The arguments on both sides are well summarised in his further letter to Herbert in 1849. Its final, ringing prophecy has been fulfilled:

. . . A word about Education. I think the subject in a very mischevious position. The Committee of Council and the National Society have suspended their correspondence on account of disagreement.

The National Society has already gone beyond the sense of the Church at large, and is in a middle position which the Government will not accept nor the Church ratify. I am afraid we shall have mischief either way. A break with government would be most mischevious; only less so than a giving in to them. My belief is that the Minutes of Council at this moment, if accepted by the Church will in due time transfer the whole 'material' of the Church education to the control of the government of the day. This we can never yield. Unhappily 'practical men' will look at nothing but money, efficiency, and the facts of today. They will not examine principles, tendencies and future consequences. Therefore some of our best men are, if not approving at least assenting parties to the government schemes.

Now for my own part I am where I was ten years ago . . . The state refuses to build churches, found bishoprics, support missions. I am more than content at its refusal. I would rather it were consistent and would refuse to give money for Church schools except upon the laws and principles of the Church . . . The theory of 'joint foundation' will I believe, bring us into future entanglements out of which the Church, or a portion of it, will escape with the portion and fortunes of the weaker party; and the remainder will be secularised.[5]

Manning himself at the stormy eight hour Annual Meeting of the National Society in May 1849 unwittingly assisted the fulfilment of his own forebodings.

There is no evidence in the records of the Ripon and York college to suggest that Committee members were alert to this historic confrontation. They might have been better occupied devoting more attention to it and less to the liturgical irregularities of Reed and Hodgkinson.

The National Society meeting was chaired by the Archbishop of Canterbury and attended by 12 bishops, numerous peers and Gladstone. The debate has been well documented,[6] the crucial issue being the unresolved 'Management Clauses'. Denison had proposed uncompromising rejection of all the government proposals and appeared to have overwhelming support. Manning bided his time and, almost at the end of the meeting intervened in conciliatory style and secured acceptance of his amendment which, instead of dismissing outright any co-operation with government, implied the willingness of the National Society to consider any scheme of government support for schools and colleges which

> . . . shall allow the clergy and laity full freedom to constitute upon such principles and models as are both sanctioned and recommended by the order and the practice of the Church of England.

He persuaded Denison not to press his further amendment which had added uncompromisingly and in particular when they should desire to put the management of their schools solely in the hands of the Clergy and Bishops of the Diocese.

It seems curious now that Manning, so close to the authoritarianism of Rome, should have urged such a vulnerable Anglican compromise. He may have persuaded himself that he was not emasculating Denison's demands but rephrasing them diplomatically. He must have hoped that the government would interpret his formulation favourably. But he did not convince his confidant Bishop Wilberforce, who saw that Manning had counselled the National Society towards capitulation:

> My venerable relative I fear, is making a hollow truce, introducing a unanimity in words which does not in reality exist.[7]

That feeling will be familiar to those who 120 years later, were involved in the various college negotiations with government which led to wholesale closures.

Perception came slowly to Denison, and bitterly. Forty years later he wrote to Manning's biographer:

> I have never ceased to regard that day as the beginning of the surrender of the Church school into the hands of the Civil Power. It is impossible for me now, so long afterwards, to call it anything else, and the recollections cannot be otherwise than very painful to me. What the Cardinal may regard the cause I contended for now to be, I have no concern with, all I know is that it was *first* by his hand that the Church school in England was destroyed.[8]

The arguments for and against acceptance of government grants for church schools were to simmer on until the 1870 Education Act, but serious dispute about grant for the Training Colleges virtually ended with the National Society's acceptance of Manning's proposition. Kay-Shuttleworth had reluctantly concluded in 1843, at the end of his educationally successful Battersea experiment, that it was not possible for a Voluntary agency to maintain a substantial institution without grant-aid. In the 1850s the Roman Catholic and Methodist churches, with much smaller investment in schools than was possible for the Church of England, accepted the management conditions required in return for grant, not only for their schools but also for their first training colleges, the Catholic Notre Dame College in Liverpool and the Methodist's Westminster College. The Congregationalists held out against school grants throughout the 1840s and in 1852, with support from some Wesleyans, Baptists and Independents, founded Homerton College which for a few years flourished unaided. It then ran into increasing difficulties and finally applied successfully for grant in 1867.

Robinson's first full year, 1855, seems to have passed uneventfully with a small increase in student numbers. Financial support was still far from satisfactory however; student success in the certificate examinations was modest and so brought in little increase in fee payments. The two dioceses were still each having to find at least £300 annually to keep the colleges solvent and a pastoral letter from the Archbishop early in 1856 produced only £100. The Annual Meeting of the York Diocesan Society in April 1856 was a gloomy occasion. Canon George Trevor protested against the failure to organise proper financial support and pointed out that only a solitary layman was present. The May meeting of the Committee of the two Dioceses agreed that having dismissed Charlton the Master of the Practising School at the end of the previous year to save money, they must now dismiss two more tutors, some of whose duties could be undertaken by 'occasional lecturers'. They also proposed to reduce the Principal's salary from £500 to £400.

These draconian measures – which were never in fact implemented – stung Robinson into action. The management structure was obviously failing and a special meeting of some 30 members of the two Dioceses was convened in November with the Earl of Carlisle in the chair. It seems to have been carefully planned. The Headmaster of St Peter's School proposed that a sub-committee be immediately appointed to oversee the affairs of the two Training Schools for a year. In spite of protests that the constitution did not permit such delegation – which was true – the proposal was carried. Lord Wenlock immediately moved a prepared list of members of the new committee including the Archbishop and the Bishop of Ripon, four Archdeacons, two active laymen and the redoubtable Vernon Harcourt who had had little to do with the college since its early years. This group had met by mid-December and, having elected Vernon Harcourt as its permanent chairman, became known as 'Mr Harcourt's Committee'. It virtually conducted the business of the College for the next four years.

In January 1857 it circulated a report of the financial position, revealing that the combined overdraft was £926 and bound to increase by the end of the year. The York Board owed Ripon £185 and would become increasingly indebted unless the shares of financial obligation were made proportional to population, Ripon being the more populous Diocese. Running expenses had increased by £720 a year since 1851 but staff salaries had taken up little of this. Food and coal costs alone accounted for an additional £520. When the report was presented to a meeting of the two Dioceses in April, Vernon Harcourt was severe on the previous administration. From 1842 to 1849 control seems to have been shared by monthly meetings held at York and quarterly meetings alternating between York and Ripon; the smaller monthly committee did most of the work. In 1849, after several disagreements, the monthly meetings had ceased, but the quarterly meetings then seem to have lost their grip on college business. By 1856, said Vernon Harcourt,

> The results of this administration were, the Bank overdrawn and charging interest, the institution involved in heavy liabilities which it had no means of paying, the debt increasing annually, the Annual subscriptions in the Diocese of York reduced to the extent of £100 in two years, the Yorkshire Queen's scholars emigrating to other schools, the Managing Committee without any purpose and having lost the confidence of all within the institution and without.

It was a fierce indictment but the constitutional opposition was not yet quelled. A rump of the deposed Committee convened a quarterly meeting at Ripon as the terms of the November coup did not prohibit it. They soon recognised however that they had no power and only a formidable overdraft to discuss. Their last throw was to try to associate the two factions with the perennial Tractarian/Evangelical split; the Yorkshire press had several field days.

The Ripon meeting was denounced as the Tractarians trying to regain control; the rump responded by blaming the Evangelicals for ever having left the Committee and condemning the proposals of the new Harcourt Committee as likely to abandon sound religous training 'in subserviency to the secularising effect of government gold'. The high church Canon Trevor claimed that his quarrel with Vernon Harcourt was not about shades of churchmanship but whether the management of the colleges should be 'representative or official and aristocratical'. He then spoilt his case by confiding to the *Yorkshire Gazette* that, whereas the committee had known where they stood with Hodgkinson, who had been appointed by the Archbishop and the Bishop of Ripon, Robinson had been selected by a balanced committee but

> . . . no one on the committee knows at this moment whether he is a High, Low or Broad church man.

Robinson responded in the next edition:

> I have no wish either to conceal or disavow my theological predilections and I believe the majority of the committee of management are by this time fully aware that I do not very strongly sympathise with that class of churchmen of which Canon Trevor is himself a distinguished ornament.

This did not dissuade Trevor and his party from questioning the legality of some severe cuts in College morning and evening prayers which Robinson had made with the Archbishop's permission. They claimed that prayers were being sacrificed to leave more time for the pursuit of certificates, and revived the allegation, from which most colleges suffered periodically, that men were being sent out too highly qualified to be willing to stay long in village schools.

But Vernon Harcourt had made a formidable case and the April meeting of 41 members approved the financial report by a small majority. It also accepted Harcourt's recommendation – crucial in the history of the college – that on the present and predictable financial base, only the Men's Training School could be supported at York. He insisted that if the Women's Training School was to survive it must be in a completely new building and that this should be in the Ripon diocese though managed by representatives from both Ripon and York. The vote in favour of Harcourt's report ended the long altercation and the chairman of the meeting, Robert Bickersteth the new Bishop of Ripon, ruled that no further quarterly meetings were to be held. In May 70 members attended the Annual Meeting of the York Diocesan Society and elected a strongly evangelical list of members to the Committee of the two Dioceses. Trevor lost his seat and the rout was complete.

The College could now look ahead with confidence, not least because Vernon Harcourt had so enthused his committee and other subscribers that by the end of 1857 the large debt had been paid off. The Archbishop contributed £200, Lord Wenlock £100 and there were many smaller contributions, again mostly from clergy. As there was also a rapid fall in the cost of food during the year, the college's financial position was transformed. So apparently were the attitudes of potential recruits, particularly those good enough to gain Queen's Scholarships. In 1856 there had been 39 men in residence in a college building with accommodation for 55; 23 of them were Queen's Scholars. In autumn 1857, with news no doubt abroad that the college's future seemed more promising, the figures were, Total Roll 60, Queen's Scholars 44. In 1858 recruitment reached an unsurpassable peak with 75 students in residence, all of them Queen's Scholars. It was held close to this level through the rest of Robinson's principalship, the figures for 1862, for example, being 77 on roll, 76 Queen's Scholars.

Robinson was therefore able to propose a substantial programme of building and improvements which the Harcourt Committee at once approved. A new cloister wing with bell turret (long since removed) was completed by November 1858, providing an additional lecture room and 29 new dormitory cubicles. The sick rooms were then restored to their proper use, having been taken over for student accommodation, and 25 men who had been boarded out in nearby houses could reside in the college which now had room for 82 students. They could luxuriate in a heating system installed at the same time, in response to HMI comment in 1857 that the college was 'fearfully cold'. The cost of these substantial extensions was £875, of which the Committee of Council paid £425 in grant. The two dioceses divided the remainder between them and might have been relieved had they known that this was to be the last capital project at York for the rest of the century. As soon as it was complete, Vernon Harcourt resigned from the committee which he had led so successfully. Throughout his career he was an originator of projects rather than a sustainer and the quieter life now in prospect for the college probably had little attraction for him.

The college was now dependent on government funding to an extent which made the ongoing argument about the wisdom and morality of accepting State support seem superfluous. In 1854 the average level of government funding to the colleges had been 30%. By 1859 it was over 70% and the York and Ripon college figure was a startling 89%. This was partly because student success in the national certificate examinations increased greatly throughout Robinson's principalship. In 1858 it brought in an additional £709 which rose by 1861 to £1,230. The contribution required from the Diocesan Boards was therefore much reduced and it seemed that for the first time in 20 years the Boards would be able to concentrate on the funding of schools.

That hope was shortlived, yet the rising standards in the college must have been gratifying. They owed something to Robinson and his colleagues, but probably more to HMI Moseley and his. By 1855 Moseley had ensured that the curriculum was standardised throughout the colleges. He had regularly complained that too many college courses were superficial and irrelevant to the needs of elementary school teachers. He circulated to the colleges a draft curriculum closely resembling what had normally been advertised at York and elsewhere with the variation that second year students dropped Catechism, Liturgy, Euclid and Algebra, and took up Physical Science and Higher Mathematics. Contrary to Hodgkinson's policy, Robinson at first increased the number of students taking Latin, but then in response to Moseley's scepticism, reduced it again. He strongly favoured the introduction of English Literature as a major study and wrote a spirited article about it, much in advance of most educational thinking at the time, for *MacMillan's Magazine* in 1860. Yet he did not press the issue in the college, contenting himself with establishing a Literary Society.

By 1861 the Committee of Council Minutes show York results as well above the national average, and particularly good in Teaching Method and Geography. The improvement in Teaching Method may have been due to the reorganisation of the college and the provision of a Model

School. In 1856, HMI Frederick Temple, the future Archbishop, had reported adversely on the national emphasis on oral methods, with little support from written and pictorial course material – maps, books and apparatus. Robinson had already carried the point with the College Committee at York, increased the book and map stock, and set up a small museum. In 1857 Temple and Watkins, in a favourable report on the college pressed for the provision of a Model School in which students could closely observe good classroom practice. They criticised the standard of the Practising School, suggesting that with a continuous procession of student-teachers providing most of the tuition no Practising School could be expected to produce high quality education. The collapse of the Yeoman School in 1858 gave Robinson the chance to act on the HMIs advice. The school had failed to attract the expected numbers of pupils into residence, in spite of a lowering of fees, and in 1858 was merged with the Archbishop Holgate's Grammar School, to form an entirely separate institution on the Lord Mayor's Walk site. This released the former Middle School classrooms in the college for use as a new Model School; it was run as a department of the college until 1903 when a separate new building was provided.

Such Model Schools were intended to provide good examples of ordinary elementary schools but at York, and elsewhere, very soon attracted an above average middle-class clientele. As Robinson subsequently observed to the Schools Enquiry Commissioners,

> The fee was a little above the fee charged in elementary schools in York, and the consequence was that boys of a better class came, they stayed longer and were more regular and we carried the education higher.[9]

By 1861 the school had 111 pupils; 65 of their fathers were in business on their own account, and 17 were in professions. Only 29 were employed by others. Not surprisingly, HMI Cowie 'did not know a more promising school anywhere' but it was hardly fulfilling the National Society's aspiration 'to educate the poor . . .' and appeared for a while to be in danger of losing its grant. Robinson stressed that students were never allowed to teach in the Model School,

> although I always used to make them attend during their second year's residence . . . and observe the processes, take notes, and make abstracts and send in, either to myself or the Master of Method, a written account of the organisation and working of the school.

As well as pressing for the establishment of Model Schools HMI Temple had demanded a higher status for the 'Normal Master', a post which Moseley had required all colleges to institute, to improve classroom practice. Reports on York in the late 1850s speak highly of the work of Revd E. B. Biddick the Normal Master, and in 1859 he received the unusual accolade of having his Teaching Practice Notes for Students reproduced in full in the Committee of Council's Annual Report, as a model for other colleges. Robinson's own high value for the careful preparation of students in classroom skills probably influenced the appointment of Biddick to the Vice-Principalship in 1862.

The high standards in Geography were owed to Revd G. Rowe, who had been Vice-Principal for a brief period in the early 50s but gave up that post when he married and moved out of college residence, in 1855. After Temple's national report every college tutor was required to present at least one lecture a year before HMI, and the reports on Rowe's Geography sessions were always enthusiastic. He also produced a series of four Geography text books on *The Colonial Empire of Great Britain*, published by the SPCK for Training Colleges. Another able tutor was James Birchall, originally appointed as Drawing Master but later specialising in History, who also published a sucessful series of text books.

The production of such specialised texts reflected the rapid expansion of the Training Colleges. Whereas in 1845 the Committee of Council had listed 22 colleges with a total of nearly 700 students, by 1858 there were 33 colleges with over 2,000 students, 1,675 being Queen's Scholars, attracting the substantial grants on which the new-found financial stability of most colleges was based.[10] Eight colleges now had more than 100 students. They were Battersea, Borough Road, Cheltenham, St Mark's Chelsea, The Home and Colonial College, Westminster, Whitelands and – combining the Men's and Women's Schools – York. Having begun with a single student in 1841, the York and Ripon College had become one of the strongest in the country. But a decade of optimistic expansion was to end on a sobering note.

In 1857 the parliamentary education vote had risen to £541,233 and reactionary voices questioned how much more could be afforded. In 1858 a Royal Commission was announced under the chairmanship of the Duke of Newcastle,

> To enquire into the present state of education in England and to consider and report what measures, if any, are required for the extension of sound and cheap elementary instruction to all classes of people.

The Newcastle Commission is important to the history of the college partly because of the drastic effect of the legislation which followed its report, and partly because Robinson gave evidence. He is quoted at such length in the Newcastle Report as to suggest that he may have had an influence on the recommendations and saved the colleges from even sterner subsequent measures. The Report was the first comprehensive survey of English elementary education and it ended a decade in which a succession of education bills had been wrecked on the denominational issue and no conclusive legislation achieved. This had probably been bad for the schools, but the colleges had prospered under larger grants and a system of surveillance which guaranteed inspection by HMI of the college's own religious denomination. In 1860, the year before the Newcastle Report was published, a parliamentary exchange occurred which could not have cheered the colleges. Robert Lowe, Vice-President of the Committee of Council for Education and effectively Chairman of the Education Department as it was now called, was asked by Sir John Pakington during a Commons debate whether he could trust the judgement of his inspectors. 'Certainly not' he replied and added his opinion that, partly because of the good nature of the inspectors, government grants could not be equitably distributed solely on their recommendations. Lowe's predecessor had already perturbed the Commons by assuring the House that he had never known an inspector report a school to be so bad that it ought not to receive State aid. This, he said, was entirely predictable under a denominational system, since no HMI would wish to penalise the schools of his own religious persuasion.[11]

Robinson seems to have been questioned searchingly by the Commissioners about the accusations levelled from the earliest days of the Training Colleges, that their products were arrogant and educated beyond the needs of the elementary school classroom. He was staunch but perceptive in defence of the students:

> They naturally think more of what education has made them than of what it first found them. They easily lose sight of the fact that they have risen from a very humble social position and they crave for that status which education seems generally to secure. I think too that in some cases they are too apt to forget that they owe the culture they have to the public provision made for them . . .
>
> It is not unlikely that the position of a pupil-teacher may tend to generate a somewhat pretentious manner of thinking and acting; and still more true is it that self-sufficiency is the inherent and constitutional fault of youth, and the great majority of our trained and certificated teachers are very young. It would however be unjust to stigmatise trained teachers as *specially* and *par excellence* a conceited set of men. I can bear testimony to the fact that the present class of pupils are a very manageable body of young men. They are not free of some of the follies of youth, but

they have little opportunity and, with very few exceptions, no great tendency, to indulge in its vices . . .

I believe this body of men to be sound at heart, anxious to do their duty faithfully, loyal to their country and in sympathy with those they have to instruct. Time will mellow the roughnesses and singularities of the class, and those who best know the disadvantages against which they have had to struggle, and the trials and difficulties of the work they have to do, will be most ready to acknowledge their merits and most willing to excuse their failings . . . They are mostly selected from a class which has been very little in contact with refinement and self-control, or delicate appreciation of what is elevated and honourable.[12]

Until the College magazine was started in the 1890s there were few recorded impressions of the quality of student life. Robinson's Newcastle Commission evidence is the most valuable single source. The routine he describes was oppressively gregarious. The first year and second year students were taught quite separately, each in their own lecture room; there was a Common Room 'for collective musters and for general purposes' and all meals were taken together in the dining hall, with resident staff dining at a high table. Each student had a separate 'dormitory' (cubicle) but was not allowed into it during the day. Robinson obviously regretted this, realising that many students would have welcomed the opportunity for private study.

They study together, they take all their meals together, they occupy a common room in the intervals of recreation, they have no privacy, they are scarcely ever alone, except when in bed.

The timetable had not changed since the 1840s, still running from 5.30 am to 10.00 pm, with virtually every hour occupied. Discipline was maintained through monitors appointed by the Principal, who told the Newcastle Commissioners:

No set of young men of the same age, as far as I know, are kept under such close restraint . . . Nowhere probably among a body of young men preparing for the business of life is there so little idleness and dissipation . . . It cannot be good for young men to be made to pass through this phase of schoolboy life . . . There is little opportunity for self-recollection or private meditation; little opportunity for the practice of private religious exercises. They would be grievously disappointed who expected to find in the majority any settled habits of devotion or any great religious earnestness.

Robinson's own most formative educational experience had been at Cambridge, and it is not surprising that he thought that his York students lacked interest in political argument, secular or religious. He believed that they suffered from a passive regime in which they spent too much time listening and transcribing. There was, for instance, a lecture course on School Management in which copious notes were dictated about timetabling, choosing textbooks, rewards and punishments, and the various subject methods. Robinson was sceptical:

> As the disquisitions of ancient philosophers on the nature of Virtue did little to make men virtuous, so it is possible that the lectures of a Normal Master on the art of teaching may sometimes be found of little avail to make men teachers . . . The Master has been 'crammed' himself and so he 'crams' his pupils . . . Vast demands are made on the memory, little is done for the improvement of the judgement or reasoning powers . . .
>
> In very few cases is a taste for reading formed among trained pupils. It will not I suspect be found that schoolmasters are a very studious or a very literary body. They themselves say that the weary round of textbooks, note-books, technical manuals etc which forms the main part of their intellectual nutriment at college has the effect of destroying their appetite for study.

The Newcastle Commissioners seem to have been persuaded by their more generous witnesses, among whom Robinson was outstanding, that the nation's teaching force deserved at least moderate respect. But the pressure for economy implicit in their very terms of reference, as well as in wider government attitudes offered little hope for the more liberal curriculum and daily routine which Robinson advocated. Their General Report pronounced the teachers sent out from the Training Colleges to be 'Quite good enough' but stressed the need

> to find some constant and stringent motive to induce them to do that part of their duty which is at once most important.

They felt that many teachers transmitted too much irrelevant information and did not give enough attention to the repetitious routine skills needed by younger pupils.

> Whilst it appears to be proved that the character of the teachers is greatly raised by their training, and that they are altogether a superior class to those who preceded them, it is equally clear that they fail to a considerable extent, in some of the most important duties of elementary school teachers . . . The children do not generally obtain the mastery over elementary subjects which the school ought to give. They neither read well nor write well . . . They learn their arithmetic in such a way as to be of little practical use in common life.

The report rejected the accusation most frequently levelled against the teachers trained by the colleges:

> Other complaints are that the trained teachers are conceited and dissatisfied. The first we do not believe . . . The second we admit to a certain degree.[13]

And as Robinson had testified, the teachers had much to be dissatisfied about.

The Newcastle Report was published in 1861, debated in Parliament in 1862 and translated into new legislation for the education service in 1863, by which time other major changes were in train for the York and Ripon Colleges. Robinson did not wait for the new order. In August 1863 he accepted from the Duke of Devonshire the incumbency of Bolton Abbey. HMI Cowie's report for the year paid tribute to his 'broad and liberal views, carried into practice with vigour and determination'. His Newcastle Commission evidence enhanced his national reputation as an educator, and he was subsequently an outspoken witness to the Taunton Commission[14] which enquired into endowed schools from 1864 to 1868. When legislation followed he was selected, in 1869, as one of the three national Endowed Schools Commissioners and was the only one to be appointed a Charity Commissioner when the Endowed Commission was abolished in 1874. Like his two predecessors at York he still had much of his best work before him when he resigned from the College.

Meanwhile the Women's Training School had progressed steadily throughout Robinson's principalship. Miss Cruse seems to have worked amicably with him and standards improved in spite of the inadequate premises and staffing. The number of students in residence varied from 1854 to 1862, between 25 and 33 but the number of Queen's Scholars built up rapidly. In 1854 there were 11 Queen's Scholars and 11 second year students obtained certificates: by 1857 there were 25 Queen's Scholars and in 1860 there were 30. In response to continuous complaints from HMI, staffing was gradually improved. In 1854, Miss Sampson, who had gained a first class certificate the previous year, was retained as an assistant mistress, Catherine Cruse having been for some time wholly occupied with the Middle School. This was closed in 1858, at the same time as the collapse of the Yeoman School enabled the closure of the Middle School at the Men's College. But the demise of the Female Middle School seems to have been entirely on account of the resignation of Catherine Cruse, cryptically recorded in the Minutes of the Diocesan Board as 'due to broken health'. Successive reports make clear that the main teaching load continued to fall on Winifred Cruse, though the Committee of Council seems not to have regarded pedagogic skills as a high priority for Lady Superintendents, who were expected to look upon the formation of womanly character, the inculcation of habits of neatness and economy, the discouragement of all tendencies to vanity, love of dress, levity of demeanour, the establishment of fixed principles resting upon a basis of religious conviction, as the most important of all objects.

By 1859 however, HMI Cooke reported that the 30 Queen's Scholars in residence now had more variety in tuition, with Revd Rowe making a large contribution.

They are instructed by a superintendent who is head governess, a clergyman who lectures in divinity, geography and arithmetic, an assistant governoress, two masters – one for writing and drawing, one for music – a mistress of the practising school, and a housekeeper who teaches needlework (Miss M. Cruse). The instruction is thoroughly good.

Miss Cruse had now endured the Monkgate premises for 14 years and better prospects lay ahead. It had taken the York Diocesan Board a full year to convince the Ripon Board of the wisdom of Vernon Harcourt's scheme but in 1858 a suitable site was selected on the outskirts of Ripon and outline plans submitted, with requests for grant, to the Committee of Council. HMI accelerated the process with the last of many adverse reports on the Monkgate School, from which they actually threatened to withdraw grant on account of

the gross inadequacy of the premises in which the Female School was accommodated . . . quite without privacy and totally unfit for Queen's Scholars.

In 1859 the Committee of Council approved the plans by the Architects J. B. and W. Atkinson of York, for the new Women's College at Ripon and on 4 December 1860, after a dedication service in Ripon Cathedral, a Civic Procession led by the band of the Yorkshire Hussars moved, in steady rain, out to the new site where Bishop Bickersteth laid the foundation stone. The new building, which was to be ready for occupation by the summer of 1862, was described as

in the Italian style of architecture and has a centre, three floors in height, and two wings. It affords accommodation with separate bedrooms, for sixty students besides apartments for the Lady Superintendent, the governesses and the servants; and includes a large dining room, a lecture room, a committee room and classrooms.

HMI thought the design as good as any provincial college in the country and the building remained unaltered for the next 35 years. The total cost was £8,347.

Committee minutes show that much thought was given to the staffing adjustments that would be needed in both colleges when the women moved to Ripon. But the long-serving Lady Superintendent was not to see this promised land. In February 1862 the College committee was informed of the

> severe and alarming illness of Miss Cruse. She was at present in such a condition that no steps could be taken to provide for the future requirements of the school.

and in April the York Diocesan Board announced

> with the most sincere regret that the Lady Superintendent who had presided over the institution for the period of sixteen years had lately been visited with a severe and dangerous illness from which she had at the date of the report only partially recovered, and feeling herself unequal to the task of organising and arranging the new and enlarged institution she had given notice of her intention to resign her office at the end of the current quarter. . . . The Board added that she had been eminently successful in her influence on the young persons entrusted to her charge and had been instrumental in rearing an efficient painstaking and conscientious body of teachers.

The college had, at last, in 1859 increased her salary by £20 – to one fifth of that paid to the Principal – but there is no record of any retirement gratuity, nor any evidence that she received a pension though, having served more than the required 15 years she presumably did. Not surprisingly, Mary Cruse, having seen her two elder sisters broken in health, informed the committee that she did not, after all, wish to join the staff of the new college at Ripon. With that brief statement all trace of the family which had served the Women's College so well, disappears from the record. We know that Winifred Cruse died near Bristol in 1868.

The 32 students moved to the new Ripon College in September 1862, to be greeted by the newly appointed Principal and Chaplain, Revd George Sheffield. He had been Chaplain and Secretary of a 'public institution in London' and his wife was also appointed 'to take charge of the domestic concerns of the establishment as Lady Superintendent'. They seem to have made an energetic and popular start, but in October Sheffield was taken ill and died within a few days. The first City ceremony the students of the new college attended was the funeral of their Principal. It was a sombre start.

CHAPTER IV

Separate Colleges 1863-1880

THE RIPON GOVERNORS MOVED swiftly to appoint a new Principal, the Revd Baynes Badcock, who took up his post in January 1863 at the age of 36. He came from Wells, Somerset, had graduated from St John's College, Cambridge in 1852, been ordained in 1853 and served a curacy at Harpurhey in Lancashire. He had then, from 1854 to 1863 been curate at St Mary's Battersea, where he became familiar with the work of St John's Training College which Kay-Shuttleworth had founded. He stayed at Ripon for 28 years and led the college through steady growth untypical of a difficult period for the colleges, especially in the 1860s. His strength appears to have been in cheerful steadfastness rather than originality and he maintained the severe regime in which Miss Cruse had persisted, without any significant alteration. The rising bell remained at 5.45 am and the day ran, well filled with organised activity, until 9.30 pm. The first HMI report repeated the customary criticism that the teaching staff was too small and insisted that 'above all a third governess is indispensible'. Badcock seems to have ensured this appointment without much fuss so that in the mid-1860s the staff for a college of 57 students, 49 of whom had been pupil-teachers, was recorded by the Committee of Council as:

Principal, Revd Baynes Badcock, £250 pa. Lived out
Lady Superintendent Mrs Sheffield, £60 pa. Lived in
Head Governess, Miss Taylor, £60 pa. Lived in
Second Governess, Miss Mustard, £56 pa. Lived in
Third Governess, Miss Wall, £43 pa. Lived in
Head of Practising School, Mrs Trinder, £90. Lived out

Mrs Trinder's remuneration resulted from the recruitment of 182 children to the Practising School, which she seems to have run with only occasional help from the governesses. Three living-in servants completed the college staff, on salaries of £20, one of them being full-time laundress.

Although the Principal received more than his four lady assistants put together, his salary was below the average for college principals

55

nationally and he was not housed. It was the combination of a relatively frugal salary bill, steady recruitment of college students and middle school pupils close to capacity, careful management, and a supportive Diocesan Board making its contributions promptly, which enabled the college to ride the storms which wrecked some colleges and seriously impeded others through the 1860s and 70s.

Among the teaching profession the new college quickly made its mark. By the end of 1865, it had sent out 151 certificated teachers, of whom 122 were known to be teaching in elementary schools in Britain; five had died in their early twenties. HMI seemed satisfied with the quality of training and predicted

> that in the course of time this Institution would supply the large important Diocese in which it was situated, with good school-mistresses.

In spite of the far-sighted suggestions made to the Newcastle Commission by Robinson and others, the syllabus at Ripon remained unadventurous throughout Badcock's long principalship. A surviving 'Government Syllabus for Female Candidates' during his last years, shows a small expansion of Miss Cruse's curriculum at Monkgate 40 years before, but little imaginative concern for its application to the education of young girls in elementary schools:

English First Year
1 The language, style and content of Milton's *Comus* and Johnson's *Life of Milton*
2 Parsing and Analysis of passages selected from *Comus*
3 An exercise in Composition on a familiar subject
   (A favourite topic being 'Good Manners')

English Second Year
The same syllabus, with Shakespeare's *Julius Caesar* and Macaulay's *Essay on Addison*

History First Year
Outlines of English History from 1066 to 1815

History Second Year
The History of England in the 18th Century with special reference to:
1 Constitutional changes and the most important laws
2 Military and Naval Enterprise
3 The industrial condition of the people
4 The Literature of the period
5 The extension of our Colonial Possessions

The syllabus for what we now call Home Economics might make modern Curriculum Developers wince. But at least it was practical, and consistent with their Lordships' advice to Miss Cruse and the governors of 1850, that 'the girls . . . have to be regarded as the future Mothers of English families.'

Domestic Economy

First Year
1 Food. Its composition and nutritive value; processes of mastication and digestion
2 Clothing: materials used. Cost, care and cleaning
3 The Home: its construction, furnishing, warming and cleansing
4 Fresh Air: ventilation; Processes of Respiration.

Second Year
1 Choice, preparation and due economy of articles of food in common use
2 Preparation of Food for the sick
3 Household Management; expenses and investment of money.

Sewing and Cutting out

First Year
1 The repair of any plain article of underclothing
2 The drawing of diagrams of a woman's chemise, and infant's shirt, a pair of drawers for a child of five years
3 The cutting out and making of these garments
4 The answering of questions on needlework

The Ripon students were given scope to exercise their domestic imaginations on their own college building, which came in for stiff HMI criticism from the first year. Poor classroom ventilation, inadequate fire-escapes and sparse provision of furniture and teaching equipment were all censured. The drainage gave problems for years; in 1863

A deputation of local residents arrived to make complaint of the injury sustained by the imperfect drainage from the institution.

and three years later, after an epidemic of sore throats, HMI ordered that

Chloride of lime be frequently poured down all the sinks and drains connected with the Institution.

HMI seem to have taken the Diocesan connection of the college seriously and to have had touching faith in episcopal intervention. Their report for 1863 recorded,

57

We brought up all these points and many others for the consideration of the Committee. The Bishop, who has always taken the greatest pains to improve the Institution, and whose Lady visits it frequently, to the great benefit of the inmates, was in the Chair, and we have reason to believe that our recommendations will be carried into effect.

The committee endorsed their reverence by deciding, in relation to another recommendation,

That the crops to be raised in the college garden be left to the decision of the Lord Bishop.

HMI Canon Tinling, the chief visitant through the 1860s, frequently complained about the lack of amenities for the students:

I shall be glad to see the students derive more benefit from the garden; at present it is used mainly for growing potatoes (presumably the episcopal choice!) whereas it might be made picturesque and be used as an exercise ground and a place of amusement.

The committee responded cautiously in 1864, resolving 'That some plants to the amount of £1 be ordered for flower beds' and more expansively in 1869, when they laid the foundation of the superb grounds which generations of later Ripon students have enjoyed, agreeing that

Walks should be laid out, the shrubs and holly bushes planted at a cost not exceeding £10.

Comparison of accounts suggests that the purchasing power of the pound in the 1860s was roughly 100 times that of the 1990s.

Tinling also criticised the domitory arrangements, insisting that each student should have a chest of drawers, should not have to hang clothes in her sleeping cublicle and

should have a bath once a week, and hip baths or sponge baths should be purchased for that purpose.

The students were still required to do much of the domestic work and all their personal washing; not until 1874 did the committee resolve that they should no longer have to wash out and clean their own cubicles, and scrub the floors and stone steps of the college.

The quiet progress at Ripon during Badcock's early years was achieved in spite of the legislative aftermath of the Newcastle Report. The Commission's terms of reference had implied that economy was in the government mind. Only four years after its formal establishment, the new Education Department already deployed 127 civil servants and a budget of almost £1 million. Robert Lowe, and Gladstone himself, had expressed concern to the House at the relative lack of financial control over the Department, and in presenting the estimates for 1861 Lowe could already claim to have slowed the rate of expenditure. In introducing to the Commons his Department's response to the Newcastle Report – the Revised Code of 1862 – he warned that the Education estimates were in danger of becoming the instrument of vested interests. The new policy was founded on a stark forecast:

> I cannot promise the House that this system will be an economical one, and I cannot promise that it will be an efficient one, but I can promise that it shall be one or the other. If it is not cheap it shall be efficient; if it is not efficient it shall be cheap.[1]

In several of their recommendations the Newcastle Commissioners showed sympathy with this aspiration. Having examined a mass of detailed evidence, they had paid tribute to the work of the Committee of Council under Kay-Shuttleworth, but advised that its system of grants must be modified if a breakdown was to be avoided. They proposed that the State should continue to pay capitation grants, with additional grants for pupil-teachers, but that new payments should also be made from local rates. County and Borough education boards should administer the rate grants on the results of examinations which they would conduct in the secular subjects. The Commissioners were satisfied that the Voluntary system should remain the channel for government aid; they considered that universal compulsory education was neither possible nor desirable.

The only major recommendation of the Commission which Lowe's Education Department accepted was the linking of grant to the examination of school pupils and college students – soon stigmatised as 'Payment by Results'. Some recent commentators have argued that, far from introducing a new policy, Lowe was building on principles established by Kay-Shuttleworth and implemented by HMI Moseley and his team. HMI J. P. Norris, in his 1860 report to the Committee of Council, had urged that at least part of each school's grant should be assessed according to work completed:

> One step in this direction would be taken if the original character of the capitation grant were restored and if it were paid on account of those children only who attained a certain fixed standard of proficiency in reading, writing and arithmetic.

The idea had been taken up in the Newcastle Report, but Lowe and his colleagues now implemented it much more severely than the Commissioners had recommended. Schools were forced to run much more cheaply, and their teachers were already feeling less respected and rewarded even before further provisions of the Revised Code began to affect the teacher training system directly.

Under the new regulations for the Colleges all capital grants for new building or extensions were immediately suspended. Only the annual maintenance grants continued, and for Queen's Scholars, who now comprised three-quarters of the colleges' recruitment, payment was to be scaled according to student success in the examination at the end of the first and second years of the course. Since the 1846 regulations the grant had been £25 per year; it was now reduced to range from £13 to £20 for first year students and from £16 to £24 for second years, according to results achieved. For many colleges this immediately lowered the income from Queen's Scholars to a dangerous level. Other new regulations made teaching a less attractive prospect: the Code introduced a lower 'Fourth class' certificate, required a two year probation period following certification – after which a raising of the grade of certificate could be recommended, as long as the teacher had not moved post more than once in the previous five years – and removed automatic increments for certificated teachers. This last penalty was in direct contradiction to the Newcastle Commissioners deduction that some of the dissatisfaction among teachers probably resulted from the fact that

> Their emoluments, though not too low, rise too soon to their highest level.[2]

The Revised Code aroused prolonged protest in the national press, in pamphlets, at public meetings and in Parliament itself, and has been a rich source of controversy in educational journals ever since. Recent scholars have presented divergent interpretations of the motives behind Lowe's reforms and of their long-term effects, but there can be no doubting how the colleges and their supporters reacted at the time. HMI Matthew Arnold had told the Newcastle Commissioners that he considered pupil-teachers to be 'the sinews of English public instruction'. Seven years later he protested that the Revised Code had

> struck its heaviest possible blow against them; and the present slack and languid condition of our elementary schools is the inevitable consequence.[3]

Kay-Shuttleworth was even swifter and sharper in his denunciation. In his second long open letter to the Earl of Granville, in November 1861, he recounted the views of many school managers and teachers that the Code would destroy the existing system by cutting off two-fifths of the annual grant to schools, by greatly reducing the income of the training colleges, and by endangering the future number and quality of Queen's Scholars. In the considered opinion of all the Voluntary bodies it was bound, he believed,

> to introduce into the elementary schools a lower class of teachers, and to degrade the instruction in the schools.

Historians of individual colleges have documented the crippling impact of the Revised Code. Gent records an immediate decline in recruitment to St Mark's,[4] and Cromwell attributes the resignation of the Principal, Derwent Coleridge, to the financial crisis which resulted.[5] Pritchard shows that, at Westminster, the Methodist College, a rapidly rising recruitment was dramatically halted, and not resumed until after the Forster Act of 1870.[6] At Chester College, as at St Mark's, the long-serving first Principal, Rigg, resigned and Bradbury relates the immediate fall in Chester recruitment to the national statistics which showed that by 1866 there were only 1,600 candidates for places in all the colleges, where in 1862 there had been 2,500.[7]

In his history of Borough Road College, Bartle takes a longer view, claiming not only that the letter of the Code was 'devastating in its immediate effects' but that its spirit of 'Payment by Results' left an imprint on the college long after the worst effects of the code had been relaxed. He identifies it as the basic cause of the 'gulf in outlook' between the undergraduate at Kings or University College and the future elementary school teacher or tutor at Borough Road;[8] it is arguable that the 'gulf' persisted for more than a century until the credibility of the Bachelor of Education degree within an all-graduate profession, was at last established in the 1980s. At Culham College, Principal Ridgeway wrote to his chairman, Bishop Wilberforce in 1868, acknowledging the alarming state of recruitment to the college.[9] For 707 first year vacancies in the whole college system there were only 224 qualified applicants. If the popular London colleges filled their places – as he thought likely – there would be nine applicants left to share between the 23 other colleges!

Burgess in his history of the National Society, catalogues the effect on other colleges. Inevitably, and unjustly, the problem was most severe in those which had attracted the highest proportion of Queen's Scholars – till now regarded as an accolade. The flourishing Highbury College decided to close at once – the only demonstrable casualty of the Code – and transferred its students to the equally successful Cheltenham College to enable it to survive. For Bishop Otter College, Chichester, already beset with difficulties, the Revised Code and the resultant loss of income was the final blow. Recruitment fell to single figures and, as a college for men, it closed in 1867, though it was later to re-open and flourish as a college for women.[10]

Some educational historians have argued that the Revised Code was a deliberate attempt to reduce further that elusive college autonomy which is one of the themes of this study, and that its successful enforcement constituted a significant victory for the State in its struggle with the churches for control over education.[11]

Hurt takes the view that Lowe's main concern was to vindicate the right of the State to adjust the content of elementary education to meet the needs of contemporary society, and that although Lowe was impatient at the unnecessary expense of the denominational system, he never declared his aim outright because to have done so would have been political suicide. Lowe's own statement points, as we have seen, to the less subtle intention of applying economic control to education. In this he was later supported by Francis Adams who, in his classic study of 1882 observed that there had been

> a strong and just presumption that the efficiency and the utility of the system were not advancing in proportion with the cost.[12]

With all the advantages of hindsight, Rich produces perhaps the best summary of the effects and intentions of the Code, in relation to the Newcastle diagnosis:

> The growing pains of English elementary education were mistaken for a chronic disease, and a drastic remedy was applied . . . On the work of the training colleges its effects were disastrous. In spite of all their deficiencies they had been reaching out towards a liberal cultivation of the teacher. For the next twenty years they were sullenly to restrict themselves to mechanical taskwork, narrow in scope and low in standard.[13]

But the steady success of the new Ripon College was not achieved entirely against the odds. For 20 years a few far-sighted pioneers had been working to change the prejudices against the education of women which had for so long limited their opportunities to the point of oppression. In the 1840s the reconstituted Governesses Benevolent Institution had begun to offer rudimentary training – and therefore better prospects and status – to governesses, of whom there were by now some 25,000 in paid employment. In 1848 a group of Anglican churchmen and women founded Queen's College, Harley Street, with F. D. Maurice of Kings College as the first Principal, to provide more advanced classes for women. The fees restricted entry to women of at least moderate means, but entry was open not only to trained or intending governesses but to 'any young ladies who wished to come'. It was therefore different from Whitelands, the successful London Training College for women, and from the colleges of London University which had forestalled the admission of women – Kings by edict and University by neglect. The non-conformist college which was to become Bedford College was founded the following year, and further impetus to advanced education for women came in the 1850s from former Queen's College students Frances Buss and Dorothea Beale who gave powerful leadership to their influential schools, the North London Collegiate and Cheltenham Ladies College.

In 1857, just as the move of the Women's Training School to Ripon was being mooted, Miss A. G. (later Baroness) Burdett-Coutts wrote to Lord Granville of the Education Department, Leader of the House of Lords, asking his support for her pamphlet entitled *Remunerative and Honourable Employment for the Daughters of the Middle Classes, and Information as to the Government Plan for Promoting Elementary Education*. She had noted from her visits to schools that most schoolmistresses 'were children chiefly of parents whose condition in life was extremely humble' and believed that if more information about teaching prospects could be made available there might be a good response from 'the less favoured members of the middle class . . . more especially . . . orphans with but slender resources'. Granville encouraged her.

> Should the effect of your notice be to attract a large number of candidate teachers from the middle classes, I anticipate benefit to many of the young women themselves, by an improved position in life, and to our schools by an increased estimation attaching to the office of teachers.[14]

This deliberate courting of middle class recruits subsequently laid several of the Women's Colleges open to charges of snobbery which persisted well into the 20th century, but it helped to swell recruitment, notably at the Ripon College and at Bishop Otter College.[15]

So did the Taunton Commission of 1864-68, which Simon later described as 'the most determined and unceremonious of all educational enquiries'. The Commission's report was democratic in tone and devastating in exposure.

> The whole country has an interest in these endowments, and has a right to know how the property is used, and whether the results are commensurate with the means. If the endowed schools are not doing good they must be doing harm by standing in the way of better institutions. The public has a right to see that they are doing good and not harm.[16]

Miss Buss and Miss Beale gave trenchant evidence, as did Robinson from his experience of both the Men's and Women's Colleges at York. The Commissioners deplored the miniscule provision for the education of women and dismissed the

> long established and inveterate prejudice that girls are less capable of mental cultivation and less in need of it than boys; that accomplishments, and what is showy and superficially attractive are what is really essential for them . . . and that as regards their

63

relations to the other sex and the probabilities of marriage more solid attainments are actually disadvantageous rather than the reverse.[17]

They were incensed at the abuse of endowments, but remained convinced of their value in maintaining the voluntary principle in education. They demanded a thorough reorganisation of the system to correct the huge preponderance of endowments appropriated solely for boys' establishments which was

> felt by a large and increasing number of men and women to be a cruel injustice.

The opinion 'of men and women' mattered to the Commissioners. Considering that the Training Colleges, including Ripon and York, were to remain cloistered and in many senses 'private' institutions for another 100 years, one ringing passage from the Taunton Report deserved a better hearing than it got at the time. It still needs more frequent quotation today:

> We are convinced that it is vain to expect thoroughly to educate the people of this country except by gradually inducing them to educate themselves. Those who have studied the subject may supply the best guidance, and Parliament may be persuaded to make laws in accordance with their advice. But the real force whereby the work is to be done, must come from the people. And every arrangement which fosters the interest of the people in the schools, which teaches the people to look upon the schools as their own, which encourages them to take a share in the management, will do at least as much service as the wisest advice and the most skilful administration . . . The task before us is great . . . But even more than skilful contrivance it will need energy; and energy can only be obtained by trusting the schools to the hearty goodwill of the people.[18]

While the Women's College at Ripon flourished in spite of the Revised Code, the York College for Men foundered on it. When Robinson left, the governors offered the Principalship to Revd George Rowe, who had already served 10 years as tutor, Vice-Principal, and tutor again. It was a cautious appointment at a nervous time and the governors were to regret it. The prospect was far less inviting than Robinson had confronted nine years before. Rowe was the son of a London tailor, had won his way to St John's College, Cambridge, as a sizar at the age of 24, had held a country curacy for 18 months after graduating, and then came to the York College, where he was to serve the rest of his career. By the time he took over as Principal in September 1863, the Revised Code had ensured that government grant could no longer exceed 75% of any college's income. As we have noted, the figure for York had risen as high as 89% in 1859, so the financial crisis was immediate. Recruitment declined almost directly in proportion to national figures, but took longer than in most other colleges to recover. In 1862 there had been 7,963 male pupil-teachers nationally; 990 of them had passed the entrance examination for a college and 64 were in residence at York. By 1865 the national figures were at their lowest with only 5,032 pupil-teachers, 450 college entrants, and 48 students at York. National numbers then slowly improved but York's did not, so that in 1869 Rowe and the York Committee found only 29 students in residence, though the national entry had climbed back to 698 and the pupil-teacher force, at 7,332 was almost back to the 1862 figure, which it surpassed the following year.

The York numbers had continued to decline in spite of some softening of the Revised Code in new regulations of 1866, which increased grants both to Queen's Scholars and direct to the colleges. At the end of 1869 the York College reached probably the lowest point in its first 150 years, when the Committee enquired of the Chester and Durham Colleges – also in financial difficulties – whether some form of amalgamation might be negotiated. Considering the relative strengths of the York and Ripon campuses of the college 120 years later, it is sobering to reflect that if Forster and his colleagues had delayed their campaign for a new Education Act by only a year or two, the York College might well have closed, while Ripon progressed steadily.

Diocesan support for the York College was actually more generous and reliable from Ripon than from York. In 1864 both dioceses paid their share of £175, and in 1866 both paid £125, but in 1868 York could offer nothing while Ripon maintained its estimated £100 for the declining numbers. In 1869 York could rise to only £50 against Ripon's £100. Things came to a head at the York Annual General Meeting when Dean Duncombe protested that £57 per head per year was far too much to be spending on 'young men who were being trained merely as village schoolmasters' and proposed that the Diocese should sever its connection with the college. Any accusation of extravagance was unjust since York's running costs were known to be below the national college average; in fact Duncombe's proposal badly misfired. After further discussion it was agreed to propose to the Ripon Diocese that in future each diocese should manage its own Training School. This arrangement seemed to favour the York Diocese which over the previous five years had contributed £875 for the Ripon College and only £475 for the men at York. Ripon Diocesan Board accepted the proposal without contention however, a new Trust Deed was drawn up, and from 1871 the two colleges went their separate ways for the next 104 years. So a proposal for the York Diocese to abandon its half-share in the college had resulted in it assuming total liability at a time when many other dioceses were increasingly resentful of the growing burden of their colleges and when the Committee of Council report for 1865 had revealed that the church-going public had become monumentally apathetic. In a year which had seen the State contribute £96,166 to the maintenance of the Training Colleges, Church and Chapel collections for the colleges had totalled £42 for the whole country. Manning's Anglican optimism of 1839 that the Church would willingly bear the entire cost of teacher education had been utterly discredited.

Throughout this period of depressing economy the York Committee was not able to support Rowe with an adequate staff. Biddick, who had proved an able Vice-Principal, left to succeed Reed as Principal at Carmarthen and from 1864 to 1872 Rowe had five different Vice-Principals, all recently graduated and ordained, none staying more than two years. Throughout the decade the staffing of the Men's College at York was less generous than that for the Women's College at Ripon – belated compensation for Miss Cruse's lean years. It comprised five members all resident:

Principal	£400 per annum
Vice-Principal	£150
Assistant Master	£80
Practising School Master	£60
Matron	£40

Rowe had to contend with an even more bewildering succession of Assistant Masters: there were 12 different appointments in his first 11 years. Nearly all were newly qualified college students who could be paid only £40 a year until they obtained their certificates after two years when they were paid £60 and encouraged to move on. Similar staffing economies prevailed at Durham, Culham and other provincial colleges. Junior staff were unlikely to stay long for such low remuneration, especially with the prospect – as soon as they had obtained the coveted certificate – of a school headship with independence, a school house and £80 or £90 a year. Staff who stayed were likely to have little time or incentive to develop a more adventurous curriculum or teaching style. In 1870 Row gave 19 lectures each week and the Vice-Principal, Revd E. H. Smart, 21. The following year HMI Cowie reported that the Principal was overworked and the Vice-Principal – referred to as 'one of the officers' but easily identifiable from the description of his duties – was

> totally unsuited to the duties he had undertaken. He had evidently no conception of the educational needs of the men he was instructing and showed no power or sympathy with his audience or with his subject.

Smart promptly moved on, but within two years his successor – prophetically named Revd O. Churchyard – was found 'wanting in enthusiasm and vigour'. This time the College Committee got it right, appointing Revd G. W. de Courcy Baldwin who was to be a power in the college for 25 years.

Etherington provides a well-documented account of the curriculum and the professional training of the Model School,[19] which finally had its recognition as an Elementary School withdrawn in 1871 because of its middle-class clientele. The record reveals a dispirited and repetitive approach, still dominated by 'Payment by Results'. St Mark's Chelsea was probably representative at this time in having 27 full days of the teaching year devoted to examinations. By 1869-70 York and several other colleges were entering students for additional May examinations in Physical Geography, Mathematics and Chemistry. In 1872 Music examinations were initiated and for 10 years York men did particularly well, under the tuition of former student Joseph Stringer. The College was commended for excellent choral work and individual instrument tuition, and gained the best second year examination marks in the country in 1872. Further examination pressure came from the National Society's own required tests in Religious Knowledge and Training, coinciding with the seminal legislation of 1870 of which we must now take note.

A conviction that schooling would be good for everyone had been growing since the Newcastle Commissioners had rejected it in 1861. The principle of rate-aid for the building of schools was strongly supported by Forster and his colleagues in their 1870 proposals. This was certain, if accepted, to provide both the demand and the resources for a big expansion of the teaching force and therefore of the training system. In advocating that continuing balance between public support and private initiative which was crucial if voluntary colleges and schools were to survive, Forster stood firmly with the Taunton Commissioners:

> . . . we must take care not to destroy in building up – not to destroy the existing system in introducing a new one. In solving this problem there must be, consistently with the attainment of our object, the least possible expenditure of public money, the utmost endeavour not to injure existing and efficient schools . . . Our object is to complete the present voluntary system, to fill up the gaps, sparing the public money where it can be done without, procuring as much as we can the assistance of the parents, and welcoming as much as we rightly can the co-operation of those benevolent men who desire to assist their neighbours.[20]

Whatever his private altruism, Forster acknowledged that the country could not afford to turn down the financial contribution of the 'voluntary agencies' ie the churches; his public defence of the Bill rested more on economic and political pragmatism than philanthropy:

> We must not delay. Upon the speedy provision of elementary education depends our industrial prosperity . . . uneducated labourers – and many of our labourers are utterly uneducated – are for the most part unskilled labourers, and if we leave our womenfolk any longer unskilled, notwithstanding their strong sinews and determined energy, they will become overmatched in the competition of the world. Upon this speedy provision depends also, I fully believe, the good, the safe working, of a constitutional system.

Churchmen seem to have been as divided over the 1870 Bill as they had been over the 1833 subvention and the 1846 regulations. Hook and Pakington, for example, had consistently asserted that a system of rate-aided education through which secular instruction became the acknowledged responsibility of the State, need not preclude the maintenance or even the extension of doctrinal religious instruction. The Tractarian Denison and the Evangelicals Buxton and Close remained vehemently opposed and were supported by Shaftesbury, who, after a change of mind on the issue, confided to his diary

> The godless non-Bible system is at hand, and the Ragged schools with all their Divine policy, with all their burning and fruitful love of the poor . . . must perish under this all-conquering march of intellectual power . . . everything for time and nothing for eternity.[21]

The Guardian seems to have expressed the view of moderate Christians of all denominations, that the Bill seemed likely to sustain religious influence in education and would offer

> . . . all we need, 'fair play and no favour'. It is our own fault if we do not make use of the fair play and prove ourselves superior to the need of favour.[22]

Manning, now Cardinal Archbishop of Westminster, agreed and wrote to Gladstone:

> The formation of men is the work you have given to the school boards. God gave it to the parents . . . Let us all start fair in this race. Let every sect, even the Huxleyites, have their grant if they fulfil the conditions.[23]

In August 1870 the Forster Education Bill emerged from 28 days of parliamentary debate to a place in the Statute Book and the history of British education. It established, formally, a 'Dual System' through which the churches and school boards might together extend the work of education, either as partners or as rivals, according to particular times and circumstances. The State, through local boards, undertook to open its own schools only where existing voluntary schools were inadequate. The 'race' to which Manning had referred, was to last six months. This was the period agreed in the Commons, within which the voluntary agencies could improve, with government grants where appropriate, both the quality and quantity of their school provision, before any need for 'board schools' was assessed in each locality.

The denominations made remarkable progress in this short time. The Church of England applied for more than 2,000 building grants, most of them through the National Society, and the Roman Catholics and Nonconformists some 500. In the decade 1870 to 1880 the National Society raised £10m for school building and maintenance, compared with the £15m it had provided in the previous 56 years of its existence. Over the same period Board of Education Reports show that the number of aided denominational schools rose from 8,000 to 14,000 and the number of their pupils virtually doubled to two million. Historians have varied in their estimates of the direct impact of the Act on the Teacher Training system but there can be no disputing two of its effects. The colleges were encouraged to respond to the increased need for teachers in an expanding school service, and the status of teachers was enhanced in the consultations which led to the Act and in the much increased lay control of schools which followed it. Moreover the continuing denominational character of the colleges was ensured by the express injunction of the Committee of Council in 1871 that they were to be free to select their students

> on their own responsibility, subject to no other conditions on the part of the Education Department than those relating to age and suitability.

But a Dual System for school provision foreshadowed eventually a similar division of spoils in Teacher Training; it took another generation to evolve.

The York Diocesan Society responded promptly to the opportunities offered. In the first five years after the Act, 30 new Church Schools were provided in the East Riding. In the City of York seven new schools with 2,700 pupils had been opened by 1877. Ironically, this generous funding of school building was probably related to the previous decline in Diocesan funding for the College. For the best part of 30 years the local landowners had seen the needs of the College pre-empt Diocesan Board appeals for funds and they gradually wearied of that. The provision of schools, especially for their own villages, seems to have enthused them at last, and for the first time Diocesan subscription lists were not dominated by clergy contributions. The insistence of the 1870 Act upon greater lay involvement in school management was reflected for a while in the colleges as well; at York by 1873, the list of Vice-Presidents comprised 14 prosperous laymen and only six clergy, though Etherington records a gradual reversion to the clergy dominated pattern of management by the 1890s.

Following the 1870 Act student numbers at York improved rapidly. There were actually 80 students in residence in 1871 and for the next 10 years numbers remained well into the 60s. But Committee of Council Reports show that, except in Music the quality of student performance was usually below the national average. The new national HMI for the colleges was Revd T. W. Sharpe, a regular visitor to York who attempted in the mid 1870s to inject more vigour and variety into all Training College syllabuses, with only modest effect. There was progress in the School Management courses towards what we would now call a Child Development approach. But Sharpe, sceptical of the permission given for foreign language teaching to be expanded, thought that most colleges already tried to teach too many subjects, that there was, as ever, too much lecturing – much of it indifferent – and that students still had little scope for private study. In 1877 he savaged the York teaching practice facilities:

> The Practising School is a disgrace to the Institution. [He reported] that the furniture is poor in quantity and worse in quality, that the maps were ragged and that the offices were filthy and the floors out of repair.

Sharpe noted that at York the second year performance of students was frequently weaker than in the first year, though most other colleges maintained steady standards. Rowe claimed that the calibre of entry was low, reporting that in 1875 for instance, only 30 out of 48 candidates for the college had qualified for Queen's Scholarships. Sharpe analysed national trends and found that in 1878 and 1879 the York entry was actually better qualified than in many other colleges. He laid the blame elsewhere. In 1878, when the college's results in first and second year French and in second year Science, were the worst in the country it seemed clear that college management was admitting too many inadequately prepared students to the examinations. Sharpe had already recorded his diagnosis:

> He considered the teaching staff weak and that the Institution was most fortunate in having Mr Baldwin as its Vice-Principal and that the Normal Master was painstaking and very efficient.

In the following year he added to his denunciation of the Practising School severe criticisms of the distribution of college duties, the timetable and the examination results, but pointedly reaffirmed his approval of Baldwin as 'an excellent lecturer and disciplinarian'.

Such reports could have done little to improve morale in the college and in 1878 the second year students threatened to resign en masse unless Rowe's choice of a 'diligent but unpopular student' as monitor was withdrawn. The issue was aired in Committee and the student leaders were in fact expelled for failing to apologise for the revolt, but HMI Sharpe was quoted in the *Yorkshire Gazette* as considering that Rowe had been too lenient. Not surprisingly the examination results at the end of the year were again poor.

Sharpe's next report on the college in October 1879, refers to Baldwin as 'Principal' and to Rowe as 'Lecturer in Divinity, Physiology and Method' and claims that

> A marked improvement was observed in the bearing and behaviour of students.

The coup seems to have been accomplished discreetly, with no reference to it in Committee minutes, local or national, but Rowe had achieved the doleful and probably unique, distinction of having been relieved, successively of the Vice-Principalship and the Principalship of the same college. The Committee, having taken the unpalatable decision, treated him well. Not only did he remain on the staff, he also continued to occupy the Principal's house being described in 1881 as 'Lecturer in Geography and Physiology and House Steward'. Baldwin too seems to have been considerate and no appointment was made to the Vice-Principalship in his place. The general embarrassment did not last very long; Rowe died in residence in October 1882.

Student feeling on one of the most depressing aspects of this period is powerfully reflected in a reminiscence of S. Mills (1875-76), which was published in the *Old Students Calendar for 1931*. As Mills later became a successful Music tutor at the college it seems unlikely that he would have overstated the strength of student resentment:

> Sunday, the Day of Rest? Early Communion at 7 am on the first and third Sundays of the month. On the other Sundays we had breakfast at 8 am followed by Litany at 8.30. Afterwards we walked about the grounds until 10 o'clock. Next we assembled for Private Study or letter writing until 11 o'clock when we had the full morning service which lasted until 12.30. Dinner followed (cold joint) and we were allowed out of the college grounds until 2.40 pm. At 3 o'clock we had the Evening Psalms etc. From 4 till 5 we could walk about the grounds but assembled at 5 for Private Study. Tea at 6 followed by chapel again. We had not done even then, for at 8 o'clock we had Oratorio singing, and

then at 9 o'clock, winter and summer, straight to our dormitories. No supper in those days. I do not think there was a single student who hated anything more than he did Sunday in college. Just fancy, the only period we could be outside the college gates was from dinner till 2.40 pm and only once in two years did we get to the Evening Service in the Minster and on that occasion our Vice-Principal was preaching and the Principal was not well enough to take the College Service. Even then we had to come straight back to the college, for Oratorio work.

The college, officially committed to Christian Education, has been a long time learning that compulsory education is ineffective, and compulsory Christianity destructive.

CHAPTER V

The Dual System Extended: 1880-1908

WHILE THE LEADERSHIP CHANGED HANDS at York, the Ripon College progressed quietly under Badcock. He seems to have fostered cordial relationships in the City and at the Cathedral, where he was appointed an Honorary Canon in 1877. The college syllabus remained virtually unchanged into the 1880s, but the quality of recruits, both Queen's Scholars and 'direct entry' seems to have been good and the certificate results were usually well above the national average. In 1888, for example, there were 2,178 candidates all over the country; the 30 Ripon students all passed, the highest being placed 49th and the lowest 1,169th. HMI often complimented the work but they continued to press for higher intellectual standards and for wider application of college teaching to practical purposes.

> The questions that entail thought are still carefully avoided . . .
> There is a great need to widen the horizons of the students and give them new interests . . . The lectures being given on School Management are good generally, but there is too little reference to the laws of thought and the constitution of the child's nature . . . In only one set of papers is there a satisfactory knowledge of drainage. It is most desirable that students should know how to meet with proper precautions the dangers that occur in both town and country . . . Too little is known of the railway routes. It would be a good thing for candidates to spend a little time studying the 'indicators' at the back of Bradshaw's Railway map.

Teaching staff were urged to keep themselves up-to-date by reading newspapers and recent travel books. The standards in needlework and in music were praised, though it should be said that Sir John Stainer, who examined at most of the Church Colleges, was a generous and appreciative music assessor. Badcock encouraged further improvement of the college gardens but HMI continued to press for other recreational provision:

Students come to be civilised as well as taught, and their surroundings in college should furnish an education in manners and taste, and the art of spending leisure gracefully and well. . . . A comely and cheerful room, free from maps and blackboards, supplied with a piano and a few drawings, books and pictures, is a pleasant recourse for Sundays and half-holidays.

HMI, most of whom were clergymen, also urged the provision of a 'separate and appropriate College Chapel'.

Intellectual and spiritual values feature more prominently in HMI reports than gastronomic advice, but the diet attracted occasional crisp comment. The introduction in the mid-70s of fruit pies for Sunday lunch and of fish as a welcome, though infrequent, alternative to beef was praised, but in 1882 there was a mild protest against the pervasive potato in the college grounds and a plea that cabbages might also be grown. The first student magazines, in the 1890s, include recollections of former students from this period; these suggest that the diet was made at least tolerable by the excellence of the home-made bread.

The 1893 magazine includes a warm tribute to Canon Badcock, just retired to a cottage in Wells, Somerset. Even allowing for Victorian duty and piety his students seem to have liked him and enjoyed his friendly manner and his repertoire of enduring jokes:

His name will be held in loving memory by all who were his pupils. How wise and able he was in counsel, how just in judgement, how courteous and kind in all our relations with him . . . And can we ever forget his genial humour, and the pleasant hours we spent with him in the classroom.

To modern educators it may seem an unctuous tribute to one who led a somewhat unimaginative regime, but as Wilkinson noted, the college was only normally repressive for its time; Girton students of the of the 1890s were driven in to lectures in Cambridge, in closed cabs with chaperones.[1] Neither the daily routine nor the academic curriculum offered students any of the choice we now think indispensible; but one indication of the college's comparative quality was that able students applied to join it, and in large numbers.

Recruitment was buoyant throughout Badcock's years, in a college system that had grown substantially since the 1870 Act. In 1846, at the end of the first period of rapid growth for the new church colleges there had been 26 separate foundations; by 1886 there were 43, of four denominations. The British and Foreign School Society had opened colleges at Swansea, Darlington and Saffron Walden, the Methodists a new college for women, Southlands in London, and the Roman Catholics a second college at Wandsworth, later moved to Roehampton as Digby

74

Stuart College. The Church of England had increased student numbers at most of its colleges and opened new ones at Oxford and Tottenham. Probably the most significant new foundation was Edgehill College, opened near Liverpool in 1885. Though it maintained strong Christian associations it was established by the Liverpool School Board, independent of any religious denomination – the first such college in England.[2]

Although employment prospects for teachers fluctuated in the decade 1875 to 1885 it became clear that even this expanded training system could not meet the demand for places. In 1866 there were 5,000 candidates, 3,379 of whom qualified for a total of 1,600 available places in the 43 colleges. In the same year yet another Royal Commission was established. Under the chairmanship of Richard Assheton, first Viscount Cross, it was enjoined to 'Enquire into the Working of the Elementary Education Acts'. Cardinal Manning, who was not satisfied that the 'fair start' for which he had appealed in 1870 had been granted, was a prime mover for the Commission and a key member of it. Other prominent members were Frederick Temple, former HMI and now Bishop of London, and Sir Bernhard Sammuelson who had chaired the Royal Commission on Technical Instruction (1882-84) The Cross Commission, which reported in 1888 took evidence from many experienced teacher-educators including Lord Lingen who had succeeded Kay-Shuttleworth at the Committee of Council, HMI Matthew Arnold and several college principals, most notably Enid Trevor of Bishop Otter College.

The Commissioners found that, though the colleges had gradually improved their intellectual standards in response to HMI's exhortations and to improved attainment levels in the schools, they had been left largely to their own devices; these, with a few exceptions, varied from the pedestrian to the pernicious. The Commissioners found living conditions often primitive and unhygienic, regimes restrictive and dictatorial, curricula archaic, and teaching methods still largely based on rote learning.[3]

The Commission had been charged to investigate whether the demands made upon various bodies by the 1870 Act for the provision of schools had been reasonably met. This required them to assess the balance between voluntary and rate-supported effort, the quality of the denominational schools, and colleges, the effects of the 1870 compromise on religious instruction, and the overall supply and training of teachers. For the Ripon College one of the most significant sections of the Cross Commission Report of 1888 was the 16,000 word interrogation of Miss Trevor, 'Lady Principal' of Bishop Otter College.[4] She staunchly defended the recruitment of middle class women, who had no experience as pupil teachers, which characterised her college and, to a lesser extent, Ripon and othe women's colleges. She was severely critical of the pupil teacher system:

Q. To what do you attribute this lamentable failure of the pupil teachers who come to you in the knowledge of history and geography?

A. I do not see how they can possibly learn them; I think it would be a miracle if they did know them. They go in at the age of fourteen, when they are too young to have acquired much knowledge, and they then teach for five hours a day, not knowing how to teach. Of course it is a terrible strain on a girl who does not know how to teach when she is at once put in charge of a lot of children whom, somehow or other, she must teach and keep in order. It looks beautiful on paper; the syllabus that is given for pupil teachers is, to look at, everything that we would wish; but they do not do it. Girl after girl whom I have questioned has told me that they have never, during the four years of pupil teachership, answered a question in history or geography. If they can do sums they will all pass through their teachership and they can all do those . . .

Q. . . . you find that they are less intelligent than those who come in from other classes, (of society) not being pupil teachers?

A. It is difficult to find the right word, they are less receptive . . . we cannot do so much with them; they go out very nearly as they came in, beyond having learned a little more by cram . . .

Q. Then do you really think that the course of training as a pupil teacher renders those students less efficient than if they had not been through that training?

A. Very much less efficient and very much less physically fit. The strain on their bodies is very great, poor girls . . .

Q. You object I see to the pupil teacher system entirely?

A. Entirely . . . and I think that any parents of better position would do anything they could to hinder their children from going through the drudgery of pupil-teachership.

Some commissioners were concerned that the motive for recruiting middle class young women direct to colleges such as Bishop Otter and Ripon was simple snobbery.

76

Q. The fact is that you are working with the object of benefiting this particular class of students?

A. No, I am not; I am working with the hope of getting a higher tone, and getting more thoroughly education people into the schools to teach the children. That is my sole motive. I do not mean to say that when one can help the orphans of clergymen, who have been left destitute, one is not glad to be able to do so, but that is not my chief motive.

The inappropriate location of the colleges was also tactfully broached by a commissioner who suggested that the colleges, if they were to offer useful exerience to future teachers, needed 'exceptional facilities for practice in good day schools'. Miss Trevor responded sharply and probably spoke for many of the colleges in quiet cathedral cities:

A. Yes, I think it is a great loss to us being at Chichester at all; it is a very dead-alive, out-of-the-way-place, if we could only get a big college, within twenty miles of London, with large practising schools, I should be very glad.

The long term influence of the Cross Commission is uncertain because there were few important issues on which the members reached consensus, and their findings were issued in majority and minority reports. They criticised the schools but did not condemn them. They upheld the voluntary principle for the provision of schools but – like most interested members of the public – could not agree whether rate-support for voluntary schools was just. They acknowledged that the denominational training colleges were doing a difficult job with some success, but both reports insisted that more training places were needed and that 'day training' should be considered because it was practical and cheap. The majority report favoured a limited experiment with 'day training colleges'. The minority report was more determined and specific; within 10 years it had prevailed:

We assent to the continuance of grants to the existing denominational colleges, partly in deference to the strenuous desire of the advocates of denominational education to preserve a strongly denominational system of training, with rigid domestic discipline, but we cannot assent to the statement in the report that the existing system of residential training colleges is the best, both for the teachers and the scholars of the public elementary schools of the country and we only acquiesce in the continuance of these grants in the hope that the system of training now in force in Scotland may be largely imitated here, in the association of training with higher education, in the great extension of facilities for day students and in the liberal recognition of the rights of conscience, and we look to the adoption of these reforms as enabling us hereafter to dispense almost entirely with the employment of untrained teachers.[5]

It was a farsighted manifesto which was to have a powerful influence on the future pattern of teacher training and on the church colleges. The commissioners might have been dismayed if they could have known that, 100 years later, a vastly expanded education service would still be employing untrained teachers and with explicit government approval.

The Commissioners were divided about the pupil teacher system. They recorded the advice of Dr Crosskey of the Education League, who condemned it as

> . . . at once the cheapest and the very worst possible system of supply . . . it should be abolished root and branch.

But the majority report nevertheless favoured retaining pupil-teaching as the most 'trustworthy source of supply' possible for the present. The minority report proposed the development of teacher training in quite different directions and demanded major modifications in pupil-teaching if it had to be retained. Miss Trevor's tones are audible:

> As for pupil-teachers we strongly dissent from the proposition . . . that there is no other equally trustworthy source . . . Indeed, bearing in mind the statement of our colleagues in an earlier part of the chapter, as to the valuable influence of women of superior social position and general culture, we can hardly reconcile the two statements, and we are certainly of the opinion that the moral securities we should look for in our future teachers are not likely to be diminished, but on the contrary greatly increased by a wider course and a prolonged period of preliminary education before students are trusted with the management of classes.

The minority commissioners considered the pupil-teacher system the weakest part of the whole education enterprise. They deplored the majority recommendation that the age of entry might be lowered to 13, proposed that no pupil-teacher should be allowed to take a class until at least 15 years old, and recommended that the first two years of teacher training should be devoted entirely to the pupils own education.

The minority report made an impact. The pupil-teacher system had already been improved in the 1880s by the introduction of Pupil Teacher Centres providing 'central classes' of what we would now call in-service training, to supplement the little that could be accommodated in the ordinary school timetable. But following the Cross Reports the Department of Education instigated a full enquiry into the pupil-teacher system in 1896. The age of entry was raised, as the commissioners had proposed, to 15, and subsequently, by the 1902 Act, to 16. The system gradually evolved towards full-time education and training, though a few pupil-teachers of the old style were still being recruited in England and Wales until the Second World War. A century later controversy about the value of the system continues, and in February 1990 a former Minister of State for Education, himself an ex-head teacher, claimed that former pupil-teachers were the best trained teachers he had known. But the spirit of Cross prevailed and he was not much supported.[6]

With the blessing of the Cross Commissioners, the direct recruitment of young middle class applicants to some of the women's colleges was extended. But the Commissioners took little notice of the claims of Miss Trevor and others on the denominational issue. They saw no reason for ecclesiastical monopoly and good reason for greater liberty of conscience. They also deplored the isolation of many of the colleges, and the narrow experience of elementary school children who, having become pupil-teachers in the same elementary schools, spent two years in restrictive colleges, in the company of fellow pupil-teachers of similar background and then returned for a lifetime's work, to the same sort of schools which had moulded them. Ninety years later the James Report of 1972 was to make a similar case against the isolation of teachers in training, but with less eloquence and more jargon.

Out of the Cross Reports came the new Education Code of 1890 which introduced two major advances for the teaching profession. The first was a radical change in the method of grant aid to schools, which gradually ended the already modified 'payment by results' surviving from Lowe's Revised Code. The second was the initiation of an alternative pattern of teacher education in newly authorised 'Day Training Colleges'. The title was odd, since the new institutions were almost all departments of universities rather than separate colleges, and all had a lot of resident students. The first to open, in 1890-91, were at London (King's College), Manchester, Birmingham, Durham, Nottingham and Cardiff. They were followed in 1892-93 by Bristol, Cambridge, Leeds, Liverpool, Oxford, Sheffield, London (University College) and Aberystwyth, and before the end of the decade by the University Colleges of Bangor, Reading, Southampton and Exeter. They were more liberal than the Church Training Colleges in at least two respects: most of them were co-educational and many of them offered students the chance to complete a university degree.

The denominational colleges suddenly found themselves confronted with an alternative route to teaching qualifications which was supported by government, patronised by universities, welcomed by the teaching profession, and attractive to applicants. The churches' 60-year monopoly was over.

With the publication of the new Education Code in 1890, Badcock decided that it was time to give way to a younger leader at Ripon and announced his retirement for December. The governors appointed Revd O. P. Whalley, lecturer at Warrington College, but he became ill during the Christmas vacation. Badcock agreed to resume his duties for the spring term at the end of which Whalley appeared to have recovered. He took up the post in April and seems to have been effective and very popular, but by the end of May he was seriously ill and resigned. He died in Norfolk in September. So two of the first three principals of the Ripon College had died within a term of taking office. Badcock, renowned for his sturdiness and calm, had not completed negotiations for his retirement home in Somerset, and again agreed to resume the principalship till another successor could be appointed.

This time the governors were luckier. They appointed Revd George Garrod, a 30 year old lecturer in mathematics at Battersea Training College who arrived at the end of November. The college owes him much; so do its historians because within six months of his arrival he had founded the Association of Old Students and initiated its annual magazine. The Association was launched in March 1892 and by June had 371 members; six years later the membership had reached 600. The magazine, a prime source of information on college developments and activities was edited for its first 25 years by Miss E. F. Palin who taught at the college from 1877 to 1917, and became 'Second Governess'. Her selection of topics for the early years reveals that Garrod brought swift and welcome changes in keeping with the Cross Report. Regulations were relaxed and the college was opened more to the influence of the local community. Garrod encouraged games and outdoor pursuits; two tennis courts were laid out, the cricket field improved, and picnics and outings regularly organised. On alternate Saturdays the students were encouraged to go rambling 'without a governess' – a concession much in advance of most women's colleges – and the subject of some local censure. The great outing of 1894 was to Brimham Rocks. A party of 80 set out in carriages, Garrod led a conducted tour of the main rock features, gave an account of the geology and, after lunch, led groups of enthusiasts in search of specimens of wild flowers and ferns while the rest of the party did as they pleased.

In his first year Garrod established a college museum, as an aid to the teaching of science and geography; each edition of the magazine chronicled recent gifts and additions. Though there was not yet a suitable common room for social events a monthly Social Evening was launched and magazine accounts convey the enthusiasm for the variety of lectures, magic lantern shows, musical evenings, poetry readings and, eventually, dramatic productions – evidence of Garrod's conviction that education should be enjoyed. He gave many of the lectures himself, and he and Miss Mercer, the Lady Superintendent, seem to have specialised in illustrated travel talks, based on their most recent holiday trips.

Garrod had married during his first year. His wife was welcomed to the college, somewhat quaintly, with a play reading of *King Lear* and the records suggest that she took a full part in the life of the college. The social event of 1893 was the birth of their son Wilfred, who was christened in Trinity Church in the presence of most of the college – the only recorded occasion in the 150 years of the college when a principal has become a father.

College reunions became a regular but not yet annual feature of the social calendar, with attendances of 300 and more. When the safety bicycle became the popular successor to the 'penny-farthing' Garrod started a cycling club, so the rambles and botanical researches went further afield. The governors purchased the field in front of the college building, to forestall a local builder's plan to erect cottages on it. Hockey pitches were then laid out and a club formed, with Garrod an occasional player. He also persuaded the governors to spend a good deal on improvements to the comfort, decor and furnishing of the main college rooms and to buy pictures to hang in them.

In 1894 the Board of Education decided that the Training College year should be brought into line with the university and school year, with students entering in September and leaving in June or July. It took two years to effect the change, but Garrod welcomed it in the 1896 magazine:

> The changes are almost entirely for the better. The extra examinations (Science, Drawing, Music, Teaching) are over soon after Easter, and the last two months of college life find us with a limited number of subjects for study, and with only one great Examination for which to prepare. This means that we are able to reduce the hours of work, and to rearrange the timetable so as to add to the comfort of students and staff. Only two hours work is done in the afternoon, and one after tea. Work for the day stops at seven and the cool of the evening is occupied with tennis or cricket or a walk. Former students will wish themselves back at college to enjoy these agreeable changes. The one drawback to the new order of things is that the Scholarship candidates have to travel to and fro in the winter . . . as a set-off against this drawback, our second year students bid us farefull in the sunny time of the year, and escape the depressing influence of a winter fog when they are looking upon their college for the last time.

So after 53 years the demands of the timetable for women students were at last reduced, but Garrod also welcomed the opportunities provided by the Board to extend the range of college studies, especially in science. In addition to his great love, botany, he himself taught courses in electricity and physiography, while the maths syllabus now included algebra. But he frequently protested against the continuing preoccupation with examinations, which had to be conducted for all subjects – there were now 18 in the Ripon College curriculum.

Throughout his time at the college there was continual national debate about the relative merits of local and central control of education. In 1895 the Bryce Commission on Secondary Education made recommendations towards a single central authority which were largely implemented in the Education Act of 1899. But the Commissioners were alert to the implicit tensions. In support of the teaching profession, the schools and the training colleges, they expressed firm convictions about the role of the teacher and the essential conditions for its proper expression. It is a statement central to any study of the constraints and freedoms of educational institutions throughout this period. It still has much to say to us at the end of the 20th century, and must have cheered Garrod at the end of the 19th:

> The fact is that the body of teachers must necessarily occupy a somewhat anomolous position in the economy of national life. The service which they render is one over which the State must in self defence retain effective oversight; the provision of teaching and the conduct of education cannot be left to private enterprise alone. Nor, on the other hand, do the teachers stand in the same relation to Government as does the Civil Service. Education is a thing too intimately concerned with individual preference and private life, for it to be desirable to throw the whole of it under government control. It needs organisation, but it would be destroyed by uniformity; it is stimulated by inspection, but it would be crushed by a code. In the public service, where the chief object is administrative efficiency, the individual officer is necessarily subordinate; in education, where a chief object is the discovery of more perfect methods of teaching, the individual teacher must be left comparatively free. Every good teacher is a discoverer, and in order to make discoveries, he must have liberty of experiment.[7]

The National Union of Elementary Teachers which had agitated for the appointment of the Commission welcomed this lofty conception of the rights and aspirations of teachers. At least as significant for Church colleges and schools was the insistence that State intervention must be limited – a reassertion of the consensus reached 30 years earlier by the Taunton Commission, of which Bryce had been a member.

Acland's leadership of the Committee of Council for Education in the 1890s did much to improve conditions, standards and attendance in schools, and so to encourage able recruits into teaching.[8] He vowed to stir into the Education Department and Inspectorate

> with a great spoon, some of the newer hopes and the fresher spirit.

He did so by liberalising not only examination procedures and inspections, but also school activities, encouraging cultural visits to museums and art galleries. He took firm action against inefficient schools. In 1894-5 for instance, 38 schools lost their grant status and 538 were put on 12 months notice. In the five years from 1890 to 1895 four fifths of the schools named were Voluntary and, predictably, the large majority Anglican. This was an unwelcome burden for the Church but a fillip for the teachers as working conditions rapidly improved. In the 25 years since the 1870 Act the Church had more than doubled the number of children in its schools, to two and a half million. But the burden was heavy and the competition unequal; in the same period the number of children in Board schools had risen from none to one and a half million. There could be no doubt any longer that the church had a formidable secular rival. As Bishop Knox of Birmingham put it

> Every child had to go to school, while no one was obliged to go to church.[9]

Fees had been abolished in the Board schools in 1891, putting the Church schools at a further disadvantage, but in 1895 Archbishop Temple led a deputation to Prime Minister Salisbury, urging statutory relief for Church schools. This was provided in a Voluntary Schools Act of 1897 which exempted Church schools from rates and increased their grants in comparison with those to Board schools. So Garrod, Baldwin and other Church College principals could be confident that improved conditions in both Church and Board schools would encourage recruits into training for teaching. Once again Church colleges benefited from important political concessions which enabled the Church to hold its own in the expanding education system.

By 1895 there were 29,000 teachers in service in England and Wales who had completed a two year college training and another 24,000 who, after rudimentary training had an Acting Teacher's Certificate. This provided one certificated teacher for every 100 children. As there were also 31,000 pupil teachers and 28,000 untrained 'Assistant' teachers, the Department could claim to be providing one 'approved' teacher for every 47 school children – a massive achievement in 25 years. Salaries too had risen slowly and by 1895 the average for a certificated master was £122, and for a certificated mistress, £81. The national economy was prospering in a peaceful decade and the national 'Dual System' of education had at last provided some sort of school place for every eligible child, as the birth rate continued to rise rapidly and the infant survival rate significantly.

It was time for confident expansion and Garrod recognised it. The Ripon governors had spent over £1,000 on the fields in front of the college, much of it donated by an anonymous 'gentleman'. There seemed little chance of further development for a few years. Garrod's account of what followed, written for the 1897 magazine, reflects the spirit of his leadership:

> On the day that matters were finally settled by the committee with regard to the fields, the gentleman already twice mentioned and the Principal of the college, were walking down Crescent Parade together. The Principal had expressed his gratitude and happiness at the way things had ended, and added, 'the next thing must be the chapel, but I'm afraid that it is a long way off'. The reply was 'Directly you start the scheme I will give you . . .' The Principal immediately answered, 'Then I will start it at once.' The promise was kept – indeed a larger sum still was given – and there was now no going back – the chapel had to be built. So the 'Chapel Fund' began its existence. And yet this is hardly fair to our old students. For . . . it virtually commenced six months earlier, when the committee of the Association made the Principal promise to carry out at a very early date his intention to issue such an appeal, and voted £30 towards two of the objects which the fund was intended to secure.
>
> The fund had a phenomenal growth but it was intended to reach a phenomenal size. For we wanted a Common Room also . . . and we wanted a Science Room too, for South Kensington 'looms formidable' these days, and we are taking a great pride in our science results for they are (we say it with gratitude and we hope due modesty) generally among the best in the country. We therefore determined we would try to get all these, Chapel, Common Room, Science Room, and we accordingly issued an appeal of £3,000 . . .
>
> This raised a very natural question as to the number of students for whom provision was to be made – if the college was ever to be enlarged any scheme of englargement would be serious interfered with by small existing rooms . . . Then came the suggestion 'Why not enlarge now?' . . . The College Committee decided to provide accommodation for about thirty-six extra students . . . The Diocese most kindly came to our aid with a proposal to buy the fields at the back of the College, to

build a hostel in the field very near to the College, to connect it with the College by a covered way . . . The architect is J. Oldrid Scott, son of Sir Gilbert Scott, and he has prepared for us most satisfactory drawings . . . The total outlay by the Diocese will probably be near £5,000; the total cost of *our* share of the work (the Chapel Building) will probably reach £3,500 so that altogether some £8,500 is to be spent . . .

The appeal fund reached its target, the work was begun in 1897, and in May 1899 the new hostel block, including the Victoria Hall (now a gymnasium) was formally opened, the Chapel (now the library) was dedicated to St Margaret of Scotland, in the presence of 400 past and present students. Though expansion was afoot in many colleges Ripon College, in the quality of its buildings and of its academic and professional achievement was probably, in 1900, among the top 10 colleges in the country. But further competition was on the way.

The majority report of the Cross Commission, whose signatories included Cardinal Manning, had guardedly recommended that rate-aid should be extended to denominational colleges and schools. Many Anglican clergy agreed, but Archbishop Benson thought the proposal 'disastrous and lowering' and certain to result in loss of real control by the Church of its 'own' institutions. As has already been argued in this study, full control had been lost with the acceptance of the very first government grants in the 1830s, by which the Church inadvertently committed itself to a long rearguard action; we are entering the latest phase in the 1990s. When Frederick Temple, former HMI, succeeded Benson at Canterbury the official Church policy changed to a firm demand for both rate-aid and increased state support. So in the debate that preceded the 1902 Education Act, as in that before 1870, the Church of England view was neither unanimous nor consistent. Meanwhile some extreme Nonconformists protested that the new rate-aid proposals for voluntary institutions would amount to 'Rome on the Rates' – though with 10 times as many schools and colleges, the Church of England stood to gain far more than Rome. Then, as now, sectarian acrimony continually provoked attempts to sweep away denominational institutions completely.

But there were voices of reason too. In January 1901, Sidney Webb highlighted the administrative confusion in education, in a Fabian pamphlet entitled *The Education Muddle and the Way Out*. It ran to 20,000 copies, was read by cabinet ministers and probably helped to shape the new legislation. Its facts were irrefutable, its analysis convincing and its idealism infectious:

> Our educational machinery in England has got into a notable mess. Some places have two or three public authorities spending

rates and taxes on different sorts of schools, whilst others have nothing at all . . . The Central organisation is as chaotic as the local. The various educational institutions in the United Kingdom – taking only those supported out of rates and taxes – are officially under the charge of no fewer than ten cabinet ministers; and their departments usually scorn to consult together. The result is that although we spend on education in the United Kingdom every year nearly twenty million pounds of public money of one sort or another, from rates, taxes or public endowments, we get a very inadequate return for it. In English education today waste and want go hand in hand.

His scenario remains sadly topical 90 years on, but he went on to expose the severe limitations on the powers of the 2,500 School Boards and the anomalies in the support system. In the year 1899-1900 the English School Boards had spent over £9m and the Voluntary Schools over £5m. But government contributions to these totals had been, respectively, £3.6m and £4.15m. The inequity should have been apparent even to the most fervent denominationalist, but to Webb's credit, rather than score points at the expense of the established Church, he preferred to make a cogent case for a new kind of local educational authority.

It is politically impossible to abolish these voluntary schools; and whatever we may think of the theological reasons for their establishment, their separate and practically individual management does incidentally, afford what ought to be, in any public system of education, most jealously safeguarded, namely variety and the opportunity for experiment. What we have to do with the voluntary schools is to put them under the control of the *local* education authority; to improve and strengthen their committees of management; to raise their efficiency and especially to provide better salaries for their teachers; to make impossible the tyrannical vagaries of foolish clergymen in village schools; and to bring these into co-ordination with the rest of the education system.

In July 1901, a joint Convocation of Canterbury and York made proposals similar to Webb's, advocating rate-aid and conceding substantial local authority control of Church schools. Given the financial statistics Webb had quoted, such a public compromise by the Church was not surprising. In the colleges it was getting an even better bargain than in the schools. In all training colleges together there was now provision for 25% of the students in Methodist, British Society or Non-denominational colleges all of which admitted Non-Conformists, for 6% in Catholic colleges and for the remaining 69% in Anglican colleges. Yet, as Lloyd

George protested, only 5% of the total maintenance costs of the Anglican colleges was borne by the Church; all the rest came from students fees and government grants.

So, when A. J. Balfour rose in the House in March 1902 it was to present a Bill incorporating much of the advice of the Fabian Society and the Convocations of Canterbury and York! He drew attention to three important ommissions of the 1870 Act: it had provided no organisation for the voluntary schools, which had remained isolated and unconnected; it had not planned for the education of the huge numbers of teachers required for a greatly expanded school system; and it had failed to develop any organic connections between primary and secondary schools and between the secondary stage and university education. His thrust on teacher education carried echoes from Cross, from Miss Trevor and from Webb:

> Any child who wishes to become a teacher gets made a pupil-teacher, and when he has reached that status half his time goes to teaching and the other half . . . to learning . . . What is the result of such a system? I find that thirty-six percent of the existing teachers have never got through the examination for the certificate, and I find that fifty-five percent of the teachers have never been to a training college of any sort . . . We spend £18 million a year on elementary education. Can anybody believe that under the system I have described, we get the best results or can expect to get the best results for so vast an expenditure?[10]

He was unabashed in his support of the voluntary schools and colleges, referring to their 'deplorable starvation' and to the unfulfilled predictions that the supportive legislation of 1897 would cause a decline in subscription support to Church colleges and schools. Such support had actually improved, so it was probably with deeper convictions than Webb's about the moral justification for denominational institutions and with similar resignation to their actual indispensibility, that Balfour assured them of their future:

> I think it is perfectly marvellous what has been done under circumstances which, as I have already told the House, were never foreseen when the Act of 1870 was brought into existence . . . But the fact remains that after all these great efforts on the part of the voluntary subscriber, and after all the aid given from the National Exchequer, the voluntary schools are in many cases not adequately equipped, and are not as well fitted as they should be to carry out the great part which they are inevitably destined to play in our system of national education. I say inevitably destined to play because the idea of the voluntary schools being

87

swept away by an Act of Parliament or by any other method, is absurd. The mere magnitude of the forces with which you have got to deal renders it impossible. The mere magnitude of the gap which would be created in the system of national education renders it impossible.

Any present-day supporters who take for granted the survival of the Church colleges into the 21st century would do well to reflect that, long before the competitive network of strong polytechnics and LEA colleges had been developed, the most powerful argument for the Voluntary colleges that so staunch a friend as Balfour could propound, rested on 'the magnitude of the forces' and 'the magnitude of the gap'. And even Balfour had a long tussle. The new Bill was 57 days before the House – longer than any previous Bill in history. Lloyd George led a fierce Nonconformist lobby against it and Robert Morant, Secretary to the Board of Education, skilfully modified it. It reached the Statute Book in December 1902, by which time Balfour was Prime Minister.

Though at face value it strengthened the Church colleges it confronted them with further stiff competition to add to the Day Training programmes at the universities. The Act established some 300 Local Education Authorities in place of the 2,500 School Boards and 800 School Attendance Committees. The new LEAs were empowered to co-ordinate all elementary, secondary and further education, to spend rate-income on secondary education and – if they wished – on the training of teachers in colleges of their own which were to be non-denominational. The new authorities assumed control over all the secular education in voluntary schools, with likely implications for that in the colleges, and the managing bodies of all voluntary institutions had to include LEA representatives. The managers retained the right to appoint teachers, subject to formal approval by the LEA and to control the religious teaching. A late amendment to the Bill, moved by Colonel Kenyon-Slaney but advised by Morant, insisted that religious teaching must be in accordance with the trust deed of the institution. This made certain that it was vested firmly with the whole management body which had to include lay members, and that it could not be controlled by the clergy. Webb's liberal aspiration for religious teaching was therefore enshrined in the Act; the diehard lobby of Anglican clergy was represented by one of its number who ungallantly claimed that

> he would rather the colonel should have seduced his wife than come to Parliament with such a proposal.[11]

As the Education Bill was making its way through parliament there were signs that Garrod's liberal attitude to the curriculum was finding support at Westminster. But hopes were short-lived and Garrod described the experience in the magazines for 1902 and 1903:

Times change and Training Colleges must change with them. So we have never been greatly surprised, although – may we confess it? – we have sometimes been a little put about – by the Departmental changes of the closing years of the old century. But those changes were but child's play, compared to what was to follow. The Board of Education all this time was only 'playin' aroun' de aidges' as Uncle Remus would say. But it was in 1901 that we discovered what Whitehall could do if it tried . . . Shortly after mid-summer a circular was issued saying that in future each college should draw up its own syllabus and examine its own students. Here was change indeed! Liberty to choose our own course of Literature, of Foreign Languages, of Mathematics of Science, of Needlework, and even of the time-honoured School Management. All this was delightful. We had always felt that a cut and dried syllabus, practically the same for all colleges, was in the highest degree undesirable.

The College responded very quickly to the offered opportunity with a much more adventurous syllabus which also enabled selected students to undertake at the same time work for the University of Durham degree of B.Litt. It was beyond the vision of the bureaucrats:

Unfortunately the Board of Education has not seen fit to adhere to its own regulations. Without giving the new scheme a single trial – much less a fair trial lasting a few years – it has taken the examination back in its own hands, and has prepared papers to suit, with slight modifications, all the colleges with their thirty or forty varying syllabuses. The result is lamentable in the extreme and there is outcry from the training colleges on all sides. In some subjects the standard has been raised in phenomenal and quite unexpected fashion. . . .

We believe the Board of Education means well by us but it was unfortunate that they were not prepared to trust us for one year at least. We mean well by them also, but it is just possible that the colleges are not understood at Whitehall. If those responsible for these changes could only look in at a provincial college (where the material is not always of the best) when one of these absurdly difficult and quite unexpected papers appears, we verily believe that they would be as grieved as we are to see how hard it hits industrious students of average intellectual power. As it is we have paid dearly for our carefully prepared syllabus with its generous scheme of work. We await the results with great misgiving and a sense of injustice.

The outcry seems to have had some effect, as in 1904 the Board issued yet another set of regulations, which were better received. They relieved students of at least some of the examination pressures and left certificate classification to the colleges. Meanwhile Garrod had worked to improve the quality and range of school experience. The practice facilities at Holy Trinity School had been expanded and re-equipped through the 1880s but HMI had reiterated their view that a small market town of 7,000 could not provide the experience of 'large schools organised on the latest systems' which student teachers needed. Garrod agreed and a series of day visits to large schools in Leeds eventually expanded into three week periods of observation and practice, with the students resident in the Leeds YWCA. These were later extended to Harrogate, Bradford, Scarborough and even York. In addition there were long day visits to rural schools at, for example, Leyburn, Middleham and Mickley.

More building followed in 1903 and 1904. Principals had lived out for the first 40 years of the Ripon College, but the spacious St Margaret's Lodge was completed in May 1903 and Garrod moved in gleefully with his wife and two sons. He suggested that Principal and students had a new challenge:

> He can have a peep at the college when he likes and the college can have a peep at him. His garden has a capital lawn and there are visions of future students bringing their tennis rackets to St Margaret's Lodge and beating the Principal on his own ground.

New chemistry and physics laboratories, a botany room and a gymnasium, all with student and staff study-bedrooms above them, completed Garrod's building schemes; residence was now available for 109 students. Two houses were then purchased in College Road, just above St Margaret's Lodge and by 1907 Garrod, now an Honorary Canon of Ripon Cathedral recorded the international impact of the college:

> We have never had better reports than we have recently received from both the Board of Education inspectors and the represent- atives of the Archbishop . . . We have enlarged our borders so that we now number one hundred and forty-one students . . . I am proud of all that Ripon girls are doing; the fruit of their labours after having left us is winning them golden opinions everywhere. I have letters from them almost daily, from New Zealand, India, China, America, Nyasa, the Cape, as well as England and there is rarely a discordant note.

In 1908, after 17 years at the college, Garrod was asked by the Bishop to accept a residentiary Canonry and lead the work of religious education in day schools and Sunday schools throughout the diocese. He was 47 and pursued the new challenge with vigour for more than 20 years. In June

1908 the biggest reunion the college had yet seen was attended by more than 600 past and present students. In his farewell speech Garrod said

> When I came to Ripon I determined to promote the happiness of students.

Many tributes that day and since leave little doubt that he succeeded. His was a distinguished principalship.

At York, through the same vicissitudes of national policy, Baldwin had a rougher ride. He was yet another Cambridge man but with exotic qualifications which enthused the college committee in 1873 when he was initially appointed Vice-Principal

> He was at one time in the army and served in the Crimea – gained both classical and mathematical honours at his university – has been a successful parish priest and has discharged with efficiency the office of Diocesan Inspector of Schools in the Diocese of Gloucester.

HMI Bowstead described him as a 'great acquisition' for the college but it was left to the early editions of *The White Rose* to reveal his literary prowess. The February 1893 edition acknowledged the Principal's permission to print

> what has never been published before, the poem which gained for him the Vice Chancellor's prize for English Verse – the same prize which Tennyson had won at Cambridge twenty seven years before for *Timbuctoo*. Our distinguished Principal received the news of his first literary triumph whilst serving with the colours during the terrible Mutiny. He had only just matriculated but left his University at the call of duty and hurried away to India where he served his country as truly and as thoroughly as he had done in the Crimea. He speaks as one with authority for he was a participator not only in the Alma but many other fierce battles on the bleak slopes of the Russian Peninsula.

Baldwin's long prize poem *The Alma* was the first of his several verse contributions to *The White Rose*.

He had, shortly after being appointed Principal, reduced the number of weaker students entered for some of the more difficult examinations, particularly languages and science, so that by 1881 HMI Sharpe rated the college's performance generally creditable. There were few distinguished results, but also few outright failures. This did not prevent the college being singled out for special criticism in a fierce attack on the Church colleges delivered in the Commons by Lyulph Stanley on 3rd April 1882. He repeated the frequently heard accusation that Church of England schools and colleges violated the consciences of non-conformist students by forcing them to receive Anglican religious instruction, and denounced the 'wretched state of things existing with regard to training colleges' particularly in Yorkshire. He claimed that at the Ripon College 'the communion was practically imposed as a test' and that at the York College

> the results were deplorably bad, for at the 1880 examinations York college came out at the bottom of the list. Whereas in the average training colleges in England, 40% of males passed in the First Division, at York only 3% passed; and instead of the average of 12% in the third division, it was there the very excessive number of 36% in the lowest rank. Yet, young Baptists from Bradford and Halifax must get baptised in dozens, like the conquered Saxons, and get up a Catechism they did not believe in, in order, if they went to a Church College, to have their intellectual ability spoiled, and come out in the third division.

Baldwin replied in *The Times* and the *Yorkshire Gazette*. Where Stanley had chosen the worst college results for 10 years, Baldwin could claim that the 1881 results – which were the best over a similar period – showed the general level of attainment to be up to the national average. He asserted that the percentage of first classes was an inadequate criterion and that the York students were

> as a rule young men of industry, teaching ability and high character.

Stanley came back to the charge, protesting the insolvency and excessive economy of the York college, but conceding that he understood Baldwin to be a liberal-minded and generous principal in respect of Non-conformist students. In the Committee of Council Report for 1883, HMI Sharpe defended the Baldwin regime, praising the York College results, particularly in relation to the levels of attainment students had shown on entry to the college. So the episode passed, probably without serious damage to the college's reputation. It reflected however the hold that the attitudes implicit in the Revised Code still had on public discussion of education; the widely held assumption was still that only examination results really mattered. The truth was that in the 20 years from 1880 to 1900 the results recorded in the Committee of Council reports show that in only five years did York achievements slightly exceed the national average; in many years they fell far below it. Ripon students were almost invariably more successful throughout this period and well into the new century.

Available records suggest that for most of this period the learning experience at York was dull and demoralising. As in most colleges – with Ripon under Garrod an honourable exception – the teaching of science was entirely theoretical with students given no practical experience at all. Even agriculture was offered for examination by hundreds of students who had studied only from textbooks. E. Hallam, a student in 1895-6 confided to *The White Rose* that science lectures had been 'rather a joke' and that he had never handled any appartus, the student joke being that the only science equipment in the college was a duster and the poker for the fire. C. H. Cooper (1891-2) recalled Baldwin's

> famous illustration explaining refraction of light – a column of men marching through a field of corn at an angle – its exposition written down in full by the students, occupied the full hour of the lesson.[12]

In spite of the claims of the Cross Commissioners that almost all colleges had laboratories, York did not acquire one until 1897. Even then an inventory recorded that most of the apparatus was antiquated and that the college possessed only two Bunsen burners. In spite of the efforts of successive HMI the timetable remained grossly overcrowded and in 1896 HMI Scott Coward was still complaining of excessive lecturing. In addition to 36 hours of timetabled lectures there were 18 hours of supervised private study. Since, as in most colleges, there was virtually no library, students relied on their few textbooks. Cooper, who had been Senior Monitor in 1892 and completed a London BA in 1898 regretted:

> Our training was little more than private swotting.

Organised games seem to have flourished sporadically from the 1870s and early editions of *The White Rose* report fixtures against local sides in the 1890s at rugby, soccer and cricket. In earlier years, it was claimed, 'football' matches were played to Association rules for the first half and Rugby rules for the second. Any 'home' games had to be played on the small and inadequate space at the back of the Lord Mayor's Walk buildings until 1899 when a playing field was rented at Wigginton. A boat race between senior and junior years was a major annual event from the early 90s and the 1899 *White Rose* reported that an annual sports day had been 'revived'.

Apart from informal Saturday evening 'concerts' there appear to have been no cultural activities planned at York, and except for a Literary and Debating Society which met irregularly from 1894, there were no college societies or clubs. Most of the 'time-honoured traditions' which *The White Rose* reported seem to have been of 'ragging' and inter-year rivalry, with elaborate initiation rites for new students and a 'college clap' for ceremonial occasions ('Three sevens and a five'). In 1896, after frequent complaints from HMI, a recreation room was improvised, but, as at most colleges, living conditions remained primitive. There were no student bathrooms until 1897, latrines were decrepit and HMI regularly bemoaned the poor state of decoration and repair. Rich dismissed the social tone of most of the colleges at this time as

That of a somewhat inferior boarding school[13]

and this seems to have been a fair assessment of York. Some of the women's colleges, including Ripon under Garrod and Bishop Otter under Miss Trevor and her successor Hammonds, attained much higher levels of culture and domestic civilisation as well as better examination results. *The White Rose* reminiscences of S. Mills (1875-6) recall that students were not allowed into the city during free time, yet were required to wear silk hats anywhere outside the college grounds. It was an offence for York students to be seen out with a young woman – a rule which endured into the 1930s. *The White Rose* for 1893 records an even more absurd restriction, in anonymous reminiscences of a former student:

> But we were not without our amusing incidents. It was a well known law that the students were not to speak to the female servants at any time. But the rule was sometimes broken. Once a master was walking in the low corridor when he heard a conversation going on. He could not locate it but on opening one of the bedroom doors he discovered a student standing on the bed and talking to one of the maids. They had made a hole in the ceiling between the water pipe and the wall and no doubt had had many conversations before. We were once again assembled to witness a public punishment. The Principal and Masters were in the study room and sentence was passed. The man was to be confined to the grounds for the rest of the term.

But if social life was meagre throughout the two year course at least it ended with a flourish. The Farewell Dinner, held outside college and in co-operation with the York Club seems to have been a prolific occasion, gastronomically and oratorically, as the 1893 menu exemplifies. There were 15 toasts and 15 responses so it may not have been an entirely welcome preparation for the more liberal life to come.

Yet HMI Scott Coward, a severe critic of the colleges, described relationships between York staff and students in 1894 as 'cordial' claiming that Principal Baldwin

allows students a reasonable amount of liberty, with good effect.

Baldwin seems to have been a patrician and distant figure and was reported to know only the senior students of each year; yet he was well-remembered by many former students, particularly at the York Club which was formed in the 1880s and had become a powerful influence by the late 90s. He was well served and complemented in his later years by

Revd W. B. Busby, MA who was Vice-Principal from 1891 and warmly commended in *The White Rose* and in individual reminiscences for his sound teaching and friendly relationships with students. All four of Baldwin's other teaching staff were former York students, reluctant to change the curriculum and college lifestyle under which they had themselves been trained.

Baldwin and his colleagues probably did not appreciate how much standards of achievement had risen in the best of the colleges throughout the 1880s and 90s, particularly after the reforms which followed the Cross Reports. York's results were nearly all below average through this period, particularly in the numbers of men obtaining First Class certificates. In the Committee of Council Report for 1892, HMI Oakeley indicated his appreciation of the general rise in the highest standards by asserting that a First Class award was now almost the equivalent of a degree. Since the average proportion of 'Firsts' in the colleges was around 40% there were apparently many able students passing through them. It is likely that this notable rise in standards reflected the swift success of the Board Schools and the high levels of preparation provided in the best of them, for pupils going on to further training. The Church Colleges, seeking to attract a share of the ablest students, needed to be alert by the 1890s, not only to the direct competition of the Day Training College, but also to the expectations created by the very good accommodation, equipment and tuition at the best Board Schools.

Baldwin seems to have been complacently oblivious to such progress elsewhere. He had no suggestions for improvements at York to offer to the Cross Commissioners, and usually ignored the recommendations of HMI towards better teaching and accommodation in the college. HMI Oakeley's general report for 1893 compared the residential colleges unfavourably with the Day Training provision at the universities and was particularly severe on Saltley and York. Scott-Coward the following year included York in a list of colleges which he believed had been virtually untouched by the 1870 Act and whose provisions were in many ways worse than those of the schools from which their students were recruited. He criticised the excessive number of tutors appointed directly by many colleges from among their own final year students, and, though appreciative of much worthy effort, insisted:

> The educational standard grows higher and cannot be neglected in the training colleges; and one of the chief ways to reach it is by strengthening their teaching staffs, by adding to them, as opportunity offers, persons with higher qualifications.

This thinly disguised pressure for more tutors recruited from the universities and fewer from the elementary school/college certificate route was repeated in the 1896 and 1897 reports, though it was publicly contested by the growingly influential National Union of Teachers, which had a powerful lobby among the membership of the York Club.

Baldwin was impervious to all criticism but the College Committee was not. By 1893 it was strongly influenced by its new secretary, F. J. Munby, a York solicitor whose firm still serves the college a century later. The Committee launched another public appeal to enable the members to

> directly promote the comfort and culture of the young men under their care, during the most important years of their lives. If their life's work is to be successful they must be more than pedagogues . . . and means must be found by which the committee may be able to encourage the Principal and his staff in sustaining the moral tone of the students by cheerful surroundings.

The appeal made slow progress and could not have been helped much by Baldwin's provocative annual reports. In 1895 he claimed

> The condition of York Training College as an Educational Institution is in every respect satisfactory

and in his report for 1896 he flung down his challenge – in case the committee had missed the force of 'as an Educational Institution':

> I have again the pleasure of being able to state that the condition of your Diocesan College continues to be in every respect satisfactory. Her Majesty's Inspectors in their reports are naturally a good deal influenced by the amount expended on buildings and furniture; but I venture to assert that the real efficiency of a training college is best measured by three tests: 1. The conduct of the students. 2. Their work as practical teachers. 3. The various public examinations.

He claimed success for the college in all three.

By now however the Committee was determined on change and was embroiled in serious dispute with Baldwin. He had received a detailed questionnaire from Munby on behalf of the Committee enquiring into all aspects of college administration. While he was considering this the Committee made searching enquiries into the Model and Practising Schools and as a result dismissed C. H. Wilson as Normal Master. A former college student, he was a staunch supporter of Baldwin, and of the York Club. The Committee allowed him to remain on the college staff as a tutor at reduced salary, and their appointment of W. P. Welpton as Normal Master was an immediate success. By 1896 Welpton had won strong approval from HMI Scott-Coward and was later appointed to the University of Leeds Day Training department in a similar capacity.

Baldwin did his best to restrict Welpton's influence; when asked by the committee to prepare a plan to give Welpton complete control over the Practising School he took more than a year to do it. He no doubt realised that the comittee was intent on radical reform of both the Model and Practising Schools, in line with recruitment advice from HMI. In the end the committee had its way.

£656 was spent on furniture and renovations to the buildings in 1895-6, in the hope that the appeal 'The Jubilee Fund' would bring in enough to build new science laboratories and an art room. But by autumn 1896 it was apparent that the appeal had failed. A temporary science room was improvised in the old committee room for £100 and plans for an Art room were shelved. The running battle between Baldwin and the Committee led to the remaining funds from the appeal being diverted to domestic purposes. Among the Committee's complaints, in addition to criticisms of students' behaviour, were similar accusations to those which had led to the parting with Reed. Baldwin and his wife were said to interfere unduly in the domestic affairs of the college – he had sacked a cook without consulting the Matron – and to have neglected to separate college bills from their own domestic expenses. Once again there was no separate kitchen for the Principal's house and meals sent in from college were supposed to be charged. In addition Baldwin was accused of not keeping any record of his receipt and disposal of the half-guinea fees paid for board and lodging at the college by candidates for Queen's Scholarships. There were other minor domestic accusations and Etherington gives a full account of the whole petty-minded episode.[14] It was decided to build a separate kitchen for the Principal's house and Munby's memorandum on some of Baldwin's reactions reflects the growing indignation of Committee members:

> My reply on the Principal's letter is that it is not in the interests of the college but of his own autocracy. This is, I hope, the last dirty corner we shall have to investigate . . . So far as the Committee are determined to understand and direct the internal economy of the place and to keep in touch with others responsible to them, so far will the Committee be resisted and those who recognise any duty to the Committee as superior to the Principal will be removed or made as uncomfortable as possible.

The last comment hinted not only at internal dissensions but at the interference of the York Club. The following year's *White Rose* actually expressed the view that the Old Students' Association was more important to the college than the Committee.

Early in 1897 Baldwin was confronted by the Committee with a list of 16 rules for the keeping of college records and accounts, signed by the

Bishop of Beverley as Chairman. He agreed to observe these and was then informed by Munby that the Committee had, in view of the 'grave charges established' decided only with great difficulty not to demand his resignation.

This he in fact tendered in February 1898, after a further year of antagonism and skirmish which must have damaged the morale and effectiveness of the whole college. To the very end there was dispute even about the precise date when Baldwin's authority ceased, and how quickly he could be expected to vacate the Principal's house.

> Baldwin retired with all the honours of battle which the York Club could bestow. In June he was presented with an address and a service of silver at a gathering of past and present students in college. The tone of the speeches . . . together with the absence of all members of the management committee . . . leave no doubt that this was the defiant salute of the old guard.[15]

Baldwin was undaunted to the end and took the opportunity to reaffirm not only his appreciation of the loyalty and efficiency of the former students who had comprised his teaching staff but also his conviction that

> now the college was one of the foremost in England.

The Committee chose as his successor the Revd E. E. Nottingham, who had been Vice-Principal of Chester College since 1895. He was 30 and a former scholar of St Catherine's Cambridge where he had taken a second in Classics. He had taught at Loughborough Grammar School and Eastbourne College. There is no doubt that the governors appointed him to reform the college; he made a brisk start. He came into residence in September 1898 and at the end of that month the Management Committee received advice from HMIs Scott-Coward and Howard, that the Model and Practising Schools within the college building, should be combined and radically improved. The Committee decided, presumably on Nottingham's advice, not to crease a free school in direct competition with the Board Schools, but to maintain a moderate fee, and obtain additional practising facilities for college students in selected local Board Schools. Welpton had already improved on the training pattern by organising up to three weeks of practice in Board Schools, and by reducing the status of the 'criticism lessons' which students were required to present in the Model School. HMI were divided about the value of such lessons; Oakeley still favoured them but Scott-Coward thought them empty demonstrations

> very like teaching people to use paper and string to make very neat parcels which contain nothing.[16]

Soon after Nottingham's arrival the assessment of student teaching was broadened to include not only model lessons, but normal lessons seen in the Practising Schools, occasional lectures on education topics, written and presented by the students, and periods of up to three weeks practice in Board Schools in York. Moreover, in 1899 the architect proposed and the Committee accepted, a plan to build a completely separate Model School at the back of the college, releasing extensive space in the main building for expansion of residence and teaching. The new Model School, still in use, 90 years later, as part of the Occupational Therapy Department, was opened by the Archbishop in November 1900. The emphasis in the new school was academic and the classrooms were designed small so that classes of more than 30 pupils were impossible. The top class specialised in Science and Art and some boys took examinations of the College of Preceptors.

But the continued charging of fees led the Board of Education to reduce its grant in 1901. Nottingham was determined that the college should not accept this injustice. He went to the Board in London, to see Kekevich in 1901 and Morant in 1905 – the first occasions in the 60 years of the college that a Principal from York or Ripon had the temerity to seek audience with 'Their Lordships'. Eventually Morant suggested an amicable agreement by which the Model School, while being designated a public elementary school, could charge a modest fee, with the York Local Authority agreeing that its staffing and special status as a college school should remain unchanged. This completed Nottingham's first effective reform and E. G. Holmes an HMI of stature, wrote in 1905:

> This is an exceptionally good Practising School and very good use is made of it.[17]

Early in his efforts to achieve better school practice, Nottingham removed former college student F. W. Cull from the headship of the school, though he allowed him to remain on the staff in his other capacity as Art tutor. At the end of his first term Nottingham addressed the staffing issue unequivocally in a special report to the Management Committee:

> The College does not at present prepare any students for the London University Examinations: in this respect it is considerably behind the best training colleges. For this reason we fail to secure the best pupil teachers of the diocese and the county. I do not see my way, with the staff now at my disposal, to remedy this most serious defect. Though I cannot speak too highly of the loyalty of my colleagues, yet I consider it my duty to inform you that, if the college is to provide such an education as the present age demands, the staff needs to be reorganised and strengthened,

both in numbers and efficiency. It is because I feel most strongly the need for this as well as for *raising the tone* of the college, that I venture to suggest that after July next, two of the present staff be replaced by men of higher qualifications and another additional tutor be engaged.

Within a month of this memorandum, in January 1899, former college students Mills and Wilson – both active members of the York Club – were given notice of dismissal.

By June when new appointments had been announced, there was unrest in the college and feelings ran high. Ten senior students were accused of having resisted college discipline throughout the year, intimidated monitors and other students, and abused college property. Nottingham took a hard line. Bishop Crosthwaite, chairman of the Management Committee made a visitation; three of the ringleaders were expelled and the other seven rusticated. In the following year, 1900, there was more trouble when 25 seniors tried to call a strike. Bishop Crosthwaite again visited and the two leaders were rusticated. Morale was not improved by Nottingham's unsuccessful first appointments. Two ordained public school men from Cambridge, both of whom had taught in public schools, left within two years. The replacement for Mills as Music tutor, was a former Battersea student who had achieved an Oxford doctorate. He could not survive the ragging of the York students and left within a year. There was satisfaction among York Club stalwarts at this failure of scholarly appointments, but Nottingham stuck to his convictions and tried again. His model was the 'public school man' who could combine scholarship with sportsmanship and readily joined students in games and in cultural societies. He backed his ideal with facilities: the first proper college sports field was rented in 1899 and the Committee actively supported the rowing club, eventually presenting it with its first 'racing four'. Etherington comments:

> This formula was successful in creating an ethos which lasted for the next half century and established a basis for relationships between the more extrovert staff and students which survived most of the strains imposed by the preservation of Victorian disciplines into the nineteen thirties.[18]

The replacement Science and Maths tutor was J. Frankland, son of a leading member of the York Club, but a graduate of both Cambridge and Manchester. The new Music tutor was G. F. Tendall, yet another Cambridge man, who stayed till 1916. Both men played rugby for the college XV. J. C. A. Borrows, who, like Nottingham, was a classical scholar of St Catherine's took over the English and History courses. He had taught at Wyggeston School, seems to have established good relationships with students, and also remained on the staff until 1916.

100

Nottingham tried to improve relationships with the York Club. At Easter 1899 a reunion of former students was attended by 250, who presented a donation of £40 to the college building fund. At Nottingham's invitation the York Reunion then became an annual event, held for many years in September, before the beginning of the new academic year. *White Rose* articles suggest that many old students took pride in the physical transformation of their college which Nottingham and the Management Committee had accomplished in 1903.

In the summer of 1899, the vacated rooms of the old Practising School were redesigned to provide 12 student bedrooms, three bathrooms and a tutors room. A College Library was formally established, the heating and lighting of the lecture rooms improved, and in 1900 the chapel was at last redecorated. The completion of the new Model School released a large part of the east wing, which by 1901 was converted into two laboratories, a lecture theatre and a workshop. Electric lighting was then introduced throughout the college, a new heating system installed and foundations laid for a new 'wing' to complete the quadrangle. This, when opened in May 1903, greatly expanded the residential capacity of the college, providing 28 new student rooms (now 'Nottingham' corridor), two student common rooms, a staff common room, two tutors' rooms and a gymnasium with changing rooms and showers.

This expansion and renovation cost £12,000. Two-thirds of it was raised by combined contributions from the Management Committee, the Bishop of Beverley and Principal Nottingham, the Dioceses of York, Ripon and Wakefield, the SPCK and the National Society. The remaining £4,000 was raised by a mortgage on the buildings.

When these radical improvements in staffing and accommodation were completed, HMI Scott-Coward pronounced the staff 'very strong' and claimed that

> The instruction given at present is on the plane of the universities in all branches.

The building improvements would, he believed

> place this institution in the front rank of the colleges for men, as regards accommodation and general equipment.[19]

and he suggested to the Committee that the college might seek affiliation to Manchester University.

In 1901 York had ranked only ninth in size of the 13 Church of England Colleges for Men. By 1904, with 112 students, it stood fourth, behind Cheltenham, Battersea and Chelsea, and so was the biggest of the Diocesan Colleges. Increased student numbers allowed a somewhat broader curriculum – within the Board of Education limits –

and individual tutors were appointed for Science and Mathematics. Nottingham's emphasis on academic distinction in staff appointments was matched by higher standards of professional training under Welpton, whose influence was praised by HMI. As we noted at Ripon the Board Syllabus for School Management had been improved and the success of the University Day Training Colleges fostered publication of good quality text-books for teacher education, to which Welpton himself contributed. He believed that the Board's vacillations in the early years of the century, which had so incensed Garrod at Ripon, had inhibited an adventurous approach to the study of Child Development and classroom practice. He campaigned for a

> psychology of development determined by logical, ethical, social, practical and physical ideals of life.[20]

Welpton moved on to the University of Leeds in 1903 and was succeeded by Nottingham's most distinguished appointment, Fred Clarke. A former pupil-teacher, Clarke had attended the Oxford Day Training College and taken a first class honours degree in history. He stayed three years at York, well reported in *White Rose* for kindness to students and willingness to encourage discussion. He then moved on to Professorships of Education at Southampton University College, in South Africa and Canada, and finally at the London University Institute where he was knighted for his services to education.

Another Oxford Day Training College graduate, with a first in history, H. P. Farrell, served as assistant Normal Master until 1908 and coached the rowing club to the great satisfaction of the students. He too had been a pupil-teacher and a succession of such graduates with pupil-teacher experience was established for the Normal Masters post, when Bright, Farrell's successor was followed by F. A. N. Wilmot who was to teach at the college for 40 years. All three were active sportsmen and exemplified the friendly relationship between tutors and staff which was one of Nottingham's ideals.

Busby, the sole survivor of the Baldwin regime, remained as Vice-Principal until 1904 and seems to have worked well with Nottingham. His successor, Revd H. Walker was to serve the college for more than 30 years. He had been a silversmith's apprentice before becoming a pupil-teacher and he then studied at Caernarvon Training College, under Fairchild, a former York tutor. After completing his training he remained eight years as tutor at Caernarvon and then went to Cambridge, where he took a degree in Natural Sciences, returning to teacher training at Carmarthen, first as lecturer, then as chaplain.

The conservative and hesitant approach of the Board of Education to the curriculum of the colleges offered little support to Nottingham in

1. *The York Diocesan Training College. The Lord Mayor's Walk Building 1845 from a print of 1864.*

2.   *Revd William Reed, first Principal at York 1841-1848 and then first Principal of Trinity College, Carmarthen.*

3. *Revd E. Baines Badcock, first Principal Ripon College 1863-1891.*

4. *Ripon College Staff, December 1862.*

5. *The Ripon College Building, 1899 after the completion of Garrod's Chapel.*

6. *Teacher Education 1900: The Criticism Room, Ripon College. Canon Garrod had joined the students to observe this demonstration lesson.*

7. *Science at Ripon College, 1908.*

8. *Three Ripon Principals, George Garrod (left), Eva Lett and Isaac Smith.*

9. *Principal Nottingham with the Senior Year, St John's College, York, 1900. Mrs Nottingham on his right is wearing probably the largest hat in the history of the College.*

10. *The triumphant Rugby XV of 1912. The Captain is John Harrison, later posthumous VC.*

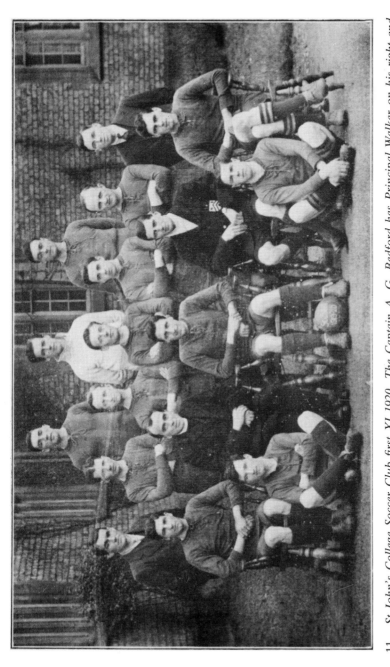

11. *St John's College Soccer Club first XI 1920. The Captain A. G. Bedford has Principal Walker on his right and Vice Principal Wilmott on his left. Note the maturity of the men, most of whom had fought in the Great War.*

12. *Archbishop Temple laying the foundation stone for the new wing, later Temple Hall, 1929.*

his drive for higher academic standards. He could not have been much cheered by the 1905 redefinition of the function of the Training College as:

> Instructing persons who are preparing to become certificated teachers in public elementary schools, in the principles and practice of teaching, and supplementing their education so far as may be necessary.[21]

This inhibited the increase Nottingham had wanted at York in the number of students sitting University of London examinations. York had rarely had more than a half-dozen entries, while Cheltenham frequently had 50. In 1906 the colleges were actually forbidden to prepare students for matriculation because this was alleged to interfere with their proper college work. The Board even attempted, unsuccessfully, to prohibit the practice of a few progressive colleges where students were encouraged to spend the final year abroad in an approved college or university. Yet over the same period the Board was pressing colleges to admit only students who had received secondary education, presumably to raise standards of achievement and potential. 1902 to 1908 were uneasy years for the Church Colleges not solely because of these curriculum aggravations. The old hostility towards the Anglican Church's large share of teacher training erupted again in parliamentary protests on behalf of non-conformists and agnostics. In fact, several Church Colleges, including Ripon and York, acknowledging both common justice and the rapidly increasing competition from LEA colleges, already offered places to non-Anglican candidates and provided acceptable accommodation for them outside the college grounds. McKenna's 1907 Board regulations insisted however that colleges must accept students regardless of their denomination. They were vehemently resisted, the National Society refusing to tolerate

> intrusion into the resident life of the colleges of religiously unsympathetic and possibly even hostile elements.[22]

Archbishop Randall Davidson took a liberal attitude, but in face of hostility from more extreme Churchmen the Board was forced to modify the regulations. They allowed Church Colleges to admit up to half Anglican students and to continue the practice of 'boarding-out' non-conformists. The impact at York, as at Ripon, seems to have been slight, with very few students exercising the right of conscience to opt out of chapel and religious instruction.

Garrod at Ripon had negotiated all these contentious issues with patience, humour and just occasional exasperation. They seem to have weighed heavily on Nottingham. He was inclined to bouts of depression and was incapacitated for most of the academic year 1907-8. In June

1908, still only 40 years of age, he resigned the principalship. He was well enough to attend and speak at a Farewell Reunion in September but did not take up another post – a living at Acaster – until 1910. He had led a successful reformation of the college courageously and at high personal cost. A former student of Baldwin's day wrote in *The White Rose*

> The present students had now no reason, as they unfortunately had in bygone years, to be ashamed of the college.[23]

and another, of Nottingham's own time, wrote in a later edition

> His zeal and efforts on behalf of the College were many times misunderstood and . . . his actions misconstrued.[24]

Nottingham seems never to have recovered fully from his later years at the college. In 1918 he became rector of Sutton-on-Derwent, but the depressions persisted and he committed suicide, aged 53, in 1921.

CHAPTER VI

A Long Survival:
War and Recession 1908-1930

ALTHOUGH TWO PREVIOUS INTERNAL appointments to the Principalship had brought little success, the York Committee members again played safe. They appointed Vice-Principal Walker to succeed Nottingham. He was to become the Colleges' longest-serving Principal through a period of almost continuous constraint.

Meanwhile the Ripon governors, as usual went for new leadership. They appointed Revd Isaac Smith, yet another Cambridge man, to succeed Garrod who remained in strong support of the college, as a Governor and in his new post of Diocesan Director of Religious Education. Smith was 44 and an experienced teacher and administrator. An Open Scholar in Maths at Sidney Sussex, he graduated in 1886 and taught at Stratford on Avon Grammar School and at Trent College before taking up the Vice-Principalship of Cheltenham Training College which he had held for 15 years. He seems at first to have been diffident and retiring with none of Garrod's gregarious high spirits. But he was a family man and with his wife and two young children, moved into St Margaret's Lodge in January 1909, and soon made an impact.

McKenna's attempt to secularise all the training colleges had failed but parliamentary antagonism to denominational colleges was to rumble on through the century. Smith made his stance clear in the College magazine for 1909:

> It is still, alas, true that our system of education is regulated by political rather than educational considerations and the longer this continues the greater the danger of an attempted solution of the question by the adoption of a purely secular system. Teachers cannot perhaps touch political mistakes, but they ought to know the educational ones and are sufficiently powerful to get them altered if made; and I have yet to meet the teacher who is not convinced that religious education is of the highest value to the

child, and few indeed who do not think that the teacher is the proper person to give it.

Competition from the Local Authority training colleges was growing fast and the National Society complained in 1911 that

> the reckless building of training colleges by local authorities with unlimited funds is already making it difficult for our colleges to be filled . . . Not only are quite unnecessary colleges being built in some places, but many local education authorities are forcing their students to enter their own institutions.[1]

LEA funds were certainly not 'unlimited' but the proliferation of teacher education institutions at a time of uncertain employment was startling. In 1900 the 'Voluntary Colleges' and Day Training colleges together had offered just over 6,000 places. By 1913, with the rise of the LEA colleges there were more than 13,000 places, and the four Northern LEA colleges for men, at Leeds, Sheffield, Sunderland and Crewe, already offered more places between them than the three long-established Church Colleges, Chester, York and Durham. What had so recently been a monopoly for the Church Colleges seemed in danger of becoming a minority interest. York, after 71 years had 120 students; Leeds LEA college in only its 12th year already had 180.

Confrontation, animosity and over-provision seemed inevitable and, as usual, the colleges were not short of unsympathetic critics who took little account of their difficulties. But there was at least one voice of reason. Retired HMI Edmund Holmes published, in 1911, an influential study of national education *What Is and What Might Be*. He considered the philosophy behind the national system to be far from idealistic, but did not pillory the 'training system'.

> Shall we blame the Training Colleges because, with an unhappy past behind them, they have yet many things to unlearn? Shall we blame the Local Education Authorities, because, with an unknown future before them, they have yet many things to learn?
>
> No, I repeat, we will blame none of these. We will lay the blame on broader shoulders. We will blame our materialistic philosophy of life, which we complacently regard – orthodox and heretic alike – as 'The Truth'; and we will blame our materialised civilisation, which we complacently regard – cultured and uncultured alike – as civilisation pure and simple, whatever lies beyond its confines being lightly dismissed as 'barbarism'. These are the forces against which every teacher, every manager, every inspector, who strives for emancipation and enlightenment, has to fight unceasingly.[2]

Contemporary readers, inured to tirades against materialism and the 'consumer society', may not readily appreciate what a jarring note

Holmes had struck for his Edwardian compatriots at the height of the Empire. He deplored the lip-service paid to the idea that education should foster the growth of the free individual, and the widespread negation of this idea in schools and colleges. The Board of Education might aspire to 'academic freedom' but Holmes believed that the hand of central control still deadened the education enterprise and that the spirit of the Revised Code endured:

> Why is the teacher so ready to do everything (or nearly everything) for the children he professes to educate? One obvious answer to this question is that for nearly a third of a century (1862 to 1895) the 'Education Department' did everything (or nearly everything) for him. For a third of a century 'My Lords' required their inspectors to examine every child in every elementary school in England on a syllabus which was binding on all schools alike. In doing this they put a bit into the mouth of the teacher and drove him, at their pleasure, in this direction and that. And what they did to him they compelled him to do to the child.[3]

Training college applicants of this period certainly were over-examined. The rise of the secondary schools had generated a plethora of tests and in the year Holmes' book was published Acland chaired a Board of Education investigation into school examinations. His Committee's wise recommendations ushered in the School Certificate Examination, but could not be implemented until after the 1914-18 War.

Garrod would have welcomed Holmes' manifesto, and Smith's leadership at Ripon began in a kindred spirit. The relaxed social events which Garrod had launched were continued and some new college societies formed. In his first year Smith inaugurated the Archaeological Society, with a programme of expeditions and lectures, and the Debating Society. Both had formal memberships of more than half the student body of 140. The Choral Society, later renamed the Musical Society gave frequent performances for the public of Ripon and district and was well served for nearly 50 years by C. H. Moody, college 'music master' and organist of Ripon Cathedral. Dramatic performances, poetry readings and occasional lectures were organised by a new Literary and Dramatic Society. Smith launched it and was patron, but the inspiration came from Miss Buysman, lecturer in English and later Vice-Principal (1903-1946), the longest serving member of the teaching staff at Ripon or York. Other societies of Smith's early years were the Art Club, the French Club and the Geographical Society.

He also gave prompt attention to the buildings and grounds. In his first year the rough track from College Road to the main building was transformed into the curving macadamed drive that still survives. An impressive entrance was formed by building a groundsman's lodge, installing wrought-iron gates, and planting young silver birch trees along the new drive. Plans were approved for a small new wing for the main building to provide rooms for four staff and a proper sick bay. The hostel was enlarged, a new laundry built behind the main block and the old laundry converted into a lecture room. The buildings were completed by the autumn of 1911, and a former lecture room was then coverted into a spacious library of which the governors were specially proud. These were to be the last major building improvements for 20 years but a spate of activity which should have given great pleasure to Smith ended in sadness with the death of his wife in January 1912.

The College now had, by the standards of the time a highly qualified staff. Two more women graduates had been appointed, and Miss Buysman had completed her external London honours degree. Many colleges were having difficulty filling places, but enrolment at Ripon was steady at 142 students of whom 31 lived in the hostel just off campus, and three lived at home in Ripon. The Church colleges continued to register formal protests about the regulation that they must be prepared to enrol up to 50% non-Anglican students, if that many applied. Non-conformists were now very unlikely to apply in larger numbers because the new non-denominational Local Authority colleges already had more places available than they could fill. In fact the legislation, though theoretically severe, caused no difficulties at Ripon or York. Moreover standards of student attainment continued to rise and the leaving class of 1911 achieved 43 First Class certificates and 25 Seconds.

In June 1912 the College celebrated its Jubilee – 50 years at the Ripon location – and over 600 former students joined the residents for a reunion at College, a Commemoration Service in the Cathedral, and lunch celebration in the City Hall, with the Archbishop of York as the guest of honour throughout. The Association of Past Students gave £150 as a Jubilee gift for furniture and books for the new Library, and the magazines of the period record several gifts of stained glass windows for the Chapel, from the 'leavers' of successive years.

Conscious of the need to keep up with the high standards of accommodation and equipment provided in the Local Authority colleges, the Ripon Committee planned a public appeal for £5,000 worth of improvements. It was to be launched in the autumn of 1914, but in November, the Committee blandly announced that it must be postponed 'until after the conclusion of the War' – little knowing how long that was to be.

Smith was understandably proud of the examination results for 1914, which were the best the college had ever achieved, and the best in the country for all colleges, Church and Local Authority. Fifty-one students gained First Class certificates, eighteen Second Class, and there was one Third. Having predominately female staff, and with Smith well beyond the age for military service, the Ripon college, like most women's colleges was able to continue its work. The 1915 Annual Report noted

> The War has brought about a very extensive dislocation of the work of many Training Colleges, but fortunately, except in the matter of working expenses, we have not been affected to any great extent. Throughout the year the students were very busy in their spare time in making comforts for the sailors, soldiers and Belgian refugees; many hundreds of articles of clothing were sent to various quarters, and splints and bandages were made for the Red Cross Society.

Smith lost a number of senior colleagues in 1915. Miss Goodacre, who had taught at Ripon for almost 40 years after qualifying there, resigned through ill-health and died at the college within a week. Miss Mander, Mistress of Method for 18 years, left for missionary work in Japan remaining in close touch for many years through letters to the magazine. Three other tutors left, one to marry and two to take up posts elsewhere. But well-qualified applicants from Newnham, Froebel College, Maria Grey College and Leicester School of Art replaced them and the Annual Report complimented the college as usual on the 'harmonious and cordial relationship

> between the various members of staff which . . . does so much to promote the happiness of college life'.

At the end of 1916, Miss Palin and Miss Woods retired after each serving 40 years, and Miss Waterhouse after 27.

The War did not diminish the enthusiasm of the Association of Past Students, which by 1917 had a remarkable membership of over 1,400. The 1918 report records continuing pressure for places:

> The number of students in training from September 1918 is 141. The applications for admission have been even more numerous than they were last year. October 1st is the first day on which applications can be received and the College could have been filled for next September by those received by the first post that day.

The cost of living had risen sharply during the War and the college had again to be assisted by the Diocese in the payment of debts. The Board of Education had announced increases in its grants which would ease pressure for the following year, but the Annual Report noted that the 'revolution taking place in the salaries paid to all teachers' would swallow up almost all the increased payments to the college.

The War had not closed the college but the 1918 Influenza epidemic did:

> . . . The College had to close for three weeks at the end of October. No nurses could be obtained but the college Teaching Staff rose to the emergency and with their assistance the Matron was able to run the college as a hospital until the last case could be sent home.

By January 1919, however, the students were all back in good health, and Ripon had survived the Great War undamaged, and with its reputation enhanced as one of the most successful and well-run colleges in the country. At York the saga had been sadly different.

Walker had been appointed in 1908 to ensure continuity. Nottingham had pressed the point at his farewell speech to the York Club:

> He could not help feeling that in a way the Committee were paying a great tribute to the efficiency of the staff and the regime of the last ten years, when they felt justified in leaving the control to be carried on by its own late Vice-Principal.

So no one was expecting sweeping changes, but Walker made a popular start and *The White Rose* for December 1908 expressed appreciation for the 'greater comfort' he had secured for students:

> The Common Rooms are vastly improved places and by the provision of lights in the studies long felt inconvenience had been remedied. Other popular improvements are the alteration of the Fives Courts, and the making of a gravel path in the inner quadrangle . . .

One surreptitious change that was now apparent was in the title of the college. There is no record of any official decision, and the magazines and reports still carried student lists headed 'York Diocesan College'. But *The White Rose* had, since the late 1890s described itself as 'The Magazine of the Past and Present Students of St John's College, York', and by 1907 the Yorkshire Press also frequently referred to 'St John's College'. Articles in *The White Rose* during the first decade of the century refer – some flippantly, some portenously – to various ceremonies which went to the initiation of a 'Sinjun'; the soubriquet 'Johnsman' was not yet current.

As at Ripon, the Association of Past Students was a powerful influence; at York it was often closely linked with the burgeoning National Union of Teachers. The annual gatherings at college were not as large as at Ripon but branch organisation throughout the country was very strong and *The White Rose* carried accounts of meetings and dinners in all the large cities of Yorkshire and in London, Manchester, Liverpool and Lowestoft. *The White Rose* was now being published with notable frequency; in 1908 there were seven editions including two in March. The contents were mostly ephemeral and the tone bantering and cheerful, but in June 1909 a sombre note appeared, that had not been needed at Ripon: having praised the quality of training at college as 'not only valuable but the most enjoyable part of our lives' the editor warned leaving students:

> Owing to the fact that at the present the supply of trained teachers is much greater than the demand, there has naturally been much anxiety felt at York, as elsewhere, as to the chances of securing suitable posts. We are glad to say that the outlook is now considerably brighter and Sinjuns are to be congratulated on having gained a fair proportion of appointments. There is still however a lamentable lack of vacant situations and, unless we experience what is now regarded as hopeless, a boom in the teaching profession, there is reason to fear that some of our number will for a time be ranked with the unemployed.

This anxiety, and a shortfall of posts for York students, continued until 1914.

The college had acquired a considerable sporting reputation and *The White Rose* reported fully on Rugby and Association football, cricket, rowing, tennis, cross country running, swimming and fives – a good range for a college of 100 students. The June 1910 edition records the shock and grief at the death of the Captain of Boats, Harry Webster, who overturned a skiff in blustery conditions on the Ouse in the middle of York and was drowned while fellow oarsmen and York citizens looked on. He was unable to swim and though students got him out of the water they could not revive him. The Cornoner's judgement of bystanders was severe:

> Had one or two persons who were present earlier acted with as much promptitude as his fellow students the unfortunate young man's life might have been saved. Whether from failure to realise the situation however or from loss of presence of mind they did not assist in any way and precious moments were lost.

In sad contrast the same edition reported the death of former Principal Baldwin, full of years, with a brief remembrance of his better days, from one of his former students:

> . . . A striking and impressive personality. Standing six feet three or four inches high his figure used to tower above them all. His had been an adventurous career before he came to York and few could rival him in dramatic narrative of hairsbreadth escapes by flood or field . . . He had a great fund of humour too and witty repartee and a power of bringing home to his hearers the lighter side of things . . .

Baldwin had been better loved by his students than by his successive college committees which, with hindsight, was understandable.

Neither humour nor sensitivity seems to have been Walker's strong suit and in 1912 a college sporting triumph was marred by his inflexible discipline. The college Rugby XV had been undefeated in the Lent Term under the captaincy of John Harrison and in February, had beaten Bede College Durham in the annual 'needle' match, with Harrison scoring all the points. Walker ruled, for no stated reason, that the returning team was not to be met at York Station and that no triumphal celebration was to be staged. Virtually the whole junior year defied the ban, and the triumphal procession through the city was avidly reported by the national press as a college 'strike'. The March edition of *The White Rose* quietly conveyed the resentment felt at the punishment of the whole junior year.

The editorial began:

> The Spring Term is now rapidly drawing to a close. What a trying time it has proved! Without doubt it has been the most eventful period of our residence, that is providing no further eccentricities occur during the remaining few months we are to stay here. It is a matter for wonder, how we, though isolated to some extent from the industrial world, have entered into the present unrest. We wish to record the above more for the benefit of '10, '11, '12 students, so that the magazine may remind them of not the pleasantest occurences of their college career . . . Bede Rugger day will doubtless be remembered by all of us, and will be perhaps the chief of our delights, when producing our reminiscences in years to come.

The episode may or may not have been related to national agitation but it was to have a tragic sequel.

A few liberal indications in *The White Rose* off-set an overall impression of narrow repressiveness under Walker's regime. There are student articles on visits to France and one in French on the poetry of Hugo, accounts of German and French Teachers' Colleges, descriptions of convivial reunions and of social and musical events in the 'Smoke Room'. A 1913 edition carries an account of the inaugural meeting of the college branch of the Students Christian Union, followed later in the year by an article by Bishop Gore 'What is an Educated Man'. These are the first clear reflections in the magazine, after 20 years of publication, of the Christian associations of the York College. This is in marked contrast to Ripon, where the magazines carried frequent articles relating to Christian activities in the college, to chapel life and to the support of missionary work overseas – some of it being done by former students and staff.

Many of the long-established colleges – Chelsea, Battersea, Chester and Durham for example – prided themselves on producing men of particular qualities, but *The White Rose* published in October 1912 an unflattering estimate of the local product, by a former student of Dudley College which, founded only in 1909, could not draw on great experience:

> Men of York lack originality. Hardworking, diligent and disciplined, they follow the lead of another with appreciation and criticism, but fail to generate new ideas, or fresh points of view . . . Speculative contingencies lie outside their thought circle, but in practical application the are adepts . . . Staunch reliability is one of their great assets . . . With less routine, more relaxed effort, with freer expression and greater discussion, the mind of the Yorker would expand and he would excel.

The editor may have included it as much to enlighten the Principal as the students.

In the summer of 1914 work began on the building of a pavilion at a newly rented playing field out at Clifton, two miles from Lord Mayor's Walk. The editorial farewell in the July *White Rose* was as hearty as ever:

> From comparative seclusion within the walls of our Alma Mater, we are soon to be plunged in 'the busy time of men' to carry on a life's work for which our two years here have been the preparation. To our juniors' keeping we leave the honour and prestige of St Johns, the upholding of her best traditions. Yet, though soon of the past we shall be Sinjuns still; the Yorkist Club claims us all as members; the 'signs of Brotherhood' must still exist.

Three weeks later the War broke out. Many of these leavers never took up their profession or sampled the pleasures of the York Club. *The White Rose* for July 1915 carried a Roll of Honour of 121 'Past or present men who are already serving with the Colours' and announced that many more seniors and juniors were about to join them. D. C. Joy (1900-2) had been the first St John's man killed in action. The simple War Memorial in the College Chapel lists 84 former students who were killed, 1914 to 1918, from a college with just over 100 places and no more than 500 ex-students below the age for military service. A poignant loss was that of Second Lieutenant John Harrison – the Rugby hero of 1912. After a successful start in school-teaching Harrison had won a fine reputation as a professional 'Northern Union' Rugby three-quarter, before enlisting in the East Yorkshire Regiment.

He had been awarded the Military Cross and – posthumously – the Victoria Cross. The Official VC Citation illustrated, like so many others before and since, the bravery, madness and waste of war.

> For most conspicuous bravery and self sacrifice in an attack. Owing to darkness and to smoke from the enemy barrage and our own and to the fact that our objective was in a dark wood, it was impossible to see when our barrage had lifted off the enemy front line. Nevertheless, Second Lieutenant Harrison led his company against the enemy trench under heavy rifle and machine gun fire, but was repulsed. Reorganising his command as best he could in No Mans Land, he again attacked in darkness under terrific fire, but with no success. Then, turning round, this gallant officer, single-handed, made a dash at the machine gun, hoping to knock out the gun and so save the lives of many of his company. His self-sacrifice and absolute disregard of danger was an inspiring example to all.

The college was closed in 1916 when even a small entry of qualified men could no longer be recruited. The remaining few students were transferred to St Johns Battersea, the College was requisitioned as a military hospital and Walker became chaplain to the military at both the College and York hospital until early 1919. The Church Colleges that remained open were surveyed by an Archbishops Commission of Enquiry in 1916. It reported an urgent need for the colleges to work in closer co-operation and as a result, in 1917 a Church Colleges Federation was formed to co-ordinate their work under a Board of Supervision.

National planning for the future of education was impressive during the later years of a draining war that Britain was by no means assured of winning. Committees of Parliament and the Education Department were at work on post-war developments and in 1917 the Lewis Report on *Juvenile Education in Relation to Employment After the War* recommended that the school leaving age should be raised to 14 and all half-time school attendance abolished. The Education Bill of the same year was skilfully piloted through parliament by the Chairman of the Board of Education, H. Fisher, former Vice-Chancellor of Sheffield University. When the Bill became the 1918 Education Act it authorised policies which were certain to increase the demand for trained teachers once the war was over. The Lewis recommendation was accepted and the further intention announced to raise the leaving age to 15 as soon as possible. The grants system was reformed so that at least half of all education expenditure was to be provided by central government. All elementary school fees were finally abolished and the range of ancillary and continuation services to be provided by local authorities was much enlarged.

Other related legislation also seemed auspicious for the colleges as they looked forward to peaceful conditions. The Superannuation Act of 1918 was shortly followed by the establishment of the Burnham Committee and improved salary scales for teachers. The Board also announced its intention of funding selected students for a third year of 'advanced study' immediately following a successful two year certificate course. In spite of the growing number of rival institutions, the Church Colleges still formed the largest and probably most influential sector of the teacher training system. At the end of 1919 there were 50 denominational colleges, 30 of them Anglican, with a total of 6,200 students. The 22 local authority colleges had just over 4,000 students and the 18 university training departments just over 5,000.[4]

But none of the colleges could afford to be complacent. In 1918 they were severely criticised in a series of articles in the *Times Educational Supplement* which accused them of being out of touch with reality and the daily work of the schools.[5] The denominational colleges still faced particular problems. Their 'providing bodies' had very limited resources compared with the Local Authorities, and the 1918 Act, progressive in many respects, had failed to improve on the uneasy 1902 regulations for religious teaching in schools. In the 1917 debates many prominent Anglicans had been ready to give up denominational schools in exchange for greater influence over the whole education system exercised largely through the Church Training Colleges, which, they believed could be greatly expanded and improved with the resources no longer needed for Church schools. But Roman Catholic and Non-Conformist policy strongly opposed this and the attempt to work out such a 'solution' was abandoned. The denominational schools and colleges therefore continued vulnerable to criticism not only for their sectarianism but – in many instances – for their underfunded inadequacy. It was an opportunity lost for the Anglican colleges; Fisher's consistent view exposed the continuing anomaly:

> . . . almost any form of settlement which provided safeguards against the imposition of religious tests on teachers and against the enforcement of religious teaching unpalatable to the parents of the child, would be preferable to the continuance of the present arrangement.[6]

St John's York re-opened in the autumn term of 1919. Supplies were precarious and transport and communications not yet restored to pre-war regularity. Yet spirits were high among returning students with little thought of national difficulties ahead. Only Principal Walker appeared unaware that the post-war college entry would be much changed and merit a more liberal regime. But the students would not be ridden roughshod. A. J. Copps who had enlisted in 1915, survived the war and been demobilised in January 1919, was one of the entry of September. Fifty years later his account of an early confrontation with Walker, was published in *Spread Eagle*, the magazine of the Old Students Association:

> The Principal, the Revd H. Walker (referred to as Taggy) was very watchful of our morals and put such areas as Coney Street out of bounds for some stupid reason. He was as sour and as dour a specimen of the cloth as I have ever met . . . We had quite a job to reform him, or to make him understand that we were not young lads but men who had come out of tribulation and having wives and families. So we objected to many petty regulations. Particularly did we criticise the dietary and one Sunday evening at the supper – save the mark – of half a cup of watered milk and a half-penny bun, we struck. Taggy, the VP and the other masters were sitting at a table on the dias, when we filed in to get our thick mugs half filled – if there happened to be sufficient in the ewer to accomplish this. Then, after a hurried Grace, we raised our mugs and let them crash to the table. There was a sound of smashing crockery, followed by a deadly silence, broken by the Principal's tensely uttered order 'You may go to your studies'.
>
> There he hinted at sending us all down for insubordination, but our chosen speakers pointed out that we had not disobeyed any order in making our protest against conditions that could not be tolerated and savoured too closely of Dickensian times. This seemed to hit him between the eyes and he began to temporise. Finally he asked our representatives to meet him in his study to state their case. When they did go he tried to browbeat them without success. Our men had a good deal of practice in calling bluffs. Besides, the VP sympathised with us, so much against his inclination and with evident chagrin he gave in, but before capitulating he enquired what we would do if he turned down our requests. Our leaders diplomatically replied that, in that case the students intended to send a petition to the Archbishop. Poor Taggy raved, but our 8 pm meal became a late dinner that even exceeded our expectations.[7]

It was hard on Walker that 14 years of leadership through difficult times should have been followed by the economic crisis of 1920-21. The rapid growth of the teaching profession made it a worthwhile target of the 'Geddes Axe' and, in spite of the best efforts of the NUT – well supported by the York Club – the government forced through a five percent reduction of the new Burnham scales. Worse still, the Geddes Committee warned that staffing must be reduced in all elementary schools and the intakes of students to the Training Colleges would therefore be cut for 1923. Yet *The White Rose* maintained a cheery tone, with accounts of occasional visiting lecturers, of musical evenings and of public productions of Shakespeare, Shaw and Gilbert and Sullivan – well received by York audiences. Some whimsical 1922 guidance from seniors to juniors on how to prepare for a 'Criticism Lesson' suggests that student views of tutors have not changed much in 70 years:

Aim (in the mind) To appease the lecturer criticising and to secure, either by bluff or by tactful subservience, a mark better than might be expected.

Statement of Aim (as set down in notebook) To teach the children to appreciate all that is noble, virtuous and admirable, and in the space of half an hour to accomplish the regeneration of fifty youngsters and therefore indirectly the regeneration of England . . .

Procedure. Section I Go to the lecturer who will criticise the lesson, declare that you are in great difficulty, listen to his wisdom with open-mouthed admiration, and bring a hand-cart to borrow twenty of his books (which need not be used) . . .

Section III Get up the material for the lesson from some twopenny-halfpenny handbook.

Section IV This will vary according to the lecturer who comes to hear the lesson:

For the Master of Method: Prepare a quarter of the lesson carefully. At this point make some unimportant error of procedure. He will then butt in and relieve you for the rest of the lesson. At the end express fervent admiration and comprehension of the skill with which he rescued you from a dangerous situation.

For the Assistant Master of Method: Assume a deep interest in the psychological study of each child in the class. Prepare carefully for a slight discussion with the lecturer at the end of the lesson, inter-larding your conversation with airy references to appreciation and epiphenomenalism. Remember that in regard to arithmetic he has a mental complex.

For the lecturer in English: Change from the Northern to the Oxford dialect as soon as he enters the room. Try to keep the class from being unduly amused at his stature; and be comforted throughout by the reflection that, after all, he will probably forget to tell you what he thought about the lesson . . .

117

Section V Have a shower, change your underclothing, take three aspirin tablets and apply for a theatre pass.

College sport continued successfully and not always too seriously. The 1923 Regatta was a fancy dress affair which drew a large crowd of local folk to the river, raised over £30 for hospital charities and was applauded in the Yorkshire press.

Through the early 1920s the college maintained student numbers above 100 and by 1925 there was at last some encouragement from government. The *Report of the Departmental Committee on the Training of Teachers for Public Elementary Schools* expressed the determination of Lord Burnham and his members to work for parity of esteem between teachers in elementary and secondary schools. It proposed that, in future, intending teachers for all schools should themselves have been educated in secondary schools, and that the Training Colleges should be drawn into close co-operation with the Universities – in which most of the country's secondary teachers were trained. This would be achieved through the establishment of Joint Examination Boards, to replace the examination procedures of the government's Board of Education. The proposal was to prove one of the most far-reaching in the entire history of the colleges, and its influence is still at work for Ripon and York. The Committee's argument includes a reference – rare in official reports – to the idea of collegiate independence which is one of the themes of this study:

> We think this mode might be further developed not only with the object of interesting the universities more generally in the training of teachers outside their precincts, but incidentally as a means of giving the training colleges a greater measure of autonomy, and of relating the examination, upon which students qualify for certification, more closely to particular colleges or groups of colleges . . . We feel satisfied also that such arrangements . . . if carefully planned and undertaken with good will by all parties concerned, in the interests of greater educational efficiency, need not lead to friction or interference or to any objectionable increase of inspection.[8]

The Council of Principals of the Colleges supported the proposal and urged that the university connection should extend beyond examining, that the colleges needed freedom from interference and that, in the new arrangements, the 'separate individuality of each college should be preserved'.

St John's York had begun a working relationship with the University of Leeds in 1921 when attendance at certain college courses was recognised as conferring exemption from part of the Leeds BA and BSc degree courses.[9] The Joint Examination Board of the Universities of

Leeds and Sheffield, University College, Hull and the neighbouring colleges became fully functional in 1929, and both the York and Ripon Colleges have worked with the University of Leeds ever since. Other academic liaisons have been explored from time to time but have not supplanted the Leeds relationship.

The 1926 Hadow Report on *The Education of the Adolescent* raised hopes again for an improvement in the status and supply of teachers – a perennial theme in the college magazine at York, Ripon and most other colleges. The report resulted from a remit of the first Labour Government and reflected the influence of R. H. Tawney who, in *Secondary Education for All* had elaborated

> . . . a widespread opinion among persons of experience that a great deal of educable capacity misses education.[10]

With Tawney a key member, the Hadow Committee recommended that the school leaving age be raised to 15, secondary education provided for all children after six years of 'primary' schooling, and secondary education expanded beyond the limited concept of the grammar school, in 'modern secondary schools' and 'practical and realistic' curricula.

By the time the Hadow Report was published, Baldwin's Conservative government had replaced Ramsay McDonald's, but the main recommendations were accepted in principle, with no commitment to specific dates. This was just as well, since the further economic slump and then the Second World War, ensured that it actually took 21 years to raise the school leaving age again. It was significant that later reports – notably Spens (1938) and Norwood (1943) – endorsed the expansion of secondary education through three types of school – 'Grammar, Technical and Modern'. The Hadow advice was substantially followed

> treating the age of eleven to twelve as the beginning of a new phase in education, presenting new problems of its own, and requiring a fresh departure in educational methods and organisation in order to solve them.[11]

The key recommendation for the Training Colleges was that, in the Secondary Modern Schools

> the qualifications of the teachers and the standard of staffing in proportion to the number of pupils in the school, should approximate to those required in the corresponding forms of Grammar Schools. More teachers however, will be required in practical subjects.[12]

Ironically the firm classification of schools as 'primary' or 'secondary' which resulted from the Hadow Report, faced the Training Colleges with the difficulty of specialisation for age ranges and subjects. They were expected to produce instant responses, and in January 1928 the Annual Conference of Directors of Education severely censured the Colleges for not preparing students for the actual conditions in schools, claiming that

> an increasing number of young teachers from college could only teach a very few subjects, instead of being prepared to teach all subjects.

As usual in education, yesterday's solution had created today's problem.

The difficult decade of the 1920s ended well for the York College. The Church Central Board of Finance in 1928 commissioned a report on all the colleges and it was published in July 1929. The Board's inspector, R. G. Mayor took a realistic view of the prospects of the colleges and urged that all should be comprehensively renovated and expanded if resources could be found. In the light of later events in the 1930s and 1970s, his comments on possible mergers seem especially prescient:

> I do not see any present reason for advising further measures of concentration or the closing of any college . . . Amalgamation of two colleges may in special cases be carried out, on terms preserving the continuity of each, as in the case of St Mark and St John in Chelsea. But schemes of amalgamation on these lines would not be easy to devise and I have not found myself able to suggest any further case in which this method could be applied with advantage.

His reports on individual colleges were brief and pointed. Of York he noted that there were 107 students resident on Lord Mayor's Walk and 28 in a nearby hostel and that the Archbishops Commission Report of 1916 had judged its buildings 'fairly well designed and well equipped for its purpose'. The several deficiencies noted were now all about to be remedied:

> A scheme has been approved by the Board of Education and is now being carried out, under which the present gymnasium will be converted into an Art Room and provision will be made for a larger gymnasium, to serve also as an Assembly Hall, and for 25 study bed rooms.

These were the first buildings to be added to the college since Nottingham's extensions of 1902, and the foundation stone of the new Hall/Gymnasium was laid in January 1929 by the new Archbishop of York, William Temple. It was his first public appearance as Chairman of the College Governors and he left a large audience in no doubt of his loyalties. *The White Rose* summarised his address:

> 'I do not think that the general membership of the Church as a body has paid anything like the attention which it ought to, to the

importance of our training colleges' said the Archbishop. There had been so much controversy about schools to attract attention that very often this entirely vital part of their educational equipment had escaped the attention of the great masses of the people.

Certainly for himself if he had to choose between the schools and the training colleges he would have no hesitation in choosing the training colleges . . . 'Training Colleges are surely more than anything else the absolute key of the situation' said the Archbishop 'and it is our bounden duty at all costs to maintain these colleges and, if possible in later years to increase their number.'

The York College had never had stronger public support, and though, as we shall see, Temple was to be hard pressed to sustain this conviction through the 1930s, it eventually enabled him, at Canterbury, to negotiate the religious clauses of the 1944 Education Act. In 1986 when the college renovated and extended the building he had inaugurated, it was named the Temple Hall.

The final sentence of Mayor's 1929 report on the college was to prove prophetic of its next 60 years.

The situation and buildings of this college offer good prospects of successful work in the future, with the possibility of establishing closer relations with Leeds University.

At the Ripon College the 1920s proved relatively stable and successful though – like any normal educational institution – it frequently complained of being subjected to incessant and unnecessary change. Smith wrote frequently and fervently about the Christian witness which was a prime purpose of the college. He and his colleagues cultivated relationships with Yorkshire parishes and schools, with the City and with Ripon Cathedral, of which he was made an Honorary Canon in 1920. At the reunion in June of that year, to which many former staff returned, he anticipated Temple and spoke out plainly in favour of developing the Church Colleges and abandoning denominational schools, if such a choice had to be made:

It was natural that the 'Fisher Proposals' should be referred to in the speeches. No one can deny the sacrifice which such a change would involve to the friends of Church Schools, but at the same time, if effectively carried out, there would be a great gain with regard to religious education. It is a pity that the question cannot always be considered on its merits, and the old catchwords and shibboleths such as 'tests for teachers' and 'right of entry' which no one in his senses wants, and which the proposals do not involve, be obliterated; it sometimes seems that facts and arguments are powerless against all such catchwords.

He had little patience with the common view among church members, that the purpose of Church Colleges was to produce Christian teachers for Church Schools. There was a greater need in the council schools:

> If the development of character is the chief end of education, then religious education must be the supreme educational interest of the State, and the most honourable work of the teacher; and the children whose parents are careless in the matter of religion are the very children whom it is most desirable to bring under its influence. If only the teachers themselves . . . would grapple with it and state boldly that they wish to solve it in the true interests of education, then we could see visions and dream dreams . . .

There seemed little chance of that in the government turmoil and industrial strife of 1921. The coal strike forced the postponement of the summer term for almost a month, but there was no discussion of national problems in the college reports or magazines, and the customary round of society meetings, plays, concerts, field trips, outings, lectures and sporting events was uninterrupted and fully reported. The Director of Music was now something of a national figure as Dr Moody, CBE, FRCO, and his lectures and musical events were big occasions in the city as well as the college. Sport was keen and successful, with regular fixtures in hockey, netball, athletics and tennis, and periodic revivals of cricket. The college often hosted the Northern Colleges Tennis Tournament between six women's colleges and won it five times through the 1920s.

Magazine articles sent from many countries showed that the international impact of which Garrod had been proud, was continuing, both in teaching and in mission work. The 1923 magazine also carried a first article on Ripon College Wisconsin and a visit from friends of that college to Ripon, Yorkshire. They reported a warm welcome from Smith

> a genial scholastic gentleman whose college is only for young ladies but its reputation has gone to the four corners of the globe.

The first link eventually developed into the strong student and staff exchange which operated between the two colleges through the 1980s and continues to grow.

In his 1925 Presidential Report to the Association, Smith feared the outcome of the Burnham Committee Report. Its minority recommendation that the college course be reduced to one year had narrowly failed, but there were still fierce critics of the colleges who thought their training should be professional only and not concerned with continuing the higher education of the students. Smith was adamant:

> Quite as many teachers fail from lack of material to present to their pupils as from lack of technical skills. Moreover the two year course at colleges like ours is planned for those who will not receive a University training, and the care of the general culture of the student is, to my mind, our most important work.

Throughout his time at the college, which he had acknowledged from the outset as a competent institution, he had been willing to support careful change, but was irritated by hasty and uninformed demands from distant bureaucrats. He quoted with approval some words of Francis Bacon, which epitomise his own years at Ripon:

> It were good that men in their innovations would follow the example of time itself; which indeed innovateth greatly, but quietly, and by degrees scarcely to be perceived.

Characteristically, he did not welcome the Hadow recommendations for closer association with the universities, and regretted the withdrawal of the Board of Education from the certificate examination. This he claimed had already been changed too often but had been fairly examined by HMI and Board staff with sound knowledge of the colleges and of the abilities of their students.

By 1928 the membership of the Association had reached 2,000 and more than half of them assembled in June for the biggest reunion yet held. It was known that Smith would reach retirement age at the end of 1929, before the next reunion and very generous presentations to him were the focus of the occasion. But he was not short of work or problems during his last 18 months. The East Wing and Art Room had given trouble almost since they were erected in 1904. They had been reinforced and repaired but eventually, at Easter 1929 the whole Wing was condemned as unsafe and the decision taken on the advice of Sir Giles Gilbert Scott, to demolish it. The Governors planned another Appeal, and a two phase rebuilding scheme which would cost £25,000. The first phase, for £13,000 was to begin as soon as possible and incorporate in a new block to the west of the main building, a new Hall/Gymnasium to seat 400, changing rooms, cloakrooms, store rooms and a staff sitting room, all on the ground floor and more than 20 student bedrooms above. A new main college entrance was to link the new wing to the old main building, with a spacious courtyard beyond.

In his final Presidential address to the Association in 1930 Smith had to report that the new building had not yet begun, that the college was having to use the Drill Hall in Ripon for some activities and that the Annual Play – a notable event for the City – could not be presented. The same 1930 magazine published a warm tribute from Garrod, with whom Smith had worked happily for 22 years – which says much for both of them.

> He has made the College move with the times. And with it all, he has kept up the good old college traditions of the past . . . it is marvellous how little the 'heart' of Ripon has changed through all this National experimenting, which must have been a constant difficulty and anxiety to the Principal . . . and now he can hand over to his successor a College which can in many respects challenge comparison with any college of its kind.

It was a considered compliment from one successful Principal to another – and well deserved.

CHAPTER VII

Through Depression and War to Butler and McNair 1930 to 1945

THE BOARD OF EDUCATION HAD DECREED IN 1919, that Training Colleges for Women should normally appoint women to their Principalships, and several colleges had been led with distinction by women through the 20s, as indeed they had in the previous century. In 1930 the governors of the Ripon College therefore appointed, after 68 years, their first woman Principal. Miss Eva Lett maintained the Cambridge tradition at York and Ripon, being a Newnham College graduate. She had taught in Church, Local Authority and Independent Colleges, having first been a lecturer in English at St Hild's College, Durham, then Vice-Principal of Dudley Training College and, since 1922, Principal of the Bergman Osterberg College of Physical Education at Dartford. She had been the first woman Principal at Osterberg so she could face the Ripon innovation with some confidence. But she may well have been startled to find that her predecessor Smith had joined his predecessor Garrod on the college governing body, which had also appointed Miss Buysman, in her 28th year at the college, to the new post of Vice-Principal. There was therefore a formidable reserve of experienced leadership to advise on change – or to resist it. Miss Lett made a swift first move, occupying rooms in the main college building, and offering St Margaret's Lodge as accommodation for several other staff, and later as a Chaplain's house.

During her first year the second report of the Consultative Committee under Hadow's chairmanship was published. *Primary Education* was ultimately one of the most important government reports produced between the wars; it contained many suggestions on which the Plowden Committee were to build in the 1960s and so was to have a strong influence on primary schooling for the next 50 years. It entrenched the Burnham and first Hadow Committees' proposals for the structure of secondary education, the age of transfer being 11 years. It also extrapolated from current psychological research, the division of children into 'ability groups' which became familiar as 'streaming'. Its convictions about primary education were inspiring, not only for schools but for the Teacher Training establishments:

> . . . any curriculum, if it is not to be arbitrary and artificial must make use of certain elements of experience because they are part of the common life of mankind. The aim of the school is to introduce its pupils to such experience in an orderly and intelligent manner, so as to develop their innate powers and to awaken them to the basic interests of civilised existence . . . Hitherto the general tendency has been to take for granted the existence of certain traditional 'subjects' and to present them to the pupil as lessons to be mastered . . . What is required, at least so far as much of the curriculum is concerned, is to substitute for it methods which take as the starting point of the work of the primary school, the experience, the curiosity and the awakening powers and interests of the children themselves.[1]

The report also made generous proposals for the design and equipment of future primary schools and for the range of services they might offer.

It came at a time when several Church Colleges were undertaking ambitious expansion and renovation, and by the end of her second year Miss Lett had seen the new West Wing at Ripon completed. It improved on and added to the facilities of the demolished East Wing and was the first college building to be equipped with electric light and power. The opportunity was taken at the same time to electrify the rest of the college buildings. The new wing was dedicated by the Bishop and formally opened by Earl Grey, chairman of the Church Board of Finance, in September 1932. Lord Grey paid special tribute to the efforts of the Dean of Ripon, Mansfield Owen, who, at the age of 87, had led a vigorous fund-raising campaign and had badgered the Church Commissioners into approving a large loan.

> For the last three years the Dean has been a perfect thorn in my flesh. Whatever happened to other colleges, Ripon must get what it deserved.

Though praising this local achievement Lord Grey warned that 'the position of all Training Colleges was grave and anxious'. He urged the Church Colleges to work together as much as possible, without sacrificing individuality.

Once again crisis was normality for teacher education. This one had been precipitated mainly by the economic recession of 1931, and by the failure throughout the 1920s to resolve the denominational schools issue – on which Fisher, Temple and Smith had all pronounced unequivocally –

in a way that would leave the Church of England with manageable financial obligations to its work in education. After the series of college surveys which had resulted in approval for new buildings at York, Ripon and Chichester, the Church Board of Finance had over-committed itself. It approved complete rebuilding programmes for Whitelands College, London, and for Warrington College which was to be relocated as St Katherine's College, Liverpool. The total cost of the two new colleges was to be £350,000 and the excellent facilities planned for them aroused envy and emulation among the older foundations. By the end of 1931 however, the new National Government had ordered retrenchment in every field of public expenditure; student allocations at all colleges for September 1932 were reduced by an average of 10%. Even more threatening was a government circular of April 1932 predicting that the number of school age children in England and Wales would fall by over a million during the next 15 years. In the event, this forecast proved wildly inaccurate, but its influence at the time was doleful for the colleges and convenient for a government bent on economies. Furthermore, the morale of the teaching profession had been dealt a severe blow by the 'Geddes Axe' which again arbitrarily reduced teachers' salaries, by 10%.

Only six weeks after the formal opening of the new wing at Ripon, the Council of the Church Colleges held a confused and anxious meeting, in November 1932. What follows deserves attention in a study of an individual college, not least because the Church Colleges were later justifiably incensed at government attitudes to closure and contraction and may need to be reminded that the Church's own record of negotiation with its colleges is not unblemished.

The November meeting reluctantly resolved

> That in the highest interest of the group of Church Colleges, this Council approves and will support a policy of concentration.

Bureaucrats need euphemisms. In the 1970s the cloak for 'closure' was 'rationalisation'; in the '30s it was 'concentration'. The meeting also resolved that alternative methods of meeting the national crisis should be explored. The following day, the Board of Supervision of the Colleges, not lingering for any such exploration, decided that three colleges must close forthwith and selected Chester, Lincoln and Bristol. Telegrams were dispatched to the colleges the same afternoon inviting representatives of their governors, 'if they wished to contest the decision', to wait upon the Board of Supervision in London in four days time.

It was an astonishing procedure, and Geoffrey Fisher, who had been consecrated Bishop of Chester only the previous month, intervened on behalf of his Diocesan College. He denounced the Board's actions in a letter to *The Times*.

Our complaint is that the Board did not in this matter act as the representative of the Training Colleges; it did not obtain their approval to its detailed proposals. It did not even consult those most intimately concerned. It acted as though it had independent authority to settle the fate of colleges over their heads. Whatever the merits of its policy may be, its method of action must appear to others, as it appears to its victims, callous and autocratic.[2]

Two months later, in February 1933, when the issue was debated in the Church Assembly, the Board of Supervision's proposals were supported by a powerful group of senior churchmen, including Archbishop Temple, who, only four years before, at York, had urged the importance of preserving all the colleges. Fisher deployed his eloquence and wit in a tightly argued maiden speech to the Assembly. It was known that one of the prime movers of the Board's proposals was Canon Partridge of Chichester, and in a debate that generated more heat than light, Fisher probably won the day with his reminder to members that the lesson for the morning – Jeremiah 18 – included the timely verse,

The Partridge sitteth upon her eggs and hatcheth them not.

The motion for the closure of the three colleges was lost. It later emerged that several colleges, Ripon and York among them, had been ruled out of consideration for closure by the Board solely because of the heavy debts recently incurred for their new buildings. A Board pamphlet naively claimed that

. . . to close a college which was committed to pay considerable sums annually on account of capital expenditure would obviously not assist the solution of the difficulties for the group. To close such a college would only create fresh debts.

It seems not to have occurred to the Board that some comparison of quality and potential among the colleges might have been fair and prudent before particular closures were decreed. The historian of Lincoln College observed tartly that since it appeared that owing a large sum of money guaranteed survival it was obviously wise for any board of governors to put their college heavily into debt as soon as possible.[3]

The Assembly's reprieve was temporary. A Committee was established, including representatives of the Board of Supervision, the Board of Finance and four College Principals, to review all the colleges and advise whether efficiency could be secured without closures. It reported in December in an 80 page document which is a good summary of the state of the colleges, collectively and individually. It cautiously recommended the attempt to retain all colleges provided they would all agree to raise fees from £35 or £40 per year, to £50, government could be persuaded to maintain existing levels of support in spite of recession, and a central pool of finance could be set up by the Church Board, to guarantee existing loans for up to 25 years. The report concluded that unless these three steps could be taken promptly, 'concentration' was inevitable. Most colleges backed the measures, though two women's colleges, Ripon and Bishop Otter declined to raise their fees to the proposed level. Ripon governors argued that their college was in direct competition not with other Church Colleges, but with LEA Colleges in the North, none of which were raising fees, and some of which actually charged less than the present Ripon fee of £40. The 'pool' was established and further drastic measures postponed.

In spite of the building extensions 1932 proved an uneasy year at Ripon. With a heavy capital debt and a tight annual budget the College was informed that numbers for the following year must be reduced from 140 to 122, with a further cut to follow. A deficit was inevitable. There was also a sad staff loss: previous Principals had combined their administrative duties with those of chaplaincy, but when Miss Lett arrived, Revd Dr E. J. Martin had been appointed resident chaplain and lecturer in Divinity. Magazine references suggest that he quickly proved effective and popular in both capacities, but he died in may 1932 after only a year and a half in office. It was a difficult enough period of adjustment for the college, seeking new patterns of staffing and authority; to add to the anxieties already created by economic crisis and the vagaries of the Board of Supervision, the year brought criticism of the colleges from an unexpected quarter.

In the third issue of the new Cambridge journal *Scrutiny*, L. C. Knights, the co-editor, who was subsequently Professor of English at Sheffield, Bristol and Cambridge, contributed a scathing analysis of the quality and methods of the colleges, drawing evidence from a questionnaire distributed among their past and present students and staff. His answer to the interrogative title *Will the Training Colleges stand Scrutiny?* was an emphatic 'No':

> . . . amongst the 'trained' – those at least who retain some critical independence after a systematic numbing of the faculties – the Training College has become a byword for futility, or worse.[4]

Knights conceded that the colleges were only part of a circular 'educational machine' – school to university or college and back to school – and was also critical of the university training departments. For all students in training, his respondents had complained, timetables were grossly overcrowded, with too many compulsory lectures – many of them poor. In academic studies there seemed little attempt to encourage that 'critical discrimination' which was the pursuit – and became the hallmark – of *Scrutiny*. In the study of literature, for example, the colleges seemed preoccupied with pedestrian historical background and alleged 'visual imagery', instead of trying to engage students with the 'quality of mind'.

Many of these charges were justified, and they were laid out of concern for the quality of English life. Knights was severe on colleges, universities and schools, but, like Holmes 20 years before, he acknowledged that the causes of cultural and educational inadequacy lay deeper:

> ... responsibility does not end with them. Behind the educational system stands the cinema, newspapers, book societies, and 'Big Business' – the whole machinery of 'democracy' and standardisation. So that the main charge against the Training Colleges is that they do nothing to check an 'increasing inattention', nothing to foster such interest as their students may possess, nothing to encourage an adult sense of responsibility.

Knights expected to be counter-attacked for not having 'mentioned the one or two decent exceptions to the general rule'. There is little evidence to qualify York for such exemption from his censures, one of the sharpest of which was directed against the mass of petty college restrictions which reduced student life to the level of a 'prolonged and hopeless childhood'.

An extreme example – not quoted by Knights – was the Lincoln Diocesan College. Among its rules at the time of the *Scrutiny* questionnaire were:

1   No new acquaintance must be made in Lincoln.
2   The names and addresses of relations and friends living in Lincoln are to be given to the Head Governess. No visit must ever be paid without leave having been previously given by the Principal or the Head Governess.
3   Any student receiving a visitor must at once inform the Principal or Head Governess.
4   No student may walk out alone without special leave.

and, with reference to the geographical location of the college but carrying delicious moral overtones

7   Students may go downhill on Tuesday and Saturday afternoons; at other times only with special leave.

The rules themselves were bad enough; even worse was the unctuous enjoinder that students should

> ... remember that the perfect confidence and trust with which they have always been treated, must necessarily depend upon their earnest endeavour to show themselves worthy of it.[5]

York could rise a little above that and Ripon a good deal, but HMI reports of the period suggest that both had far to go in creating adult comunities. A former York student from Walker's post-war period reminisced 50 years later in *The Spreadeagle* of 1973. He seems to have formed little sense of an 'academic community' but continual agitation against Walker's regime was an abiding impression.

> I cannot claim that my junior year was one of unalloyed bliss. There was a small group of roughnecks among the seniors who boiled up and went berserk occasionally. They are probably pillars of respectability now – maybe JPs deploring the antics of today's 'skinheads'. In fact, one senior rebel, a leader in a Black Monday silent demonstration against some decree of 'Taggie's' became President of the NUT.

The HMI report of a full inspection at York during the 1931-2 academic year describes a daily timetable hardly changed from Reed's first prescription of 1841:

7.45 am	Chapel
8.00 am	Breakfast
9.10 to 12.40	Lectures
12.45	Lunch
2.05 to 3.55	Lectures
4.00 pm	Tea
4.30 to 6.25	Lectures
6.30	Chapel
6.45	Dinner
7.30 to 9.30	Private Study
10.15	Lights Out

HMI A. L. Thornton simply recorded this primitive routine, but made some crisp observations on the student body

> Students: There are 180 students in residence, 132 in the college itself, 28 in Dean's Park and 20 at Heworth Croft. Most of them are 'North Country' men, with the virtues and defects of their kind. Examination results and other records show that with few exceptions they possess determination and grit, that they are loyal to their college and value what it does for them. Most of them enter with a School Certificate Qualification, a fair proportion with Matriculation and a few with sucess in the Higher Certificate Examination.

He noted that the College had the privileged position of 'affiliation' to the University of Leeds in addition to its links as one of the seven Yorkshire colleges in the Joint Examination Board. He regretted that, in spite of the high proportion of matriculated entry, there was at this time not a single student taking the opportunity to follow a four year course of training to obtain a degree from the university as well as recognition as a certificated teacher from the Board of Education.

HMI noted that for 10 years hostel accommodation for 18 students had been provided in Dean's Park, a rented house, close to the Minster, a few minutes walk from Lord Mayor's Walk, and that the College had just acquired the spacious house and grounds of Heworth Croft half a mile north of the main college. This already gave accommodation for 20 students, and was later to be much extended. By far the most enthusiastic section of the report continued:

> But the great value of Heworth Croft lies in the admirable facilities it gives for instruction in gardening. . . . An Old-world garden is used for the practical instruction. This, with its attractive lay-out, its lawns and shrubberies, rose beds, herbaceous and alpine borders, plots for vegetables, fruit trees and bushes, greenhouses and frames, and specimens of forest trees, provides abundant opportunities . . . Part of the adjoining meadow has been broken up to increase the space available for the culture of vegetables and annual flowers and to provide each student with scope for the exercise of initiative and definite responsibility.

This appeared to be the outstanding example in the whole college programme of 'scope for the exercise of initiative'. The detailed criticism of the teaching of English might have come straight from *Scrutiny*.

> While a good many of the men have some taste for the broader literary effects, the main obstacle to their study of literature, as in their writing of really good composition, lies in their lack of accuracy and sensitiveness in dealing with language. This defect becomes specially obvious of course in respect of poetry; here they sometimes give the impression of not regarding poetry as making any particular sense of any sort; occasionally they do not even know the bare dictionary meaning of essential words and phrases. Better and closer habits of study must be acquired before many of the men can hope to profit from their texts as much as they might . . . It would be well also if a larger proportion of the time available could be devoted to class discussion, during which the students themselves bear the brunt of textual elucidation and commentary. At present they seem too often to limit their efforts to noting down the explanations of their tutors.[6]

The quality of History teaching is commended; so are the efforts of the tutor in French, though the results were so discouraging 'with poor material' that

> the major problem remains whether the weaker students of French are getting anything of value out of the French course.

Shortly after the inspection French was withdrawn from the curriculum. Geography was described as taught in 'a sound and stimulating way' but the facilities provided were 'the barest minimum in the way of standard reference books, wall maps, specimens and geographical appliances'.

The course on Principles of Teaching was directed by Vice-Principal F. A. N. Wilmot who though not specially qualified – being a history graduate – was credited with 'long and useful experience to go on'. Again however the method was unimaginative

> . . . 180 students is a large number for two lecturers to deal with and there is apparently some shortage of accommodation. As a result the students are taken in large groups and opportunities for discussion and written work are necessarily restricted . . . In the circumstances good work is being done. It is unfortunate that the facilities are not better for more frequent written exercises, study circles, discussion groups or tutorial classes.

Walker's role is civilly acknowledged:

> The Principal has held his post for over twenty years. In addition he is mainly responsible for tuition in Hygiene and shares with a visiting cleric the teaching of Divinity. His leadership and stimulus are valuable assets. The staff give him loyal support.

Set alongside contemporary reports on other colleges the 1931-32 York inspection report suggests a mediocre institution, dutiful and sound, but dull, inward-looking, and tightly controlled.

Walker and the Governors responded promptly however to the criticisms of the accommodation. In spite of the reduction in student numbers a new block was planned to provide a modern kitchen and larger dining hall, behind the Temple Wing, with student bedrooms above. This released the old kitchen and dining room for conversion into lecture rooms, and the whole project was completed in 1933.

At Ripon, an HMI General Inspection Report for 1933-34 was more positive but in one respect, supported the *Scrutiny* censure. The standard of accommodation and maintenance was obviously considered better than at York:

> The fabric is unusually well kept and the general atmosphere of cleanliness and brightness provides an environment which has much to recommend it.

HMI praised the 'harmonious relationships' among the staff, the high quality of work done in schools by the students and, 'a good deal of very wholesome activity' throughout the curriculum. But they condemned the poor quality of library provision which, except in science, was 'seriously defective and quite unworthy of a college of this standing'. They stressed the disadvantages of 'the comparative isolation of the college' and asked that the range of outside activities should be widened. Finally they echoed Knights' demand for more freedom for the students and urged that the 'prefect system' be replaced by a more mature form of student representative council.

> It would seem desirable to give the students a fuller measure of self-government and self-determination in order to foster initiative, latent powers of leadership, and experience in thinking and acting for themselves.[7]

Miss Lett seems to have responded promptly. A Student Council was established, a student-run play centre for children was launched in the Ripon Cathedral school, the dramatic and musical societies were revitalised and a broader programme of guest lectures provided. A significant initiative was the founding of a vigorous branch of the League of Nations Union which fostered awareness of international affairs through meetings and debates in the college and the city and involved students in preparing representations to parliament on the growing political crisis in Europe.

Meanwhile economic recession continued to take its toll. By 1933 student numbers were down to 112, the hostel in College Road had to be closed and, as at York, tuition in French was abandoned, which meant the much regretted dismissal of the French tutor and long-serving hostel warden. Two new advanced courses were introduced however, in Geography and Handwork, and the Annual Report for 1934 indicates that staff were becoming more involved outside college, attending in-service courses and offering lectures in other institutions. The 1935 report mentions the first staff exchange with a college in the United States and a continuing high rate of employment for Ripon students in spite of the recession; all but five of the 49 leaving students obtained posts for the start of the school year.

1936 saw a successful reunion, with 700 of the 2,100 members of the Association returning to college. Later in the year they mourned the death of Canon Garrod who had served the college as Principal and Governor for 45 years. Though numbers remained depressed at 113 the range of student activities increased and the building of the Ripon City Swimming Pool lifted the standard and popularity of the student-run college swimming club. The library had been improved, partly through donations from governors and friends of the college, and the opening of the first Ripon City library in 1937 as a branch of the County service provided additional facilities for students and staff. Social life seems to have become more varied and relaxed. The 1937 report praises the range of student drama, music and fund-raising activities for charity and records a social breakthrough:

> They have twice successfully organised subscription dances in the college hall to which their men friends were invited.

Occasional events, including dances, were now being held jointly with St John's, York.

For three years the shadow of contraction had hung over the Church colleges and in 1937 the Board of Supervision announced that the postponed 'concentration' must be effected by 1938 with the closure of three of the women's colleges, Brighton, Peterborough and Truro. The opening paragraph of the Ripon Annual Report pays tribute to the unfortunate three

> . . . and our sensibility of the sacrifice which they are about to make for the benefit of the Church Training Colleges as a whole . . .

but it concluded with an opportunist addendum from the new Honorary Treasurer warning that the college deficit had increased over the year from £137 to £806. He suggested immediate economies and longer term prospects:

> It will be obvious that something had to be done to 'make ends meet'. Accordingly the Principal and the teaching staff are contributing the total sum of £400 per annum for Board; part of the hostel has been let as a Nurses Home to the Ripon Cottage Hospital; £100 has been saved on pensions, while another £100 has been made on conferences etc. besides what is being derived from other economies. It is estimated that the effect of all these steps will be to reduce the annual deficit to £28 by the end of the year.
>
> The only satisfactory solution to our difficulties will be a real increase in the number of students allocated to us. At the present time there are 112 students in residence while there is accommodation for many more. If the Board of Supervision in their wisdom see fit to send us some thirty additional students, I shall have little doubt about the state of our finances in future. The closing of three training colleges for women in other parts of England should make this possible.

In fact the college was allocated only 18 additional places as a result of the 'concentration' and, to avoid an imbalance between the years, decided to fill only 10 of them for 1938. But stringent economies ensured that the books were balanced at the end of that year.

Meanwhile the 1936 Education Act had brought assistance and better prospects for Church colleges and schools. It made available capital funding of between 50% and 75% of the total cost of building new voluntary denominational schools where this was by agreement with the Local Authority. This concession was intended to apply only for the three years to 1939, which the Act proposed as the target date for the raising of the school leaving age to 15. In the event that long-awaited improvement was frustrated by the declaration of war in the very week in which it was to have been introduced, but the capital opportunity was seized by the churches. Between July 1936 and September 1939 the Anglicans and Roman Catholics each made more than 200 proposals for denominational schools, with obvious implications for the expansion of teacher training. The new Act had achieved its intention of removing from the church 'providing bodies' the burdens of expense and of competition with LEAs which had been imposed by the Hadow recommendations. Opinion has since been divided on whether this represented enlightenment and attempted reconciliation between government and denominations or merely growing national indifference to religious issues and to church involvement in education.[8]

1938 was a successful and optimistic year for Ripon. With 122 students in residence the governors felt justified in re-opening the hostel; the junior year had 72 students so with examination results and employment success continuing high, recruitment remained strong, and prospects for 1939 seemed good. A well qualified staff had remained stable through the 1930s, and the governors began to plan building extensions to include a new dining hall and kitchen, new lecture rooms and new, or converted individual study bedrooms for all students.

Such confidence was encouraged nationally by the farsighted Spens Report of 1938, on *Secondary Education with Special reference to the Grammar Schools and Technical High Schools*. This deplored the 'conservative and imitative tendency' which it claimed was 'so salient a characteristic of English political and social institutions' particularly as manifested in the traditional Grammar School curriculum. It took the Board of Education to task for failing to develop since the 1902 Act

> secondary schools of quasi-vocational type designed to meet the needs of boys and girls who desired to enter industry and commerce at the age of sixteen.

The Committee recommended a wide extension of technical education and also exemplified the educational philosophy of the first Hadow Report in directions congenial to an expanding teaching profession.

> The Multilateral idea, though it may not be expressed by means of the multilateral school, should in effect permeate the system of secondary education as we conceive it. Each type of secondary school will have its appropriate place in the national system with its educational task clearly in view . . . The establishment of parity between all types of secondary school is a fundamental requirement . . . The salary of the teacher will no longer depend directly upon the type of school in which he is serving . . . The maximum size of classes in the Grammar School and the Modern School should be the same.[9]

This was another challenge for teacher education. Most of the new secondary schools would, however, be provided by the Local Education Authorities and it was the LEA Colleges, secure in their funding, and the University Education Departments training the majority of secondary teachers which could be assured of expansion. The Church Board having just succumbed to concentrating its colleges found the implications of the Spens Report even more daunting than those of Hadow, in spite of the capital concessions of the 1936 Act. To provide and staff a significant proportion of the new secondary schools needed for the longer and more varied Spens curriculum, and to fund a complementary expansion of its teacher training colleges was beyond the means of the Church Board of Finance.

Yet official statistics of the period convey a misleading impression of comparative strength in Church sponsored teacher education. There were now in England and Wales 105 recognised teacher training institutions – 22 university departments and 83 colleges. The colleges trained just over 5,000 teachers a year, more than half of them in the 55 voluntary colleges, among which the largest group was still the 25 Church of England colleges. In September 1938 they seemed poised to share in the implementation of the Spens Report. Within a year they were rising to a different challenge.

The Ripon College report for 1939 recorded an increase to 131 students in residence but in spite of the additional income, the events of September forced the governors to suspend the development plan and also – as the Board's threat of 'concentration' had failed to in 1934 – to raise the fees.

> Unfortunately the outbreak of war has not only postponed the development of this building scheme but has created fresh

financial problems for us to face in the shape of increases in the cost of living and of wages, and an added charge of Air Raid Precautions. This unexpected expediture seems likely to absorb most, if not the whole of our estimated surplus. In consequence the Council has taken the step of raising the fee chargeable to students from £40 to £45 per annum from September 1940.

For a later generation, inured to annual inflation, it seems remarkable that this was the first increase for 12 years. The 1939 report described college routine much as usual

Ripon being scheduled as a reception area the college has been able to function remarkably normally since the war so far as ordinary work is concerned, including teaching practice. The 'blackout' has limited facilities in travelling, and other restrictions have altered considerably the character of the students social life, including their games organisation but they have adapted themselves well.

The 71 students who left in July 1940 had achieved good results and all obtained teaching posts. Most of them also did some kind of war work throughout the long vacation – in hospitals, on the land, at Air Raid Precaution posts and First Aid centres, with refugees or with evacuee children. Air raids were rare in North Yorkshire and the 1941 report noted that only about 20 hours had been lost from the timetable in the air raid shelters – the college cellars suitably reinforced. Many urban colleges had suffered bomb damage and after the blitz of 1941 Ripon welcomed 30 students and four staff from Hull Training College who took over the hostel and parts of the main building. The arrangement continued through 1942 and 1943 and seems to have worked amicably, but in the summer of 1943 the Hull Authority decided it must close its college for the duration of the war.

Meanwhile Ripon had offered St Margaret's Lodge as a refuge for children under five from bombed areas, in co-operation with the Waifs and Strays Society. A matron, nurses, a nursery teacher and 25 children came into residence in April 1941 and the 'Ripon War Nursery' functioned with strong student support until 1944. Throughout the war there were very few changes on the staff; an unusual recruit in 1942 was Miss M. Saunders, a member of the Women's Land Army who was

engaged to help in the production of vegetables . . . The front lawn and borders of the playing field have been ploughed up and used for growing vegetables. The supply during the year has been very good.

Because of the shortage of domestic help the students had to do some of the cleaning and household chores but the 1942 report claimed that they had organised this so well that 'no individual was having to give undue time to it'. Miss Lett was away on two months sick leave during the early summer of 1943, but Miss Buysman took over and the Annual Report compliments her and the staff on a smooth continuation.

As in the years 1915-18, when MPs and Civil Servants had worked at the legislation which became the Fisher Act, so the study of educational activity from 1941 to 1944 yields striking evidence of the foresight and faith with which planning for the post-war period proceeded, before there could be any assurance of victory.[10] Church and State were both determined to create new opportunities. Archbishop Temple, after 11 years at York, moved to Canterbury in 1942, and, in the two years that were left to him, exerted a powerful influence, appreciated at the time by Christians and agnostics, and more so since.[11] In 1942 the National Society published his presidential address, entitled *Our Trust and Our Task*. Already involved in the discussions which were to lead to the 1944 Act, Temple spoke of the present and future role of the Church in education and defended the anomolous relationship it had developed with government since 1870

> I would daringly suggest that one value of the dual system is its duality. I wish to suggest that there is a very great advantage in the educational field, in maintaining real variety of type, with a considerable measure of individual liberty and autonomy . . . I do not think our administration desires mechanical uniformity; but there is an inherent and inevitable tendency in any bureaucratic control, towards mechanical uniformity; with the best will in the world the administration cannot prevent it increasing. In face of what has been happening in Europe the importance of regaining the real independence of the several schools ought surely to be obvious to all of us. If we wish to avoid Totalitarianism, there is merit in the very duality of the dual system. I should not in the least mind it becoming triplicity; but I should regret it becoming a mere unity.[12]

He ended his address with a firm commitment to the Church's continuing involvement in education and to making sensible changes in the inherited 'dual system' to suit changing needs and conditions. His aim was to secure, in a reasonable and conciliatory style, increasingly effective Christian religious education for the children of the county, and this had stiffened his resolve on Church Schools since his 1929 statement as Chairman of the York College governors

> Anything like the wholesale surrender or transfer of our Church Schools we should have to resist

It was a strong lead to cheer the Church Training Colleges, and was shortly followed by two reports from the Church Board of Supervision stressing the need for planning that was both 'Professional' and 'Christian'. The Board offered evidence on behalf of the colleges to a government committee, chaired by Sir Arnold McNair, which was considering *The Supply, Recruitment and Training of Teachers and Youth Leaders*.

The Church reports ranged widely. They made specific estimates of the scale of expansion required of the Church Colleges to meet the expected challenge of a three-year course; they dealt frankly with the shortcomings of the colleges, their position in the overall provision of higher education, with staffing, religious education and with the structure of governing bodies, which they expected would include LEA members and school teachers. They recommended improved staff salary scales and conditions of service, including sabbatical leave and support for research, and they pressed for closer relationships between the colleges and universities.

> The time for this Christian planning is now. In the Church Colleges the Church still possesses an instrument of priceless value, for it is first and last the teachers who matter. We have got to set ourselves, Colleges, Governing Bodies and members of the Council, to the task of seeing that the opportunity is not lost. It will be a costly undertaking . . .[13]

While McNair's committee was at work, yet another influential planning document emerged from a committee under the chairmanship of Sir Cyril Norwood. An enthusiasm for order and system was becoming apparent among all the groups at work – Temple's address had revealed his concern that this should not be pressed too far – so Norwood might have seemed an odd choice to chair a committee charged 'To consider suggested changes in the secondary school curriculum and the question of school examinations in relation thereto'. Some years before, he had claimed that one of the strengths of English education was

> its capacity for making an illogical compromise work in practice and for getting things done without bothering overmuch about theory. We are tolerant of anomalies and patient with survivals so long as they produce results that are worth while. The history of our education is full of instances of this genius for action and indifference to theory.[14]

This is a view of more than historic interest to those who now wrestle with the aftermath of the 1988 Education Act. Yet the Norwood Committee's 1943 report itself smacked of the more prescriptive style of government pronouncement to which we became accustomed in the

1980s. It contained the most explicit theorising yet published on a tripartite system of secondary schooling and revealed that its own 'patience with survivals' was severely stretched by the existing Grammar School curriculum. This, it believed, had 'often been asked to do too much'.

The Norwood Report, with the White Paper of 1943 was the last of a powerful series of enabling recommendations, beginning with the Burnham and Hadow reports of 1925 and leading to the Butler Act of 1944, which guided the English schools system through recession and World War at least some way towards the earlier vision of Webb and Tawney.

The religious education clauses of the Butler Act, which Temple helped to negotiate, provided new opportunity for Church schools, and for teachers of religious education in all schools. The McNair Report, which also appeared in 1944 proposed most of what the Church Board had requested: a three year course of teacher training followed by a supported probationary year; more specialist courses in, for example music, physical education and the arts; and better salaries and conditions for teachers and college tutors. From two closely argued alternative proposals it settled for Area Training Organisation, based on largely autonomous University Schools of Education, each with its own group of Training Colleges. All this was recommended with keen awareness of what it implied:

> Three things in particular must be done, if the number and quality of teachers required to match the reforms proposed in the White Paper are to be obtained. The field of recruitment must be widened; conditions of service which deter people from becoming teachers must be abolished; and the standing of education must be improved so that a sufficient number of men and women of quality will be attracted to teaching as a profession.[15]

All three aspirations remain as valid – and as unfulfilled – in 1991 as in 1944 – or 1841.

In spite of the constraints of war, the governors of Ripon College were also thinking purposefully. The annual report for 1944 describes a proposal to draw the two colleges of Ripon and York together again:

> The original proposal for the future of the Ripon College was that it should have a separate Hall of Residence in York to which students could be sent for the purpose of broadening their experience and outlook, not only by enjoying the richer life of York, but also by facilitating contacts with St John's Training College whose traditions, aims and ideals are broadly the same.

With full co-operation of St John's College Standing Committee it is now proposed that the Hall of Residence shall be built upon the main site of the new St John's College, an independent and self-contained unit but so planned as to make possible the sharing of a corporate life with St John's College as and when desired. The siting committee has now made definite and somewhat detailed proposals . . . the scheme in general outline has been submitted to the Minister for Education. It is supplementary to any building additions and improvements which may be made in Ripon and for which plans were approved in 1939.

The 'new St John's College' was a project of the York governors to move the whole college from Lord Mayor's Walk and Heworth Croft, to a spacious site available on the Hull Road, next to the college playing fields. But, as the final sentence of the reports hints, Ripon governors were less than enthusiastic about integration with the Men's College and, as we shall see, the scheme foundered.

There were 152 students in residence at Ripon in September 1944 and the governors had reluctantly to terminate the War Nursery's lease of St Margaret's Lodge, which was reoccupied for teaching and student residence. The health of staff and students remained good, though Miss Buysman was away seriously ill, for a term. Finances too were healthy and the treasurer reported a further £500 added to an accumulated reserve of £5,284 available for development, re-equipment and arrears of maintainance after the war.

The relief of victory in Europe, in May, and in the Far East in August, was shadowed for the Ripon College, by the illness and eventual resignation in August of Miss Lett, who had cancer. She died in a Winchester Nursing Home in November. She had led the college, with patience and skill, through the most constrained period in its history and had to resign her post just as new freedoms and opportunities were assured. Students and staff praised her courage and sympathy, and her care for the beauty and colour of the college's interiors and the civilised style of its daily life. Miss Buysman, now recovered, was appointed Acting Principal for the rest of the academic year 1945-6.

At York, Walker had reached retirement age in 1935. His had hardly been a popular regime, but, like Miss Lett, he had endured some of the college's most restricted years including the closure during the First War. His last two years, which followed the full HMI inspection, seem to have been relatively untroubled, and *The White Rose* of 1935 paid measured tribute to him:

. . . a big little man . . . He never spared himself and would not begin a scheme or introduce anything new until he had worked it out fully and carefully . . . He spent himself to further the interests of the College and certainly never used his position for his own advantage.

The same edition applauded the first decisions of his successor.

The Revd Dr James Welch took up his appointment on 1 May 1935. He was yet another Cambridge man, having graduated from Sidney Sussex College in History in 1925, and subsequently taken a Master of Education degree at Durham and a PhD at Cambridge. He was ordained Priest at Durham in 1927 after serving as a Deacon at Jarrow, and was Curate at Gateshead 1926-29, before going as a CMS missionary to Oleh, Nigeria, where he taught and was also involved in the administration of the mission school system. He had come to York from Nigeria and though his was to be the shortest tenure of the York principalship – only four years – he made a deep impression – and a dramatic start. In his first term he introduced two major innovations – freedom and films. *The White Rose* records his impact vividly:

> This last term has been the most eventful in the life of the college for very many years. Old Johnsmen returning this term find the rule of the new Principal much different from what they remember of their former experiences . .
>
> During the term a modified form of self-government has been established in the college. All old rules were abolished; but no new regulations were made. The students were left to build up their own body of law. The College organisation is now Principal, Senior Common Room and Junior Common Room; the latter being composed of all the students, the former of all the tutors.
>
> Ultimate power resides in the JCR; the basic principle involved being that everything passed in the JCR automatically comes into force providing it does not interfere with Work, Health or Expense . . . Monitors have been abolished . . . Members of the SCR have given up many of their powers so that the students may be less restricted in their actions and more free to develop along their own lines . . . The Principal reserves the right to veto any resolution that he considers eminently undesirable.

In the July edition of the *Old Students Calendar,* Welch introduced himself, appealed for funds to renovate and 'beautify' the college chapel, and shared his convictions about student freedom, to which he had not entirely converted his new colleagues:

> The next great change, debated long and earnestly by the Senior Common Room, is the introduction of a controlled system of self-government by the students, who, with necessary limits, will make their own laws and punish their own offenders. To break laws made by the 'powers that be' is to win social approval; to break laws made by the community of students is to offend against the family and to win social disapproval. Chiefly however we are setting ourselves to this high adventure because the most valuable part of a college training, for one who is to educate future citizens, must lie in the practice of government and the assumption of responsibility.

Cinema shows in college might seem a trivial manifestation of this new freedom, but they made a great impression. Again, *The White Rose* enthused:

> June 13th 1935 was certainly a memorable day in the history of the college. The Gymnasium was used as a cinema and from 10 pm until midnight we were entertained by the celluloid. The main feature of the programme was 'Jack Ahoy' starring Jack Hulbert.
>
> True the apparatus did not work too well and it was with great difficulty that the dialogue was heard at first. But the sound improved in the latter part of the film and it was possible to hear most of the words . . . We hope that the cinema will be increasingly used in college life . . . it is a great entertainer and it has immense educational potentiality. Both these aspects of the Cinema should be welcomed by the student who wants to have his educational outlook broadened and yet desires hours of recreation which will keep him fresh for further study.

Throughout Welch's first year every small concession to student responsibility was recorded. In a short account of improvements to the chapel services *The White Rose* exulted

> At the end of the service the students no longer emerge like the animals out of the Ark, but in a manner less efficient but more agreeable. Nor do we any longer lift our united voices in the psalm in the very early morning.

A 1936 edition praised the quality of three political addresses given in college by guest speakers, and printed a long poem *Communism – Fascism – Christianity* which set a new standard for the magazine's verse, hitherto mostly doggerel. It was contributed by Kenneth Muir, lecturer

144

in English, who was later Professor at Liverpool University and a distinguished critic and poet. Muir and Mrs Welch directed a production of *King Lear* at the Rowntree Theatre in which several St John's students took small parts.

The magazines of 1937 celebrate the range of visiting lecturers and cultural activities in college, the refurnishing of the dining hall and JCR, the repainting of the junior corridors and the arrival of a new tutor who was to win the affection of 30 years of Johnsmen:

> Mr J. R. Copping, late of Manor School, has come as lecturer in teaching methods and as a guide philosopher and friend in matters 'School Practical'. His name will go down to posterity if only because of the reams of cyclostyled notes he has already distributed.

Self Government remained a hot topic, easier to write about than to achieve. A senior reflected on the roots of the difficulty:

> There is bound to be in any community a certain percentage who are utterly incapable of imposing any form of self restraint on themselves. This may be partly due to early training and partly to the autocratically restrictive influences of the secondary school. The present generation suffers from a lack of character training in early life, they have not been trained in a sense of responsibility . . . One cannot expect a person coming straight from school, with no idea of the value of communal life or of the psychology of personal freedom . . . to live in harmony with an idea which is utterly strange . . .

The Standing Committee had different anxieties. Student numbers were still depressed to 135 for economic reasons and the governors were obliged to let the recently acquired Heworth Croft for two years. Teaching jobs were hard to find – 20 of the 1936 leavers were unemployed – and, on Welch's suggestion the governors authorised him to tour Local Authorities in the south of England 'to endeavour to find places for the men'. The minute book reveals that he had quickly won the governors' confidence and though funds were tight they authorised a large sum for an innovation to widen students' experience:

> The Principal asked for authority to spend up to £500 a year for the purpose of sending students to schools outside the York area for practice in teaching. He considered it essential that the students should have experience in the most modern and best equipped schools, and when these did not exist in York he wished to send the students further afield.

The wonder is that it had taken 96 years; in fact the total extra cost for the first year was only £160.

145

In 1937 the college purchased 13 acres of playing field on the Hull Road. The design for a pavilion, incorporating a groundsman's house was approved in 1938 and, fortunately, completed by the summer of 1939. The field at Clifton was sold. The college's reputation for sport and physical education had grown and it had been awarded one of the new specialist third year courses in 'Physical Training'. Welch's enthusiasm for the college did not blind him to its shortcomings however, and the April 1939 minutes record a comment to make later generations of PE Johnsmen wince.

> The Principal reported that the new arrangements for School Practice were working admirably. He also reported that he had done his best with the third year men who were taking the Physical Training Course but he felt the college could not do enough for them in comparison with the Carnegie Course and he suggested that the course be abandoned.

The governors left the decision 'to the discretion of the Principal' and in fact the course survived.

Applications were down for 1938; the colllege had hoped to recruit 82 first years but admitted only 64. Welch was now a force in the General Council of the Church Colleges and had spoken strongly in defence of Culham College, which had originally been proposed by the Council for closure along with the three women's colleges. He then adroitly obtained six of the 'redistributed' places for York, in spite of the fact that only women's places had been lost in the closures. In the summer of 1938 he persuaded the governors to lay a running track on the new playing field, to bid a for a grant of £5,000 from the National Fitness Council towards a swimming pool and to accept a loan of £5,000 from the Church Board to complete the second storey of the north-east wing, which would add 32 student rooms. The Board had offered to loan York up to £45,000 for more ambitious buildings, but Welch advised that the interest charges would cripple the college. The request to the Fitness Council was turned down and the college had to wait another 30 years for its swimming pool.

Welch had brought to the college fresh energy, vision, sympathy with student needs, skilful communication and a Christian conviction which influenced many students and staff. Of all the principals of the first 100 years he seems to have given most thought to what a Christian college of higher education should aim for and how it might become a community of scholars. It was no suprise that his talents should be sought after and in October 1938 the governors accepted six months notice of his resignation to take up the post of Director of Religious Broadcasting at the BBC. His farewell message to the students in the 1939 *White Rose* returned to the theme of self-government:

I still believe it is the only possible system for a community of future teachers. To learn in practice the necessity of law and rules; to deal with the lawbreaker; to place the group above one's individual desires; to be, each man, his brother's keeper – these are lessons to be learned in these days when civilisation is cracking . . . It is a system which is at the mercy of a minority and can be ruined by selfishness; it makes heavier demands than authoritarian government; and students, often ignorant of the fact that self-government is an art which has painfully to be learned, are slow to look to the tutors as 'elder brothers' for the guidance their maturity and experience can supply. But it has more than justified itself – in a freer and happier atmosphere, in more sincere, because voluntary, chapel worship, in the way in which students mature during their two years, and in the better quality of work of those who are adult enough to work when left to themselves. I hope the system has come to stay; and I hope the system will be altered and added to by each generation.

At the governors meeting in April 1939, Archbishop Temple, not given to gushing tributes, moved

That this Committee bids farewell to the Revd Dr Welch with very great regret. It desires to place on record its sense of the great service which he has rendered to the college during his tenure of the post of Principal, especially in respect of the religious life of the college, for the sake of which the Church maintains its Training Colleges.

Temple advised his fellow governors not to advertise the post of Principal. He considered the choice of a successor to Welch crucial and difficult but believed he knew the man for the job and recommended the governors to invite him for interview. They did so, confirmed Temple's judgement and appointed, from September 1939, Professor Albert Cock of University College, Southampton, who was ordained priest by the Archbishop before taking up the appointment. He broke the College's Cambridge tradition, having taken First Class Honours in Philosophy at London University in 1914 and been made a Fellow of King's College, London in 1930, before moving to Southampton, a University College affiliated to London.

The students were keenly disappointed to be losing Welch so soon, and anxious to maintain the benefits he had brought them.

We wish him as much success in his new post as he has had during the years he has been Principal of the College. We hope that the coming Principal will maintain the same happy relationship with the students.

In the same edition of *The White Rose* Cock sent greetings to the young men he was shortly to join. He was sure they must realise that it was a 'great wrench' for him to come to the north of England after serving a university in the south for so many years.

> But I come North under a very distinct sense of vocation and am looking forward to my stay with you with very great enthusiasm.

The students might have suspected he was coming with missionary zeal from the 'civilised south' but were probably relieved to read on and discover that he had a sense of humour. The editor had asked him for a photograph. If he decided not to print it

> doubtless it is because he wants to save you from a shock. If he does think fit I can accept no responsibility. Photographs often tell fibs – but often also they tell the truth.

As Cock joined the college in September it was losing part of its history. A demolition gang was at work on 'Blenheim House' in Monkgate, the former Manchester College in which the York college had begun in 1841. By the time the new Principal arrived the original 'college' had disappeared. So too had many of the assumptions of the previous year. Wilmott had acted as Principal during the summer term and though Cock had attended a cheerful July meeting of the governors which discussed increased numbers, the possible recruitment of ordinands – still occasionally discussed 50 years later with no visible progress – and second thoughts on the £45,000 loan from the Church Board, his first meeting as Principal was on 7 September. Four days after the declaration of war the governors were relieved to have received permission from the War Office for the college to reopen on the 19th. Like Ripon, York was part of the designated north-eastern 'reception area' and so could expect evacuees of various kinds.

Black-out and Air Raid Precautions exercised the governors but having negotiated these they agreed to accept 40 men from St Paul's College Cheltenham, with their Principal and Vice-Principal, for the first year of the war. 184 students were therefore in residence, the college and Principal's house were overpopulated and some students were boarded out in the city. No extra staff were taken on, except to replace those called up for military service, who included Stanley Watkin the newly appointed Bursar. Cock had continued Welch's support for a vigorous Students' Union on similar lines to university unions. This was unusual for a Training College and the advantage was apparent in the governors congratualtions to Student Union and Chapel Officers for their

> conspicuous personal services in promoting the very satisfactory and harmonious fellowship of the whole body of the students.

Although teaching was one of the 'reserved occupations' many students were liable for conscription. Cock went to London and successfully lobbied the Board of Education and MPs for guarantees that special final examinations would be made available for men whose courses were cut short in their second year. The college received unwelcome publicity when allegations were made by the chairman of the Exemptions Tribunal that staff were influencing students towards conscientious objection. Cock protested that there were 157 York men and 51 Cheltenham men in residence in October 1940 and only 11 – nine York and two Cheltenham – had registered objection, eight of them being willing to accept non-combatant duties to assist the war effort. He reminded governors that four of the present senior staff had served in the First War and several had already volunteered in 1940. There was, he insisted, no instruction given in college on how to conduct a pacificst case, nor was there, as had been alleged, any contact with the Peace Pledge Union. Archbishop Temple wrote to the Court and the Press on behalf of the college demanding 'a public withdrawal of the aspersions on the college'.

By April 1941 applications to the surviving men's colleges had been so reduced by conscription that it seemed doubtful that any would survive. The Board of Education met with the Church Board in May to settle the issue and the governors asked Temple and Welch – now a member of the Church Board – to speak for York. The college survived and readily agreed that men from Bede College, Durham, which was to close for the duration of the war, and from Saltley College, Birmingham, which had been bombed, should be accommodated at York. The St Paul's men returned to Cheltenham; their college too had been selected for survival and asked to take in the remnants of Culham and St Luke's, Exeter.

But the war was not all high drama for the governors; the same minutes which celebrated the reprieve recorded

> That Heworth Croft be offered as accommodation for officers of the ATS (the Women's Army Corps) . . . that the late tenant be released from his rent . . . and that the college take over the black-out blinds at a cost of £4.10s, the lawn mower at a cost of £8 and the draining board at a cost of £1.

The augmented college now had over 200 students in residence for the rest of the war and could support strong branches of the University of Leeds Air Squadron and of the Home Guard. In May 1942 the war struck directly when, in a rare air raid on the city Joe Copping was badly injured and his wife killed – two of York's very few civilian casualties. Deaths of former students were reported too frequently from the various fronts.

In spite of war conditions, normal Education Department regulations were enforced. In an attempt to economise on heating and household expenses the governors extended the Christmas vacation in 1942. The minutes for January 1943 recorded a reprimand from the Board of Education, which insisted that a further week's residence be added to the spring term. Cock had to report that the continuance of the college after July 1943 had not yet been confirmed. Yet he, like the bureaucrats in Whitehall, was thinking about the post-war propects of the college and thinking big. He had already advised the governors that the Lord Mayor's Walk site, hemmed in by houses on the one side and Archbishop Holgate's Grammar School on the other, would not be adequate to the demands of post-war expansion. A special sub-committee had been set up to discuss long term action.

Cock's ambition for St John's was a much larger, wholly residential college on a greenfield site outside the city and he pursued it forcefully. The sub-committee considered the possibilities of Heslington Hall but judged it unsuitable for academic purposes. At the time – badly run-down – it probably was, but 20 years later, splendidly restored, it was to become the administrative centre of the new University of York. Temple's successor when he moved to Canterbury was Archbishop Garbett. He took little apparent interest in the college and though he remained titular chairman of governors the effective chairmanship passed to the Dean of York, Eric Milner-White. Cock, deluded by his vision of a new St John's, wrote to Garbett suggesting that as he was a bachelor he might like to consider moving to more modest quarters from the spacious Bishopthorpe Palace beside the River Ouse, allowing the college to take it over. Garbett's reply was brief, frosty and conclusive. Archbishops have continued to reside, unharassed, at Bishopthorpe.

Through 1943 and '44 however, the college gradually negotiated an option on an open site beyond the playing fields on Hull Road, eventually purchasing at reasonable cost just over 50 acres. This offered scope for an imaginative project and the talks with Ripon governors began. Nothing could be approved by the Board in London until the war was over, but when *The White Rose* appeared again in May 1944 – the first edition for five years – Cock dropped hints of exciting possibilities 'on another site'.

In a later account of the war years he described how staff had built on Welch's more adventurous approach to work in schools, particularly beyond Yorkshire

New forms of teaching experience were also found in such places as the Lord Wandsworth College, Basingstoke, the Kingham Hill School, Oxfordshire, the famous St George's Boys' Club, under Mr Basil Henriques, and Mr Noel Moor's remarkable Social Centre at Slough.

St John's in war-time was a more exciting community than in the 'peaceful' early 30s, and *The White Rose* reported in 1944 and '45 a surprising range of sporting and social events in which Cock took pride:

> The games activities of the college were carried on with conspicuous energy and success; its social life was broadened so that the Saturday and Sunday nights, so finely inspired by Mr Copping, achieved an ever widening frame . . . The Chapel, despite the blackout, remained the heart and spiritual centre of the college life.

In his leadership of the Christian life of the college he gladly acknowledged fine support from successive assistant chaplains Peter Wansey – also a devotee of physical education – and Leonard Poore who had been a colleague of Cock's at Southampton.

The war had brought another change to the male enclave on Lord Mayor's Walk, which Cock celebrated in his quaint style:

> We have a lady on our staff. What a shock to the first generation of Johnsmen! Miss Pearson brings all kinds of creepy things to the Biology Lab, and with great difficulty we keep the creepy things away from High Table. I do believe however that having a lady on the staff is very good fun and does help the students.

Throughout the war St John's students and staff had only one year, 1940-41, on their own. Bede's staff and students remained till 1946 and Saltley's till July 1945. By this time Cock's health was poor and he asked the governors to accept his resignation with effect from May. They did so with genuine regret at a special meeting held in March, the first that Archbishop Garbett had chaired. Tributes from governors and students were warm. Cock had recently led the governors in a consideration of the McNair recommendations, advising them to support the closer relationship of the college with the University of Leeds. In this he was well supported by Professor Frank Smith, a long-serving co-opted governor from the university – author of the definitive study of Kay-Shuttleworth – and Cock seems to have felt that St John's was a 'university quality' institution. In his farewell message to the college he praised the work of the Students' Union officers throughout his principalship

> A very fine set of men, more than worthy of comparison with their opposite numbers in University Unions.

The Union President admired the achievements and innovations through which Cock had led the college but thanked him 'above all for the friendship, kindness and interest he has shown to all'.

Wilmott again acted as Principal during the summer term. Within a month of Cock's departure the War in Europe was over and colleges all over the country were being derequisitioned at astonishing speed. At the end of July the governors interviewed four applicants for the Principalship. Three weeks later the War in the Far East was over and Cock's successor could be sure that new opportunities lay ahead for the college. The men of St John's had paid a high price for them. The Chapel War Memorial records the names of 54 former students who had been killed, 1939-45.

CHAPTER VIII

Expansion towards Maturity 1945 to 1971

THE NEW PRINCIPAL OF ST JOHN'S, YORK, was Philip Lamb. An Oxford man, he had graduated in Theology from Magdalen College in 1928 and after studies at Cuddesdon was ordained and served curacies in Carlisle and Leeds 1929-35. He was appointed Vicar of the large parish of St Aidan's Leeds in 1935 and served it for 10 years. Though acquainted with the work of the college he was the first Principal since Reed in 1841 to be appointed without formal teaching experience. In the July 1946 edition of *The White Rose* he reflected on his first year. He had already acquired three convictions. The first was

> There is too much to do in too short a time. A man comes from school with his School Certificate having spent perhaps one year in the Sixth Form. At college he must learn the teacher's art, its theory and practice, including physical education and hygiene. He must attain an examinable proficiency in three or four subjects . . . Education demands that he shall somehow learn to organise the information he acquires into something that can be called wisdom – an understanding of the world in which he lives that can lay claim to some degree of wholeness and integration. To do this he must have at least a general understanding of The Bible ; for apart from the inhumanity of Communism there is no focus but the Christian that can claim the attention of intelligent men in the world today.

> The clash of opinion in organised or informal debate, mere lounging among good books, social contacts, the chance to make and be moved by music, to see and act plays, to rub up against the minds of first-class lecturers, the opportunity for exercise, the practice of worship – time needs to be found for all these An impossible requirement. At least it means that all of us must be on our toes, knowing the fix we are in . . .

The key to the problem, he told his students, was 'discipline' – coming from a root to do with learning, instruction and discipleship; this was his second 'conviction':

> It is the name of the chief problem in the story of humanity – how to induce a man to behave rightly without taking away his freedom. It is all too easy for laxity to encourage license; it is all too easy for paternalism to undermine responsibility. Fortunately the right trail has been blazed already . . . The more the student body can learn to regulate and administer its own corporate life, the healthier the discipline.

Lamb's third impression was that the colleges confronted an 'unprecedented opportunity'. The new financial regulations from the Ministry of Education suggested that at last economy was not to dominate every decision.

> At the price of more detailed administrative control, more money is to be made available, and more money means a higher staff ratio, better equipment, a whole list of advantages for which our predecessors sighed in vain. To whom much is given, from him shall much be required; and difficulties are less hard to deal with than opportunities. It is at this point perhaps more urgently than at any other, that we need the prayers of our friends, as we enter upon the second century of the life of our college.

Government plans had already been announced for a great increase in teacher training which would necessitate the opening of a number of 'Emergency Training Colleges' to provide 'crash' programmes alongside the long-established Church and Local Authority Colleges. One was actually established half a mile from St John's, at Marygate, York, and was to continue for three years, with tutors from St John's assisting its staff and Lamb having titular responsibility for it. The strategy raised, even more sharply than the 1890s emergence of the university 'Day Training Colleges' or the 1902 establishment of LEA Colleges, the question 'What is different about a Church College?' It is a question which still exercises us in the 1990s – and should do as long as Church Colleges and Schools exist – but in 1946 it received a firm answer from a leading Churchman and college governor. George Bell, Bishop of Chichester and a leader of the Ecumenical movement throughout the war, preached at a Thanksgiving Service for the return of Bishop Otter College, of which he was chairman, to its Chichester campus which had been requisitioned in 1943 as a planning base for the liberation of Nazi-occupied Europe.

> A Church College stands for Truth, as other colleges do, and Truth is offered at the altar. It stands for Friendship like other

colleges and Friendship is hallowed by Communion. Its point of view, its atmosphere, its tradition, are distinctive. And the sign of its distinctive atmosphere is most clearly seen in its possession of a Chapel, with a Church of England chaplain as its minister, ready at all times to help all members of the college, irrespective of creed, by teaching or counsel or fellowship.

All these particular features make it different from a Local Authority college which, with the best will in the world on the part of the Principal and lecturers, is prevented by law from providing a chapel or a chaplain, or tradition or atmosphere of a similar kind. I would also make bold to say that a Church of England Training College for Teachers, when it is true to its ideal, does make love the inspiration of everything. I do not claim that it is unique in this. But a Church college does try, with the help of the Church, to develop in its students the sense that it is motive that matters, and that it is the attitude you bring to your profession that is all important. The end of the charge is Love . . .[1]

It was a considerate assertion of distinctiveness but one which laid special responsibilities on the Principals and staffs of the Church Colleges at a time when the professional challenge alone was formidable. Lamb's early statements and decisions at York show that he took the Church foundation of the college seriously and was keen to keep its Christian life vigorous. Bell had promised the 'help of the Church', though for St John's, as for most of the Church Colleges, Church support over the first 100 years had been sporadic and inconsistent. In October 1947 however the Church made up its mind in public, that the post-war opportunity must be grasped. In a seminal report the Central Board of Finance confronted the Church Assembly:

Members of the Church Assembly will have noticed that earlier reports in reference to the training colleges bear witness to a constant demand for improvement and extension. No college seems to have been able really to keep pace with these incessant calls. The post-war situation is therefore no change and the Church must face the new challenge.[2]

Through the new grant regulations of 1946, to which Lamb had referred, the Ministry of Education undertook to finance half the cost of approved capital developments in the Church Colleges. The colleges had to look to some 'Providing Body' if they were to raise the other half and take a full share in the proposed expansion of Teacher Training. The Church Assembly responded

that this Assembly accepts in principle the responsibility of the Church for securing the future of the Church Training Colleges and asked its Board of Finance to prepare a specific programme to re-equip and extend the colleges. The Board prepared a scheme to be underwritten by the Church; Assembly members would have been relieved at the Board's cautious tone:

> It is well to remember how far-reaching the plan is. In view of the present position of the building trade there can be no expectation of the speedy completion of the whole scheme. Money raising can be an extended task.

The last sentence could serve as a motif for the first 150 years of the Church Colleges.

The 1948 expansion plan was in three phases; the first was to be finished within five years, but the third might take 20. Such a long-term vote of confidence from the Church Assembly strengthened the Council of Church Colleges, well served by Canon Cockin, later Bishop of Bristol, and then by Robert Stopford, later Bishop of London. The information and enthusiasm which flowed from the Council to influential committees and officers of the Church ensured that the farsighted expansion plan was carried through into the 1960s. The colleges had been wary of their own Church Board since the Chester fracas of 1933 and the closures of 1938, but more open procedures gradually restored confidence. From the Butler Act, to the White Paper debacle of 1973, the Council, working with the Board, gave the Church of England Colleges a measure of group identity and cohesion within a fragmented national teacher training enterprise. Though its potential for co-operation was not fully developed it compensated a little for the more generous finance and services often made available to local authority colleges and university training departments.

While Lamb and his colleagues were planning the college's submission to the Church Board for a share of the expansion, HMI conducted a full inspection of St John's in the academic year 1948-49. The 26 page printed report gives an account of achievement and aspiration from which the college emerges with credit. In their 'Conclusion' HMI echo one of Lamb's own convictions from his first year:

> This is a good college. In common with other colleges it finds that there is much to be done in a short time. But the inspectors, whose visits have taken place at various times over a period of nearly a year, have been impressed by the happy spirit and keenness with which both staff and students tackle their work. The college has fine traditions and is worthily upholding them. The Principal sets a manly tone to the place but it is the happy co-operation of Principal, staff and students which creates the sense of purpose which pervades the life of the college.

HMI probed the Church connection of the college and pronounced it 'real and vital'. The 1944 Act permitted the Church colleges to reserve half of the student places for committed members of the Church of England, but HMI noted that this college took for granted that the remainder also would possess a common Christian faith and loyalty:

> No person is willingly admitted to the College either as student or lecturer who is altogether out of sympathy with this profession . . . Every student is required to receive instruction in the Bible as given by the Principal or one of the chaplains and the intention of the instruction is pastoral as well as academic . . . Attendance at College Chapel is not compulsory but most services are well attended.

There were 222 students at the college and, because many had completed their two years of National Service, average age of entry was higher than the pre-war seventeen years and three months. Most came from maintained Grammar Schools and a few from independent schools, preference being given to those who had done at least one year of Sixth Form study after School Certificate. HMI were sympathetic to the strains on a staff which they considered too small:

> The ratio of staff to students is 1 : 13. The members of staff form a generally effective team. Academically they are reasonably well qualified. The relations of the staff with the students are excellent – indeed the visitor is inclined to wonder whether, out of the goodness of their hearts, members of staff are not too accessible. They are working hard and care should be taken to see that they have time for private reading. Some of the tutorial groups are unduly large and if the tutorial system is to be fully effective more staff will be needed.

HMI approved of the system of delegated authority but considered the committee procedures unduly cumbersome. They shrewdly observed that, in some respects, the system, operating within an overloaded curriculum, might be producing a less liberal regime than was recognised. For example, lectures at the college tended to be the prime source of factual information, whereas HMI believed that students could obtain much of this on their own from well-chosen text books.

> Many students attend more than 26 lectures a week, some even as many as 33. It is for consideration whether better standards of scholarship would not be obtained if attendance at some or all lectures were optional and the students were expected to do more individual study . . . the opportunity for use and abuse of freedom from compulsory lectures would make considerable demands on the students self discipline. The question has been

considered by the College Authorities. It is however the desire of the students that lectures should be compulsory. In this case therefore there are grounds for suggesting that they are not necessarily the best judges of their own welfare.

They expressed general satisfaction with the college buildings and with the governors' plans to extend and improve them. The Limes, a substantial house with grounds, half a mile beyond Heworth Croft, had just been purchased and it was planned to extend hostel accommodation there and at Heworth Croft as soon as permission and funds were forthcoming. HMI noted that the governors had finally abandoned the grand design to move the college entirely to the Hull Road site; they supported this decision, in view of likely planning developments in the City of York. By the time large-scale building became possible on the site outside the city, much of the old housing which restricted development at Lord Mayor's Walk would probably be demolished. HMI recognised the attraction of the present site

> . . . the maintenance of tradition, the proximity of the fine buildings in the City of York, and the dignified exterior of the present college buildings are strong reasons for allowing the college to remain where it is.

They complimented the governors on all that had been done to update facilities at Lord Mayor's Walk but listed the most important short-comings of the site as

> the lack of an Assembly Hall, an adequate Library and a Swimming Bath. The governors are aware of this and intend to provide these rooms when space becomes available.

They acknowledged the governors good intentions towards students' rooms too, but thought that some improvements need not wait for a major grant:

> Many of the students' beds are hard and uncomfortable, rugs might be provided to cover the bare board floors and a general redecoration would make the rooms brighter and more attractive.

On the curriculum they raised the perennial problem of integration. Teaching was, they said, necessarily divided between the subject departments and the Principles and Practice of Teaching, which should 'dovetail closely' but did not. They praised the quality of much of the teaching, especially considering the shortage of staff. Work in Religious Education was 'of a very high order indeed' and fitted well with the services and influence of the Chapel

> deliberately planned, in the words of the Principal 'to let loose into education those same spiritual forces which have been so effective for good in the past'.

While complimenting much of the work in Principles and Practice of Teaching they made three suggestions of lasting value. First that work in schools should be jointly planned by tutors in Education and in the subject departments; secondly that teaching groups should be much smaller – preferably not more than 20; thirdly that, though the college did not offer a specific training for infant teaching, all students should be given some acquaintance with work at that level and that 'this might necessitate the appointment of a woman lecturer'.

HMI particularly noted staff strains in English, in which the equivalent of two full-time tutors taught almost 100 students. Criticism reminiscent of the *Scrutiny* attack was hardly surprising:

> There has inevitably been a tendency towards the second-hand which is aggravated by the pressure of too many subjects all being taken at once. English suffers as much as any subject from the failure of students either to read for themselves or to think for themselves. Perhaps they simply have not the time. The critical opinions which they do express show diligent labour and study and some power of selection, but they often do not seem to bear the marks of personal experience. Many of the students themselves appear well aware of this; they appreciate the tutorials which have been introduced and would greatly welcome many more.

History, Physical Education and Music all received qualified praise. Science was considered sound, with Rural Science developing well. A related subject provoked a comment which remains familiar 40 years later

> The number of students who take Mathematics at any level is small.

HMI noted the college's awareness of the importance of Art and Craft but found the Art Room 'a dreary place' and the standards of work uneven and 'on the whole not high'.

They approved the general domestic arrangements, the food, considering that rationing and restrictions continued, and the cleanliness of the college, all of which reflected well on the Matron, Mrs Collett and her staff. Finally, HMI acknowledged the sound administration of Principal and Vice-Principal. Wilmott's long service had given him a 'shrewd judgement in the assessment of students capabilities' and enabled him to maintain high standards in spite of difficulties during and since the war. Their praise of Lamb's leadership was particularly warm:

> The present Principal brings to his work a warm humanity, a firm Faith, vigour both of mind and body, sound scholarship and

considerable administrative ability. He also possesses the gift of inspiring these qualities in others . . . the team owes much to the inspiration and encouragement it receives from its Principal . . . his broadminded tolerance, good humour and firmness of purpose have also won him the respect and loyalty of his students.

On most aspects of college life the report of 1948-49 is better than that for 1931-32. In his own letter to *The White Rose* Lamb endorsed the HMI compliments to the college's work with schools, particularly Copping's twice-weekly demonstration lessons with pupils from neighbouring Park Grove School, in a model classroom in college. Because this work was carefully related to the childrens' other lessons 'the element of artificiality is reduced to a minimum'. Lamb shared HMI concern about space problems and was pleased with the gracious rooms of Gray's Court, a fine mediaeval/Georgian house, which the college had leased from York Minster to accommodate History and Social Studies.

In 1949 he commended the start of the McNair-style relationship with the University of Leeds Institute of Education which had been celebrated in an Institute Service at York Minster. Tutors grumbled about excessive committee meetings at Leeds but the relationship was giving the college a sense of being part of a greater enterprise and was reducing its 'cultural isolation'. Building progress was slow, as everywhere else, and Lamb complained that no improvements had yet been possible at Heworth or The Limes. In his letter to Old Yorkists, he proposed that the College should choose a new motto and apply to the College of Heralds for a crest.

> I make no secret that 'Floreat Ebor' with its quasi-Etonian flavour and its suggestion of ice cream seems to me, though well suited to a war-cry on the touchline, to be not quite as happy as an escutcheon.

He suggested part or all of 'Ut Vitam Habeant et Abundantius' based on St John Chapter 10 – 'That they may have life and have it more abundantly'. This, with a crest incorporating the Eagle of St John and the Crossed Keys of the Arch Diocese of York, was finally approved by the College of Heralds in 1953.

In 1950 the college agreed to add two more third-year special courses, in Rural Science and Divinity, to the established one in Physical Education. A three-year college course for all students had long been canvassed and Lamb believed that anything the college could do to hasten it would be worthwhile. The colleges were to wait another 10 years for it. Most were also still waiting for any major building projects. Lamb wrote in *The White Rose*

When I was appointed five years ago we had dreams of a £25,000 new college. Well I am grateful for £5,000 of waking reality . . . at least we have the compensation of seeing bricks and mortar at Heworth Croft and the wall of a biology laboratory rising.

He also mentioned 'one matter that lies near my heart and gives me some anxiety'. The Sunday chapel services were not well attended, though weekday 'assemblies' were. He asked for a special effort to make Sunday worship 'more like what should be expected of a Church Training College'.

To have a decent, kindly, self-disciplined life such as we lead together is worth a lot of churchgoing; no one could be more aware of that than I am . . . But we shall not be quite the powerhouse we should be . . . unless Sunday worship as well as weekday forms an inevitable part of our corporate experience. Eventually you cannot spend a pagan Sunday and a Christian week.

In 1951 three long-serving tutors retired. Wilmott had lectured at St John's for 35 years – with a break for war service in which he won an MC – and had been Vice-Principal for 22 years. Wardle, Head of English, and Howarth, Head first of Physical Education and then of Art had both served 28 years. The governors appointed Christopher Chapman, Head of Education, to the Vice-Principalship. He and the enterprising bursar, Stanley Watkin, were to be Lamb's chief aides and mentors for the next 20 years; for old students of the period both are legendary figures. As colleges grew, Vice-Principalship became a heavier responsibility and Chapman had charge of much of the discipline and daily organisation. Among an able and long-serving team which guided the expansion were Stanley Barnes, Physical Education; James Shields, Education and eventually Registrar; James Coleclough, History and Geography; Peter Wenham, History; Harold Liversidge, Art; George Baggaley, Music; Frank Disney, Physics and Agnes McCutcheon, Principal's secretary. In a small and relatively insular college some frictions and rivalries were inevitable but there was humour too. Baggaley's was renowed; when Wilmott died in retirement, the Head of Music urged students to augment the chapel choir with the lure 'You'll not get many chances to bury a Vice-Principal'. Years later, at his own retirement, he greeted David Lang – who was to prove an outstanding successor – 'Well, David, I hope you're going to be as happy here as I thought I was going to be'.

In 1952 the enlargement of the Lecture Theatre was completed and the college at last had a space in which all members could assemble together. The staff continued to grow and Lamb was able to act on another HMI recommendation when a woman tutor in Primary

Education, Sheelagh McCullagh, was seconded from the staff of the Leeds Institute to the College Education Department. On Open Day 1953 the new Library was opened by Sir Charles Morris, Vice-Chancellor of the University. It was spacious and well equipped and few present could have guessed how soon the expansion of the college would render it inadequate. The Limes hostel was opened by the Speaker of the House of Commons, Sir Harry Hylton-Foster; it provided well-equipped single study-bedrooms for another 40 students. While the college gradually expanded its staff and facilities in response to the government's commitment to train more teachers, Lamb was concerned about the supply of students. National applications for the men's colleges had declined from 5,700 in 1949 to 3,700 in 1953 and with new colleges opening and established ones expanding, even the well-reputed St John's felt the pinch. Applications to the college began to rise again by 1954, but Lamb complained that, because of the vagaries of the grant system, it was hard to sustain the three courses for third years. Fewer men were coming forward each year for such supplementary courses

> and will continue to do so I have no doubt until better financial provision is made for them. It is unequitable that students who are already qualified teachers should not only have to find all their college expenses, outside fees – except for the often exiguous help they can wring from LEAs – but should also be regarded as dependent upon their parents. I had a letter the other day about a third-year student of thirty-five saying he must still be regarded as dependent upon his parents. Help from LEAs varies unaccountably . . . some are quite generous while others refuse to contribute a penny.

St John's received just enough applicants to sustain its third year courses; most were men who suspected that before long a mere two-year training would be devalued in the profession. Lamb enveighed once more against the brevity of the course, acknowledging that it was 'a song that I have sung before'

> A period of two years – in fact it is only ninety-four weeks – is shockingly inadequate for our purpose . . . Much has to be left for the student to do on his own after he has left us if ever he is to become a mature scholar. We send many a man out to eat meat in the workaday world who is academically still unweaned, hoping that his appetite will survive, but fearing the reverse.

The college tried to ensure that the 'appetite survived' and had widened its cultural activities since the HMI encouragement of 1948. Instrumental and choral concerts, expeditions, visiting lecturers, poetry readings, variety evenings 'produced' by the ubiquitous Copping, and high quality play productions filled the evening and weekend programmes. Helen Lamb made a strong contribution to college drama, directing many plays and assisting other staff and student directors. Her 1954 *King Lear* seems to have set new standards, and there were well reviewed productions of Shaw, Synge, Eliot, Anouilh, Fry, and other Shakespeare plays including *The Tempest, The Merchant* and *The Dream*. Casts were augmented by amateur actresses from the City and from York schools and occasionally, students from Ripon. In 1957 and 1958 she directed productions of Lamb's plays *Go Down Moses* and *Sons of Adam*. The *Manchester Guardian* described the latter as 'a rare example of non-professional production that was both precise and determined'.

The quality of writing in *The White Rose* suggests a more mature community. The overgrown schoolboy tone of the 20s and 30s has given way to an unembarrassed aspiration to culture – Peter Wenham on 'Why Archaeology?', Roy Stevens' allegory of the Muse's descent to a local school, first-hand reports from former students on education overseas, and shrewd student viewpoints from the subject departments. In 1955-56 the college had students from Nigeria, Thailand, and Sudan, followed by others from South Africa, Syria and Czechoslovakia. There were visitors too from USA, Australia, New Zealand, Malaya, Germany and Russia. Lamb welcomed this growing internationalism

> In a quiet way we hold our place as a creative centre of education in the great world whose sprawling bulk the bonds of modern communication are drawing into ever denser cohesion . . . I always feel when I say goodbye that I have been privileged to show off something that was worth looking at.

At Ripon, the transition from war to peace had been simpler than at York, in spite of the death of Miss Lett. The student body had not been fragmented and Miss Buysman provided continuity for two terms as Acting Principal, retiring at Easter 1946. The new Principal, Miss Valentine Hall, had taken a Froebel Certificate, and a First in Psychology, at London University. After experience in schools she had lectured at Peterborough Training College and been Vice-Principal of Crewe Training College. She took up her appointment in September 1946. The college had 154 students and was asked to increase to 170 for the following year, so, as at York, accommodation was an immediate problem. The governors provided a prompt solution which has served the college well. They bought 'Highfield', the country house and grounds adjoining the college's north boundary, providing residential accommodation for up to 20 more students and staff as well as good teaching space in the large ground-floor rooms. The new Bishop of Ripon, Dr Chase, arrived a few months after Miss Hall and gave her strong support in planning an expanded college. The first stage was to be a new block containing a large dining hall, new kitchens and 50 study bedrooms. It took three years to negotiate the grants and various approvals but in September 1950 the Princess Royal laid the foundation stone and the students set up a Furnishings Fund to supplement the equipment grant and ensure comfortable and colourful study bedrooms. In her care for tasteful domestic provision Miss Hall was a worthy successor to Miss Lett, and made the most of expansive national policies. The college interiors were gradually transformed from their war-time austerity, a fine collection of paintings, prints and sculptures – some by college students and staff – graced the long corridor, while bright furnishings, flowers and plants from the college gardens lightened the lecture rooms and common rooms. The Ripon tradition of an agreeable lifestyle at modest cost was restored after the war by Miss Hall and her colleagues and has endured into the 1990s.

She also cultivated Ripon society, opened the college to it, and took unashamed advantage of it. Her brief account of improvements to the college grounds in 1949 exemplifies:

> It is planned to remove the hedge and to have a broad sweep of lawn extending to the front playing field, which is scheduled for cricket. Flowering shrubs along the drive will eventually take the place of laurels. The Royal Engineers are helping with this work, which involves much removal of soil to obtain the desired levels . . .

The Literary, Dramatic and Musical Societies flourished with good local support and musical standards under Dr Moody remained high. As part-time music tutor and organist he taught in the college for 50 years and was made a Freeman of the City of Ripon on his retirement in 1952. He had also tutored the young George Baggaley who took Moody's high musical standards with him to York. So there was easy co-operation with St John's and in the early 1950s joint ventures included performances of *Messiah*, Brahm's *Requiem*, Bach's *St Matthew Passion* and Elgar's *The Music Makers*. Occasional joint debates and dances were also held with St John's though Lamb had to remind Miss Hall that York also offered Johnsmen social opportunities. Ripon ladies had no monopoly.

The impact of the Korean war made building supplies uncertain again and put a break on government approval of capital projects. The new block rose slowly and the welcome conversion of the old student cubicles into modern study-bedrooms along Jervaulx and Byland corridors actually reduced student accommodation. For the first time, in 1951, 20 students were boarded out with families in Ripon; the college has never since been able to house all its students on campus. Miss Hall informed

Old Students through the magazine that throughout the training system there were some 250 unfilled places for women and even Ripon was in danger of not filling. She appealed to them to tell possible applicants about the college and its interest in older students

> Students who enter Ripon in 1952 and 1953 will have very many more amenities, and the larger number of study bedrooms, and the greater provision of common rooms and new dining room will make our buildings compare very favourably with those of most other colleges. The present qualification for entry is five passes in the General Certificate in Education, and these need not be gained at the same time. There is also the possibility of older students gaining admittance without the usual quali-fications if they can produce other evidence of their fitness to profit from the course. At the present time we have a number of older students in College.

Her timescale for the main improvements was optimistic but at least the Jervaulx and Byland conversions were complete by 1952. Each of the 30 student rooms had a different colour scheme with matching soft furnishings – adventurous for the time, with materials still in short supply

> Corridors are white, each room door painted in a different colour and some rooms have different colours on the four walls so we can compete with the most modern of school decorating schemes! Groups of students undertook to decorate some of the rooms, and hand-block printed curtains were made by the Special Art students. The results are most attractive and admired by all but the most conservative of our visitors.

In September 1952 all places were filled in the college, which had 184 students including three 'matures' on a one-year course. In 1953 there were 180 students but as this was the official 'target' number there were again technically no vacancies, which was well above the national average. Miss Hall had given strong support to chapel activities throughout her first seven years and now persuaded the governors to appoint the first full-time Chaplain and Lecturer in Divinity, who was not to have other responsibilities in the Diocese. Charles Buckmaster worked effectively with students and staff for Miss Hall's remaining seven years, before going on to become Vice-Principal of Bishop Lonsdale College, Derby and Principal of St Peter's College, Saltley, Birmingham.

The new block was at last completed early in 1954 and formally opened in May – the only occasion in the college's history when the Archbishop shared the platform with the Minister of Education. Garbett may have given little time to his chairmanship at St John's but at the dedication service at Ripon Cathedral he proclaimed his belief in the

Church Colleges in terms which echoed Temple's of 1929. He commended the million pounds which the church had given towards the expansion of its Colleges and particularly the generosity of ordinary parishioners who had contributed the bulk of it through the parish quotas.

> I have no doubt that these sacrifices are well worthwhile. If I had to choose between schools and training colleges, much as I would regret the necessity of the choice, I should unhesitatingly choose the colleges, as great and pervasive centres of Christian faith and culture . . . The Church was the pioneer of education in this country and throughout Christendom . . . and now when under changed conditions education is given by the State. the church must still continue to bear witness to the vital importance of a Christian education . . . not by passing pious resolutions . . . But if this witness is to be effective these colleges and schools must be of the best. The inefficient Church college or school is a deadly weapon in the hands of those who advocate a uniform national system of secular education.[3]

The Minister, Miss Florence Horsbrugh, chose the occasion to make a statement on government education policy, taking a different view of the creative tension between central direction and local responsibility from her successors in the 1980s. She praised the voluntary element in English education, to which the chief contributors were Church Colleges and Schools

> And I for one hope that we shall retain this idea of diversity in our education system . . . I think the more we have of this . . . rather than uniformity, and the more we leave responsibility to a great extent to Local Education Authorities and Voluntary bodies and do not centralise it, the richer will be our educational system.[4]

She acknowledged sound advice which her Ministry had received from the Church – particularly from Robert Stopford and Bishop Chase – and praised the efforts of school teachers and college tutors in expanding the school system to cope with the rising birth rate.

> It is to those people above all that we owe this increase. They have been increasing the teachers by the rate of over 5,000 a year; last year we were up to 235,000 . . . it is not fully realised that in the last two years we have had nearly half a million more children coming in, and – taking the numbers back to 1950 – between 1950 and 1954 there have been an extra 700,000 more children in our schools than ever before.

She was adamant that high teaching standards could be maintained even through such a massive expansion, again taking a generous view of the profession:

> I believe it has been done. I see a good deal of the young teachers as I go around the country in our schools, and I am perfectly convinced that the standard is high; that we have got keen, intelligent, enthusiastic young men and women coming into our schools to carry on a job that, unless you *are* keen, unless you *are* enthusiastic, unless you *are* really interested, you cannot do and succeed.

She was troubled that women did not readily come forward for headships and other posts of 'resonsibility' and urged Ripon students to do so boldly when their time came

> I would ask those who go from this college . . . to go with spirit, self reliance, enterprise, energy . . . and if they have the opportunity to take a post that they themselves may wonder 'Can I do it well?' – let them risk failure, rather than not having the courage to try to do it.

It was a speech to inspire confidence at Ripon and beyond, and there is evidence that it did. Reassured by Ministerial approval a committee of the Council of Church Colleges visited all the colleges in 1955 and recommended a further phase of planned expansion. It rejected the possibility either of confining development to only a selected group of colleges, or – as in 1938 – of closing some to concentrate resources on the rest. It advised the Church Board to limit its liability by fixing the maximum number of resident students in any college at 180, maintaining the current total numbers of nearly 5,000 in its colleges and reducing the number of shared rooms. It also offered a hostage to fortune:

> The economic size for a college, both for teaching and residence seems to lie between 180 and 240 students.[5]

We shall explore further the mythology of 'optimum size' for higher education institutions; what is noteworthy at this point is that it should have seemed reasonable to the Church Council and to the Ministry of Education, to assume that college sizes could be 'fixed' and that the approved expansion would meet foreseeable demands. The Committee advised the Church Assembly to spend another £1.5 million on its colleges and, like the 1947 Committee did not leave much scope for argument. Predicting, euphorically, that the three-year course was 'imminent', its members claimed

> Nothing that we have recommended could be called a luxury; our concern has been to secure relief from conditions which still

hamper the work of the colleges and cause frustration to teachers and students. We were frankly taken aback by what we saw, because we had not known how much was needed. It would be a tragic pity if the Church were compelled to stop short of completing all the work we have recommended. A great opportunity would be missed . . .

They justified this assertion with an extravagant claim on behalf of the colleges. It is a claim which is central to this study and demands sceptical examination by each new generation of Church College staff, students and governors:

There is no unifying inspiration and influence in the mass of the Training Colleges. In the Church Colleges there *is* this force, and the Church is responsible to the nation for maintaining a unique and vital service.[6]

There was another fillip for the colleges in 1956 when LEA grants for students were standardised and increased, and the resented and ineffectual 'pledge' for Teacher Training students was abolished. In 1957 government committed resources for the introduction of the overdue three-year course in 1960. Yet, in spite of such useful reforms there was still not much concerted national planning.

In 1939 there had been 13,000 students in the Training Colleges and University Departments in England and Wales. The opening of the Emergency Training Colleges in 1946-47 pushed the numbers to 20,000 and by 1957 they were over 26,000 with 20,000 of these in the colleges. Only then – and under pressure – was an overall national training strategy formulated. Looking back on these years with the hindsight of the late 1960s, Sir Philip Morris, Vice-Chancellor of Bristol University and Chairman of the National Advisory Council on the Training and Supply of Teachers, revealed the extent and duration of the disarray:

It took a long time, indeed until the sixth decade of the Twentieth Century, for two ideas, now taken for granted, to see the light. These were that the Training Colleges had a quantitative relationship to the needs of the schools and secondly that they needed to be institutions of advanced rather than elementary education.[7]

Miss Horsbrugh's Ripon speech of 1954 reads now like a pronouncement of the self-evident; at the time it seemed radical in relating the growth of the school population in precise statistical terms to the expansion of teacher-training colleges. The Ministry had acknowledged the second of Morris's transforming 'ideas' in announcing the start of the three-year course, which was it said intended to foster an academic and social life in the colleges more akin to that in the universities.[8]

It was Morris's National Council which pressed home the first idea in its 1958 recommendations on the *Supply of Teachers for the 1960s*. These demolished the assumption of the Ministry and the hopes of the Church Board that average college size might stabilise around 240 students. For the first time a range of conflicting factors was carefully analysed, with supporting statistics. The Council's proposals allowed for the gap in teacher supply that must result from the start of the three-year course, for a higher wastage rate than had been notified, for a higher birth rate than had been estimated, and for more school pupils staying on at school beyond the leaving age of 15. Their report predicted that all these influences would create a shortfall of at least 34,000 teachers within 10 years.

> We recommend therefore that 16,000 additional places be provided so that the total capacity of the colleges is 36,000 places, enabling 12,000 teachers a year to be trained on a three year course. We regard it as of the utmost importance that these places should be ready for occupation not later than the Autumn of 1962. In accordance with the Minister's remit, we have made no allowance in this figure for future demands for teachers that may arise from major reforms in the educational system. There is no need to fear therefore that this proposal will result in an over-supply of teachers.[9]

The Council urged the Minister – now Geoffrey Lloyd – to review the shape and location of the training system. Before any college was expanded note should be taken of its accessibility to a university and to adequate school practice facilities, of the special teacher recruitment difficulties of remote areas, of the suitability of particular sites, of the need for more co-educational colleges and of the vexed question of size:

> The optimum size of a college, for economic running both educationally and financially, will have to be taken into account. For expansion by 1962, large and medium sized colleges will be the best candidates. Some existing training colleges are too small to be able adequately to provide the appropriate educational breadth of a three-year course and too isolated to offset this deficiency by co-operation with other colleges. Such colleges should not be expanded even though the risk of their ultimate closure may be increased.[10]

This pronouncement caused anxiety at Ripon and some of the smaller women's colleges. The Church Colleges were fortunate that Lloyd's parliamentary secretary was Sir Edward Boyle, an enthusiast for the

Voluntary principle and later influential in the development of the Ripon and York Colleges. The Ministry did not go the whole way with its Advisory Council, but in September 1958 announced an expansion of 12,000 places by 1962. Both St John's and Ripon were within the size of college recommended by the Advisory Council to expand and both were invited to – St John's to 400, and Ripon to 350. Among the Church Colleges only St Luke's Exeter, with 500 places, was to be larger than St John's. A sympathetic Ministry recognised that this rapid growth would strain the finances of the Anglican, Roman Catholic, Methodist and Free Churches, which had been asking since 1956 for more favourable capital grants for the new schools urgently needed, in co-operation with the LEAs, to cope with the 'bulge' in the child population. The Education Act of 1959 offered 75% capital grants, precisely the scale which the Churches believed would enable

> the question of voluntary school finance to be taken out of politics for twenty years.[11]

Ironically the Church Training Colleges benefited quicker than the aided schools whose legislation was hedged round by qualifications about types of school and dates of submissions which created resentment and no permanent solution to the denominational school problem.

While the Church Board of Finance braced itself, the expansion of teacher education received further impetus from a report of the Ministry's Central Advisory Council. The Crowther Report *15 to 18* had been commissioned in 1956, before teacher supply had become contentious. It came out firmly for the raising of the school leaving age to 16, by 1966-68, and demanded better opportunities for pupils and teachers in expanded sixth forms and 'county colleges'. The continuity of aspiration in the major educational reports of the 20th century is epitomised in the Crowther recommendation for a fifth year of secondary schooling. It looks back explicitly, 34 years, to Tawney and the first Hadow Report.

> Our main case is not economic at all. It rests on the conviction that all boys and girls of fifteen have much to learn, and that school – in the broadest sense – and not work, is the place for this. 'Secondary Education for All' will not be a reality until it is provided for all up to the age of sixteen. We believe that this is a duty which society owes all its young citizens . . .[12]

The Church Board applauded the Crowther Report and in January 1959 put to the Assembly yet another revised expansion programme for the Church Colleges. It was for more than £4,000,000 of capital development; the Church's share under the new regulations would be £1,200,000 of which £250,000 was to be invested in an entirely new college. In its report the Board posed a series of questions which may at the time have been rhetorical, but would not have seemed so 12 years later.

> To what extent can the individual colleges be considered firmly established for an indefinite period? . . . Is there a danger that a recession may make some of this work redundant and leave colleges with empty places? Will there be another round of expansion, accompanied by additional financial demands on the Assembly? . . . When this operation has been completed, how effective and varied an educational instrument will the Church Colleges provide?[13]

It apparently answered them to the satisfaction of the Assembly, which endorsed the report. This was not a matter only of financial or strategic judgement; the Board had tried to grapple with issues of quality and to assess honestly the 'religious life and teaching of the Colleges' not as supportive Church people liked to imagine them, but as they appeared to a critical visitation. The conclusion, with judicious reservations, was confident:

> The Training Colleges are the only stake which the Church has in the State system of higher education, though their influence has hitherto been restricted almost entirely to the primary and secondary modern schools. The introduction of the three year course will open new possibilities . . . each College is likely to have certain broad fields of specialisation. Yet between them all the Church Colleges will be able to provide all training college subjects at a high level so that an able candidate with a Christian background will always be able to find a Church college which provides an appropriate course in his own subject.[14]

This vision of a group of likeminded colleges planning and working together should have been enacted in the 60s and maintained in the 70s in the face of retrenchment. In fact the leaders of the surviving Church Colleges are still struggling to achieve it in the 90s. On the credit side, it should be said that although misgivings were expressed at the time about funding the first new Church College for more than 50 years, the Board was convinced that

> as an affirmation of faith in the education work of the Church it might have an incalculable effect.

It was a conviction which 30 years have not discredited.

The Ripon College target of 350 places demanded more building. The Ministry and the Church Board agreed an imaginative scheme for a new hall of residence, assembly hall, music lecture room and practice rooms, and a new chapel, the old one to be converted into a library.

As at other Church College's, later including St John's, the decision to abandon the original chapel was taken with regret. The 1899 Ripon chapel seems to have inspired the loyalty of many students and for 50 years this had taken the positive form of gifts by leaving years – 20 stained glass windows, a marble pavement in memory of Miss Lett and much specially designed furniture. After consultations with architects and the Old Students' Association however all feasible schemes for enlarging the old chapel were rejected and a bold modern design for a new one, to be built alongside a modern hall, was widely approved. The negotation of this sensitive change was one of Miss Hall's last gifts to Ripon. In 1960 she was appointed Principal of St Mary's College, Cheltenham, where she continued to lead vigorously for another 10 years.

At Ripon she seems to have been held in some affection and much awe. The mixture was reflected in an incident after a visit by a group of 'Johnsmen' for a dance. When they returned to Lord Mayor's Walk, Vice-Principal Chapman discovered that they had appropriated as a trophy, Miss Hall's revered door-stop – a large brass lion – and had painted it in the green and yellow hoops of the St John's rugby shirt. Scenting a diplomatic crisis, Chapman phoned Miss Teasdale, the amenable Ripon Vice-Principal, who undertook to distract Miss Hall for an hour or two. The paint was stripped off, the lion repolished, and a student dispatched on a motorcycle to restore it to its dignity outside the Principal's door at Ripon before it had been missed – at least at the most exalted level. So inter-college relations remained cordial. Though Lamb and Miss Hall had sponsored a measure of social interaction between their students it seems that neither deeply regretted the 25 miles distance between them. In the 1960s however the pressures against single sex colleges were to become irresistible.

As growth and change continued at St John's, Lamb was exercised to maintain the Christian commitment of the college. He was strengthened in his efforts when Michael Ramsay, distinguished professor of divinity successively at Durham and Cambridge, became Archbishop of York in 1956. He took a keen interest in the college and regularly chaired governors meetings, with Milner-White still an active member. The college had accepted more readily than many, the Ministry's invitation to double in size but in the 1958 *White Rose* Lamb ruminated on the challenge

> With larger numbers the problem of preserving our unity will grow more acute. The greatest asset of the 'Third Force in Education', the Training Colleges, has been from the beginning, the quality of life that can flourish in a residential college where everyone knows everyone else and the whole body can meet

together for the daily act of worship, for meals, for JCR discussion and for the occasional lecture . . . if ever we grow into a multi-hostel community the question how to maintain the old coherence and esprit de corps will become perhaps the most important question of all . . . There never was a time when we were more significantly challenged to achieve the new thing which history is always demanding of everything that remains alive.

He must have sensed that the 'multi-hostel community' could not be far away.

In 1959 he reported the governors' acceptance of the requested student target of 400 – three years of just over 130 – but their postponement of any response to the Ministry's urgent request to the college to admit women. A team of architects had agreed that new accommodation must include two gymnasia at Heworth Croft, teaching rooms and laboratories for Physics and Chemistry; extensions for Maths and Rural Science; a Craft Department to be housed in a nearby vacated school; Music rooms; a general lecture room; two more residential hostels at Heworth and The Limes, and numerous conversions of existing areas. The possibility of enlarging the Chapel was 'under discussion'. Lamb acknowledged that it would be impossible for some time to accommodate all the enlarged intakes in college hostels, but pledged his own commitment to '100% residence' which he believed might be restored 'with patience'. Within a year however the Ministry announced that because of the expense no college could be permitted to sustain full residence in future.

The conversion of St Thomas' School in Lowther Street into a Craft Centre went ahead and was opened in the summer of 1960. The former craft rooms were converted into an English lecture room and a Science teaching workshop, and Lamb informed *The White Rose* that the whole project had been completed for less than £10,000

a remarkably low figure considering the magnificence of the Craft Department which it has provided.

The requirement on all the Church Colleges for 150 years to make heavy contributions to all capital projects has made them good stewards of tax-payers money as well as their own. The Lowther Street conversion was one of the many imaginative building projects at Ripon and York which have been thrifty but not frugal.

1961 brought two portentous developments. The first – widely welcomed – was the appointment of a Prime Minister's Committee, chaired by Lord Robbins, to review and make recommendations upon the pattern of Higher Education in Britain. The second, which caused consternation in the colleges, was an expected circular from the Ministry offering 'guidance' on the *Balance of Training* of teachers for the various age-ranges in schools. After what seemed to them a long struggle, the colleges had just achieved parity of length – if not esteem – for their standard training course with university degree courses. Now they found that their long-sought scope to train teachers for secondary schools was to be small. It had been tacitly assumed for 60 years that colleges offered lower level training appropriate for primary teachers, while universities dominated secondary training; now the Ministry had virtually decreed it. The colleges protested the restrictions, urged that compulsory training for all teachers should be introduced as soon as possible – a degree was still regarded as a full teaching qualification in its own right – and pinned their faith on Lord Robbins and his committee. Lamb announced the St John's strategy in the 1961 edition of the student magazine *Spread Eagle*

> We have side-stepped the Ministry's request to 'go primary' by going 'wide' instead. What the Ministry apparently did not perceive before making its dreadful pronouncement was that the Training College course contains a very wide element that is taken by all students irrespective of the age of children whom they will teach . . . What is chiefly vexing is that Sixth forms up and down the country have been given a wrong impression of the place of the Training College viz a viz the Universities just when the expansion of the latter and the lowering of the qualification required for a bursary increase the danger of University competition for good candidates.

Beyond the colleges the *Balance of Training* circular caused wide concern about the appropriate staffing of secondary schools which led to an invitation to the Central Advisory Council under the chairmanship of John Newsom 'to consider the education between the ages of thirteen and sixteen, of pupils of average or less than average ability'. The Robbins and Newsom enquiries proceeded throughout 1962, while the expansion of the training colleges continued apace. Meanwhile the Church Board of Education again fluttered the Church Assembly with a report commending participation in the further expansion of 8,000 places in the training colleges which the Ministry requested in 1961. The total expansion of numbers now sought from the autumn 1958 total was 24,000 – just short of a 100% increase. The Church Board stressed its concern both for schools and the training of teachers. It reminded the Assembly that general and technical higher education had already grown substantially. New university charters had been approved for Sussex, York, East Anglia and Essex; eight Colleges of Advanced Technology had been designated. Expansion on this scale could only succeed if places were filled by well taught pupils from well equipped schools. The Board welcomed the decision that the new Church College, at Canterbury, was to have an immediate allocation of 400 places; it proposed that 1,200 more be financed in the other colleges.

In the late 1970s some critics claimed that the Church Board of Education and the Council of Principals failed to foresee either the dangers or the best opportunities in responding to government pressure for expansion. But we noted that the Board in 1959 had asked hard questions. In 1961 it made some shrewd predictions

> The Church is seen to be willing and able to play a distinctive part in higher education at precisely the moment when attention is being given by a government enquiry to essential questions of policy. What began as a rescue operation after the war has turned into something far more important. The Assembly's support of the colleges has put them in good heart to take part in the expansion programme and to undertake the greater responsibilities and higher academic standards of the three year programme. Some of the colleges stand ready for closer co-operation with the universities: Two of those being expanded – York and Norwich – are in places chosen for new universities; several church colleges are being chosen for graduate work. Colleges not in universities but able to be strengthened and enlarged, are developing their own specialisms in such subjects as divinity, physical education, science and rural studies and so have, of their own right, their distinctive part to play in the *newly emerging picture of diversified forms of education* [my italics].[15]

Although a relationship had now been acknowledged by government between staffing needs in schools and training quotas in colleges, there were still – as there had been since the first grants of 1833 – naked financial pressures. Those of the early 1960s were frankly discussed in a subsequent book, by Lord Boyle – the former Sir Edward – who, in a reshuffle of the MacMillan cabinet found himself suddenly translated from the office of Financial Secretary to the Treasury to that of Minister of Education. Although Government had conceded Sir Philip Morris's 'two ideas' acceptance for Ministry proposals still depended on cabinet tactics and Ministerial adroitness; as Boyle admitted, conviction did not always last:

> That's what I remember most about my transfer from the Treasury to the Ministry of Education. I had abruptly to change sides on a costly issue where the case wasn't altogether easy to argue because we had this high rate of wastage among women teachers, but none the less one had to do battle – it was a matter

of deciding how to play the hand wisely . . . Looking back on it I'm not sure I was quite wise in my decision to press the Treasury all the way on the teacher supply point.[16]

It was a rare example of Education triumphing over the Treasury, and, in the long view, an unfortunate one. Boyle recognised that his predecessor at the Ministry, Sir David Eccles, had resisted a large increase in teacher training places because he was convinced it would create teacher unemployment by the late 1960s.

The Robbins Committee received written evidence from the Church Board and from the fast growing Association of Teachers in Colleges and Departments of Education. The ATCDE articulated the concensus among the 140 training colleges in favour of integrated 'concurrent' patterns of training, the upgrading of the three-year course to degree status, the strengthening of links between colleges and universities, the speedy introduction of mandatory training for all graduate entrants to teaching, the provision of higher degree and diploma awards for serving teachers, and reforms in the governance and administration of the colleges to give them more autonomy. It claimed that the colleges had far outgrown the 19th century image which still clung to them, and it reminded Lord Robbins and his colleagues that, though much had been done in 19 years towards implementing the McNair Report, there was still too much truth in its assertion

What is wrong with the majority of training colleges is their poverty and all that flows from it.

The Church Board supported all these reforms and particularly pressed the development of university relationships for the colleges. It listed the specialisations of the individual Church Colleges and, tendentiously, claimed one distinctive characteristic for all of them:

The voluntary sector of teacher education, consisting of colleges sponsored by the Churches, which accounts for some forty percent of the total numbers of students in training colleges, lays claim to an independence which should be preserved as higher education expands to embrace a larger section of the community. With the relative freedom from stereotype controls which is in its fortunate possession, it is willing and should be encouraged in the ways suggested, to experiment in new forms of personal, academic and professional education implicit in the whole of our evidence.[17]

If in the 1960s the colleges themselves had made an unsentimental analysis of the 'stereotype controls' from which they were said to be 'relatively free' their self esteem would have taken a knock, but they might have been spared some of the disillusion of the 70s. Though they were subject to less interference than those LEA colleges which were tightly controlled by autocratic authorities, the more fortunate LEA colleges enjoyed supportive relationships with their local councils and were funded more generously than the Voluntary colleges.

Institutions, however, are no more inclined than individuals to sober re-appraisal during periods of buoyant optimism. The colleges were further elated in August 1963 by the publication of the Newsom Report, *Half Our Future.* It called for

> New modes of thought, and a change of heart on the part of the community as a whole

about the needs and merits of secondary modern schools. More emphatically, it called for the right kind of training for those who would teach in them and offered in a single paragraph, an accolade to the colleges and a rebuff to the Ministry's *Balance of Training* policy:

> We are convinced that the kind of training the colleges offer, that is a 'concurrent' course in which the personal higher education of the student is combined with pedagogical studies, is likely to provide the most suitable professional preparation for teaching most of the pupils with whom we are concerned. We are also aware that current policies require the colleges to concentrate on the training of primary teachers, and that in the immediate future only a minority of teachers with this type of training, mainly specialists in certain shortage subjects, will be available to the secondary schools. While we recognise the serious teacher shortage which the primary schools face, we are concerned lest an emergency measure which does not rest on any positive assessment of the needs of the secondary schools should be retained as a long term policy.[18]

So convinced were the members that the training colleges should be entrusted with the preparation of teachers for the secondary modern schools that they had asked the Minister to make their views on the matter known, before their report was published, to the Robbins Committee. They suspected that the Robbins Report might have serious implications for the training of teachers, perhaps in new kinds of institutions. Newsom's Committee pressed its point and gave the colleges for a few months the unique experience of being publicly congratulated, by a prestigious professional group, as offering the *best* form of education for a large cadre of the teaching force:

> We are not concerned with types of institution, or with the title of the qualification that trained teachers may eventually claim, but with the preservation of a pattern of training which we are

convinced has marked value for the future teachers of large numbers of girls and boys.[19]

The report proposed that a training requirement for all graduates wishing to enter teaching should be introduced as soon as practicable and that the colleges should be offered a share in providing it; that the content of many of the current graduate courses in university departments should be re-examined, and that the in-service courses in university departments should be extended to untrained graduates. The colleges had high hopes of Robbins; the plaudits of Newsom were an unexpected bonus.

The Robbins Committee presented its report in October 1963; 28 years on, it can be confidently described as one of the three or four most influential educational reports since government was reluctantly drawn into the enterprise in 1833. It offered the colleges all that they aspired to: a change of title to 'Colleges of Education'; enhanced status as member colleges of University Schools of Education, each college with an independent governing body – a big advance for most LEA colleges – and receiving its funds through the University School. A proposed *four*-year degree programme offered parity of esteem with the 'degree plus postgraduate certificate' route. Anticipating a power struggle, the committee offered specific suggestions for the association of the Local Authorities with the University Schools and was

> convinced that immense benefit will flow from closer links with the universities and that our proposals offer the best hope of raising the status and standards of the colleges and securing their full integration into the system of higher education of the future.[20]

It took special note of the Voluntary Colleges, supported the principle that they should not be financed entirely from public funds, and saw little difficulty in routing their finance through the University Schools at roughly present levels.

The Committee recommended further expansion of teacher training. In 1963 there were 49,000 students in training at 146 colleges; the Robbins proposal for 1970 was for 82,000 students in 156 colleges of a minimum size:

> We are convinced that in the long term a college with less than 750 students should be regarded as exceptional. Indeed such a development is essential if the total number of colleges is to be kept at a reasonable figure and if the colleges claim to higher education status is to be made good.

This argument for larger colleges related not simply to financial economy but also to educational efficiency. The Committee suggested that though groups of small colleges could share some facilities they could not be afforded the generous library facilities, nor the range of staff for specialised courses which could be available to large colleges. In implementing most of the Robbins proposals governments of the 1960s used this argument constructively towards wise expansion; subsequent governments – national and local – have frequently used it speciously. The nostrum 'economies of scale' has come to be regarded as self-authenticating and justifying claims of economy for which no evidence has been produced.

These two major reports of 1963 reflected a swell of support for the work of the colleges grounded in concern for the education of the less privileged. Lord Boyle believed that the Newsom and Robbins reports represented a watershed in educational development. Both reflected and endorsed the convictions of influential sociologists such as Halsey, Vaizey and Floud, that the heavily selective system of education which had persisted into the late 50s had been inequitable in its distribution of benefits. One key assertion from each report could profitably – even 30 years later – be displayed in the entrance to every school and higher education institution in Britain, because we have still not fully responded to either. The Robbins Committee reported

> Our investigations have suggested the existence of large reservoirs of untapped ability in the population especially among girls.

The Newsom Report was commended in a brief foreword by the Minister, Sir Edward Boyle. His final sentence – for which he claimed no originality – summed up the quiet revolution in educational attitude which had begun but is not yet complete:

> The essential point is that all children should have an equal opportunity of *acquiring intelligence* and of developing their talents and abilities to the full [my italics].

For the rest of the decade Ministers of Education in successive governments of different parties, accepted social demand as a policy criterion.

The Robbins Report was acclaimed by the colleges. It offered them enhanced status, degree courses in a university context, more attention to the quality of entrants to teaching, and steady expansion for at least 15 years. Its planning figure for Colleges of Education students for 1980 was an awesome 145,000. Ripon College and St John's York were poised to respond, confidently led and with Principals and staff knowledgeably supported by Chairmen of Governors, Bishop Chase at Ripon and Archbishop Ramsay at York. When Ramsay moved on to Canterbury Lamb wrote to the Association

179

It was characteristic of him that he scarcely missed an attendance at our governing body and that he brought to our discussions not only lightning ability to size up the business in hand but also a sympathetic understanding of both the dignity and the educational potential of a training college. It is by no means always that one who enjoys the most exalted standing in the world of the universities appreciates so imaginatively what goes on in our more restricted sphere . . . His place has been taken by Dr Coggan who is also a scholar and well acquainted already with what goes on in a Church Training College. He has promised to take an active interest in St John's . . .

The promise was to be richly kept.

In her farewell letter to the Ripon Association in November 1960, Miss Hall announced that work had begun on a new hostel which should be finished within a year, in time for the first of the three-year course students. During the year the new hall and chapel would be started, to be followed by a linking building with additional common rooms and cloakrooms. There were 235 students, 40 of them living out in Ripon. The college had acquired the former Ripon Girls Secondary School building next to the front fields and this was to be renovated in time for the next year's enlarged entry. Having previously set the local Royal Engineers to work on the college grounds one of Miss Hall's valedictory gestures was to offer them a share in the social life of the college. The new '38 Club' linked college students with members of the 38th Corps Royal Engineers for activities including cinema and theatre visits, canoeing and photography clubs, lectures, games and fortnightly dances in college; Johnsmen had competition.

Miss Hall's successor, Marjorie Gage, came into residence in January 1961. She had taken a first in mathematics at London University and after varied teaching and lecturing experience had been Vice-Principal of Homerton College, Cambridge. She arrived at a time of radical and supportive change for the training colleges; she and her colleagues grasped the opportunities and the next decade was one of continuous success for Ripon. Bishop Chase retired as Miss Hall moved on to Cheltenham but his successor Bishop John Moorman also proved an excellent chairman of governors, with insight and concern for the scholarship of the college as well as its spiritual life.

In 1962 student numbers were just over 300; by September 1963 they were 370 and the academic staff had expanded to 32 with more appointments pending. By May 1963 the new chapel and hall were complete and the old chapel transformed into a fine library. Similar chapel conversions were carried out in many Church Colleges as funds were provided for new libraries and student numbers outgrew old chapels, but Ripon's is one of the most skilful and unobtrusive. These substantial additions coincided with the College's Centenary, celebrated in May when the new buildings were dedicated and in July when at College and Cathedral over 1,000 gathered for the reunion. There was satisfaction too at the success of the first students to complete the three-year course. Standards were high, external examiners complimentary, and already there were murmers – in the light of the Robbins Report – of a four-year degree course within three years. The college might have to continue for some time in the throes of building operations and policy changes, but there seemed hope that, for individual students, there would be release at last from the pressures which the McNair Report had regretted 20 years before

> Many students in Training Colleges do not mature by living, they survive by hurrying.

This had been one of Lamb's strongest concerns and St John's did not respond readily to the Ministerial demands of 1963-64. In the 1963 *White Rose* Lamb was critical of the inadequate expenditure proposed for massive college expansion compared to the sums being spent on new universities; he was sceptical of rapid growth.

> The thought that size means status must have given a wonderful incentive to colleges to squeeze the numbers in. At any rate our offer to go from 500 to 600 was considered in high places as ungenerous compared with the first thoughts of colleges in the country as a whole and we have been invited to reconsider. I face with considerable reluctance the prolongation of the experience of living like a balloon that is being blown up . . . No doubt we shall have to grow larger even than 600 . . . Every time we grow larger we lose something. Our task will be to see that our gains are still greater than our losses and when I say gains I do not mean prestige but real increases in the power of the college to influence young men and women for good.

In the same letter he announced an important change in the social style of the college – the replacement of the Staff/Student 'Constitution' by a full Students' Union with its own elected officers, committees and financial structures – a further stage towards student self-determination.

The college offered opportunity for students to contribute to debate on the curriculum and the 1974 session saw lively exchanges at the end of the first Foundation Course. Lamb relished them.

> The encouragement arose, not from any flattering words that were spoken, far from it, but from the sense one had of confronting an intelligent, critical, articulate audience of young

people with a quality that could not exactly be matched outside a university, on an occasion which no university would be likely to arrange.

Eighty places had been offered to women students for the coming session and it was expected that there would be 250 within four years. Lamb foresaw at least one advantage

> Perhaps the most difficult, and also the most worthwhile task we have ever set ourselves is to reaffirm the best values we have exhibited as a mens' college and in this different medium where the two sexes work together. I shall be disappointed if our academic standards do not rise quite sharply . . .

He was not disappointed. The first six women to sit final examinations for the certificate registered six 'A' grades between them out of a total of 41 'A's between 173 candidates; the top student of the year was Miss M. Procter. Lamb also exulted that 'Choral and dramatic activities had been transformed'. Jane Allen, senior women tutor was in post to welcome the women students and Joan Valentine had been appointed from the Headship of Osmondthorpe School Leeds as second Vice-Principal, working alongside Christopher Chapman in this role and in the Education Department. In the same year present and past students marked the retirements of Joe Copping, Head of Primary Education, and James Coleclough, Head of History and Sheriff of the City; both had served the college 35 years.

The increased student numbers were to be accommodated partly in new buildings but also in the refurbished premises of the Archbishop Holgate's Grammar School – the former Yeoman School – next door to the college on Lord Mayor's Walk. It had been designed in association with the original 1845 college building and by the same architect, G. T. Andrews. This gave the college a fine extended frontage along Lord Mayor's Walk and provided further building land on which Lamb hoped a swimming pool might be built. Meanwhile ground was being cleared in the centre of the extended site for a new chapel designed by George Pace. It was to be a large, boldly modern, multi-purpose building able to put large crowds or small groups at ease, and suitable for choral and orchestral music, drama and dance. In the changing 60s Lamb was conscious of the risk.

> We asked . . . that the chapel should be architecturally worthy of its place in the very centre of the college, and of its function as our rallying point and the symbol of what we stand for. This Chapel is intended to suggest no compromise. It will either be our banner, proudly wrought out in terms of architecturally enclosed space or it will be a white elephant reproaching us with

what we have allowed ourselves to lose. Let no-one under-estimate its significance.

Nor was the college underestimating the pace of academic change. Negotiations were well advanced with the University of Leeds for the new BEd degree, with the college determined to protect the integrated pattern of its course. Cordial discussions were also proceeding with the new University of York, in its second year, on possible areas of co-operation. Professor Harry Ree proved prophetic of many an inter-institutional scenario of the 70s, when he suggested that St John's and the new University might proceed 'through confrontation and consultation to effective co-operation and perhaps eventual conjugation'. At York events were to prove otherwise.

At Ripon the 1964-65 academic year began confidently with 400 students, 100 living out of college, but before the end of the autumn term all colleges of education had new cause for anxiety. After a long period of in-fighting by the LEAs the government rejected the administrative and financial arrangements by which the Robbins Committee had proposed to integrate the colleges with the universities. This was disappointing for the Church Colleges but a more severe setback for the LEA colleges, many of which had looked to Robbins for release from local authority dominance. It was a crucial decision.

Having forestalled a university takeover the LEAs asserted themselves to maintain their control of colleges which represented their growing participation in higher education. By the end of the academic year they had organised a strong lobby for removing the colleges altogether from university influence and linking them instead to local authority technical colleges. It was urged that their qualifications should be conferred by the Council for National Academic Awards, newly chartered in response to a Robbins Committee recommendation. One justification claimed for the strategy was that at a time of acute teacher shortage, supply and training could be more accurately monitored by a Chief Education Officer within a single local authority than by the large committee of a University School of Education 'serving' several authorities. In the end it was probably the teacher education experience and political influence of the universities which salvaged the McNair relationships, but the issue was in doubt for most of 1965, and in some Schools of Education the uncertainty postponed planning for the proposed Bachelor of Education degree.

At the same time there was concern about student numbers. The ninth report of the National Advisory Council on the Supply and Training of Teachers took an even more lugubrious view of teacher supply than the Robbins Committee and recommended to a sceptical Department and

Treasury a further doubling of numbers in training by 1983. It pressed for the Robbins targets to be brought forward by three years and all colleges to accommodate a 20% increase in the three years 1965 to 1967. It proposed that, where necessary, colleges should achieve this target by 'doubling up' in larger study bedrooms, by increasing non-resident numbers, by working a four-term year, or by organising virtually continuous school-practice work through 'Box and Cox' methods, ensuring that the whole student body was never in residence at the same time. The Church Colleges co-operated readily in attempts to recruit more non-resident students, and 'doubled up' where large rooms permitted. The four-term year proposal was not pursued and on the 'Box and Cox' proposals the Church Colleges refused to co-operate. They were determined to maintain high quality training and insisted that the ideal of an integrated college community was at the heart of their work.

This was a rare example of the assertion of that Voluntary college 'autonomy' which in the next decade was to prove illusory. The LEA colleges had to do what their Authorities required and in some of them professional and social opportunities were seriously reduced. There was resentment that the high hopes from the Robbins Report remained largely unfulfilled, and unease that the training system might be expanding too far too fast. Three years later the ATCDE surveyed conditions of service in the 10 colleges which had endured the greatest expansion. Introducing the report, Joyce Skinner, Principal of Bishop Grosseteste College, Lincoln, struck a prophetic note:

> The general impression gained from the replies received suggests that the nation is considerably indebted to the goodwill, energy and effort of staff and students in producing the required expansion of the teaching force often in adverse conditions and frequently at considerably human cost. It will be a poor repayment to both staff and students if one of the consequences of their endeavours to meet the needs of the nation's children proves to be unemployment among the nations teachers in the ensuing years.[21]

Both Ripon and York agreed to accept the 20% additional entry for 1965.

In her letter to the Association Miss Gage announced a significant variation in the entry.

> This session started with 464 students with no increase in residential places. The pattern therefore of having only about two thirds of the students actually resident in the college seems to have come to stay. It means of course that students normally have to spend at least one year in lodgings – an experience which they enjoy and which has immense value. This year we have a

group of twenty older folk, six men and fourteen women – for want of a better title called our 'mature group'.

So co-education had begun modestly at Ripon; it was to develop more gradually than at most colleges. At St John's the 1965 entry was 300, with the college's overall target reluctantly raised to 900. Lamb was aware that some college's aspired as high as 2,000 but he believed his colleagues supported his policy of 'watchful caution'. All the Church Colleges were buoyant and for the first time in autumn 1965 they published a joint prospectus advertising the range of locations, courses and life-styles offered by 27 Anglican colleges including the new Christ Church, Canterbury, and St Martin's Lancaster. It was a high-water mark in their fortunes.

As they were circulating this manifesto of Voluntary distinctiveness and direct-grant 'autonomy' the burgeoning power of the Local Authorities in higher education was inadvertently proclaimed by Secretary of State Anthony Crosland in a speech at Woolwich Polytechnic. Prompting a further step in what Lowndes described as 'the conversion of Whitehall from resignation to leadership'[22] he announced government's support for the Robbins Committee view that post-school education needed 'a system'.

> And in Britain the system must be based on the twin traditions which have created our present higher education institutions. These are broadly of two kinds. On the one hand we have what has come to be called the *autonomous sector* represented by the universities, in whose ranks I now of course include the colleges of advanced technology. On the other hand we have the *public sector* represented by the leading technical colleges *and the colleges of education*[23] [my italics].

It is some indication of the expectations the colleges had derived from Newsom and Robbins that they seem not to have appreciated the significance of this prescriptive statement or of the White Paper which followed in May 1966, proposing the designation of 27 institutions as 'polytechnics' separate from the university 'sector' of higher education. Interest later focussed on the influence of senior DES officers who write Ministerial speeches when Crosland frankly admitted that he had not really known what he was talking about when he made it.[24] For the colleges of education it was decisive because it ran counter to the formerly stated DES policy for the three-year course – to foster in the colleges an academic and social style 'more akin to that of the universities'. It placed them firmly in the 'public' i.e. the directly controllable sector of higher education along with the newly designated polytechnics.

The exhilaration of rapid growth and the prospect of the Bachelor of Education degree seem to have preoccupied the Church Colleges in 1966-67. Crosland later conceded that the timing and the terminology of his speech had been ill-chosen but affirmed his belief in the policy in words which could leave the colleges few illusions.

> When I finally mastered the subject I became a passionate believer in binary and the polytechnics . . . Most of the age group is not going on to higher education anyway and, alas, will not do so for a long time to come. And of those who are going on, not all want a university type of education. Both the demand and the need is for a pluralist, not a unitary system of higher education and for alternative institutions which offer something totally different from the traditional universities.[25]

The centralising attitude underlying the policy was to have lasting influence; Crosland himself endorsed a subsequent comment that the power which could now be exercised by the Department of Education and Science extended to

> such hitherto untouchable subjects as the future of higher education – universities and all.[26]

So the speech announced a shift of power but no new thinking about higher education. It was a notable illustration of Norwood's conviction that the English talent is for making do with what has already been done – a 'capacity for making an illogical compromise work in practice . . . without bothering overmuch with theory'. The colleges were to regret it in the 1970s.

In 1966 a Working Party under the chairmanship of the Bishop of Salisbury reported to the Board of Education on *The Communication of the Christian Faith*. They had visited all the Church Colleges during the previous year and Lamb had reflected on their visit in a letter to the *Spread Eagle*. He had found the visit 'most opportune' because of all the development and planning that was afoot; it made the college think:

> I was glad to be asked to call a staff meeting and be faced with the question 'What difference does it make to you to be in a College of the Church of England?' What matters most of all of course is that we should be a good college, doing efficiently the same job as other such colleges undertake . . . The college justifies itself as a place of Christian Education by the kind of people we are in whom it is embodied at the present moment, and of course in those teachers out in the world who are, as it were, an extension in space of the body corporate. No institution is perfect. The

186

excellence which we should like to claim is never a thing already achieved and established; we are always having to become what we are.

The Working Party reported that the huge expansion and the radically altered attitudes of students had changed the colleges. In a subsequent study, Murphy suggested that although the denominations had sustained their right to appoint to their schools and colleges staff of their own faiths, they

> now in practice often considered themselves fortunate to obtain a teacher or lecturer of any religion or none.[27]

because of the shortage of teachers, and the decline of religious commitment.

The Working Party detected a parallel change in patterns of student commitment. It rejected the hallowed assumption that a majority of students enrolling at Church Colleges did so with Christian conviction

> If ever this was true in the past it is clearly no longer true today. Most students, we discovered, chose their college for quite other reasons – because it was near home or had a good reputation for their main subject, or simply because it was the only one which would take them or the one which their school teacher had recommended. Very few chose it primarily because of its Church connection . . . We have the impression that among third year students, who have nothing to lose by frankness . . . perhaps seldom more than a quarter would call themselves active Christians.[28]

In 1966 *The White Rose* celebrated Lamb's 'coming of age' as Principal with a witty appreciation by Joe Copping. Lamb himself wrote thankfully that at last the college had ceased to resemble a builder's yard and the gardeners had been able to tidy up and plant out the spaces between new buildings. The new Chapel was dedicated by Archbishop Coggan in June, and Lamb exulted in

> a gracious harmony of angles in silver grey brick defined by precise aluminium edges singing Sursum Corda . . . I admit that I myself wanted to build the swimming bath before the chapel, since I hold that life is more important than liturgy and the thing symbolised than the symbol; but it is a wonderful thing to have such a banner.

College chaplain Ned Binks gave imaginative leadership, occasionally too imaginative for Lamb who, being himself a cleric remained ex-officio senior chaplain. Students and staff were encouraged to join in a range of

187

cultural and religious activities in the new building and Binks ruefully acknowledged an enthusiastic response:

> Anyone who serves as a chaplain at St John's these days will leave well qualified for a job either with Pickfords or the Theatre Royal. For the new chapel is proving such an adaptable building that every week presents at least one exercise in furniture removal or scene shifting. This year Institute Day was the busiest day, with five different events: a secular oration; a programme of readings on student life; some children's opera; a Greek tragedy and finally the evening service. Fortunately few days are quite as hectic but the same variety has continued throughout the year.

The following year the chapel lost a staunch supporter with the retirement of Leonard Poore, Head of Religious Studies, renowned for 25 years for his scholarship, gentle care for students and colleagues and a sense of fun which extended to loaning his deaf-aids and dog-collars to students impersonating him at variety shows.

Women applicants to St John's outnumbered men after only three years and the college abandoned its intention to maintain a ratio of 5:3 in favour of men. The women were, on average, better qualified, and there were 'empty places' for men throughout the whole college network. An extended programme of sport, drama and music now included college contributions to the York Festival, with staff and students taking part in the performance of the Mystery Plays. The music programme owed much to 'that seasoned impresario' Joan Valentine, who enrolled the college as one of the original patrons of the Leeds International Piano Competition. Lamb confessed to *The White Rose*

> Perhaps also a tiny grain of emulation has helped to stimulate the vigour of our contribution to the life of the City – the hope perhaps that amid the thunder of welcome to achievements at Heslington there might be an occasional whisper about an older place of education situated nearer the heart of the city. Certainly it is stimulating in more ways than one to have a university in our neighbourood.

In the same edition he struck an untypically doleful note on the decline of co-operation between students and staff following the establishment of the Students' Union. He appealed, not for any limitation of students responsibility but for a 'friendly re-think' of ways in which the Senior Common Room could support student activity. The Students' Union President endorsed Lamb's comments on the importance of honouring fixtures – variety and apathy were taking their toll even at St John's. But he was confident that students were content with the new situation and was appreciative of Lamb's support and advice. For much of the 1970s enthusiastic staff at universities and colleges felt that Students' Unions no longer wanted their involvement, so they took less interest in student activities. For St John's this was a drastic change.

On the credit side the college was one of the first to gain Ministry approval for new Articles of Government which formalised participation of students and staff in the making of policy and decisions. Stanley Watkin, popular and ingenious bursar for almost 30 years, welcomed the changes in an article for *Spread Eagle*, pointing out that the new Instrument brought the first legal changes in college government since 1841, all powers having previously been vested in the Governing Committee and its agent, the Principal. The new arrangements distributed authority more appropriately, with curriculum matters largely in the hands of the new Academic Board and with Principal, Vice-Principal and two elected staff joining the Governors. The Ministry took a more cautious view than the college about student membership of Governing Body and Academic Board, which were not yet conceded. Watkin reminded former students that the college's activities were now distributed on four major sites in York – Lord Mayor's Walk, Gray's Court, Heworth Croft and Hull Road, with the large hostel at Limes forming a fifth and the Lowther Street Craft Centre a sixth. Though staff could still meet together in a re-located, spacious Senior Common Room, there was inevitably more fragmentation with 92 academic staff. The college now had close to 1,000 students so this allocation was

> within the staff/student ratio of 1/11 which has been long established

but was to be a casualty of the 1980s.

School Practice arrangements too had necessarily become more complex for a larger student body and a wider range of trainings. Watkin noted that only a third of the students could now be located in schools close to or in the City; a third were away in lodgings up to 60 miles from college, and the remaining third were transported daily in hired buses all over Yorkshire. Summarising the building projects being considered he added with pride that

> The old college was last year scheduled as a building of historic importance – not to be altered without much argument.

In the 1969 *White Rose* Lamb announced that the swimming pool would open in the autumn term; it was just in time. Subsequent generations at York have been grateful that this fine amenity, with adjacent squash courts, was completed before the axe came down on further major building projects, in the colleges. Following the new Instrument of Government the college responded to Lamb's concern about deteriorating co-operation by setting up a Staff/Student Council, with equal numbers of staff and students, chaired alternatively by the Union President and the Principal. There was satisfaction at the balanced recommendations it had made so far, for example, about student dress and involvement in departmental decisions. St John's seems to have weathered a stormy period of national student agitation with little damage and a fair degree of tolerance, and Lamb wrote in the 1969 *White Rose*

> Open discussion of this kind offers an antidote to the prevailing malaise of young people today, which seems to me to relate closely to the insecurity bred in them by the disappearance of a firm social framework . . . To attack the few restraints that remain provides an excuse for reintegration within the group, the small, aggressive group of agitators or the large mindless mob. All too often the younger generation's willingness to get up and shout grows out of an underlying fear of freedom. The only progress that matters is progress towards shared rationality.

This last phrase was to be echoed in unexpected, and perhaps unmerited attacks which were directed against the colleges at the end of a decade which had seen so much enthusiasm and achievement in higher education but was ending in disillusion and unease. Some of the criticism came from the least expected quarter, the University Schools of Education which, since McNair, had seemed so supportive of the college's work and aspirations. William Taylor's *Society and the Education of Teachers* researched from 1966 to 1968 and published in 1969, presented data on students, staff, courses and values in the colleges. Taylor drew on experience as Director, successively of two University Schools with associated colleges, but also as Head of Education at one of the Anglican Colleges, Bede College, Durham. His thesis was explicit:

> I want to argue that the dominant value orientations of teacher education during the first six decades of the present century have been those of social and literary romanticism . . . a partial rejection of the pluralism of values connected with conditions of advanced industrialisation; a suspicion of the intellect and the intellectual; a lack of interest in political and structural change; a stress upon the intuitive and the intangible, upon spontaneity and creativity; an attempt to find personal autonomy through the arts; a hunger for the satisfactions of inter-personal life within the community and small group, and *a flight from rationality*[29] [my italics].

This may have been intended as no more than a case for more realistic and rigorous preparation for teachers. It was widely interpreted however as a condemnation of the colleges of education which the government would shortly be seeking justification to dismantle. It still seems harsh 20 years on, as it did at the time, since what Taylor demanded for teacher education was what the best of the colleges had been working towards for at least a generation and – with a period of consolidation now promised – might have been close to achieving.

We have noted the perennial pleas for more time and depth for the college course. Professor Geoffrey Bantock made no concession to those when, from the security of the four-year university training pattern, he taxed the colleges with excessive emphasis on the intuitive and the sympathetic:

> The purpose of schooling is to induct young people into some important areas of understanding, certain refined modes of feeling and a few complex skills . . . Similarly the trainer of teachers is concerned with helping his students to cope with these essentially limited demands of the schools . . . it is as well to call a stop to this obsession with the spontaneous where the higher rational activities are concerned. My revolutionary suggestion is that students should be sent out not only full of friendly feelings towards their charges but actually *knowing* something. Even Facts. A profession defines itself in part in relation to the body of expertise which characterises its activities.[30]

Like most effective caricature, this was witty, unfair and dangerously timed. Taylor and Bantock were appealing – as experts and amateurs have in many generations – for the kind of assurance in the educational process which is not to be had. To counter such destructive criticism the colleges of education needed bold and articulate support to establish a position – which had seemed within reach – of acknowledged indispensability to the national education service.

By September 1967 Ripon numbers had risen to 576, including 25 men and the first six students proceeding to a fourth year for the BEd degree. Accommodation was cramped and plans were approved for a separate purpose-built Students' Union building to be ready by 1969. The new chapel continued to host a range of activities and in October 1967 BBC Television broadcast a Sunday morning service from the college. Former students still gave generously to the college, especially in response to an appeal for a memorial to former Vice-Principal Miss Buysman, in the form of furnishings for a separate School Practice Library. Another past colleague was commemorated when the college purchased a nurses hostel in South Crescent, Ripon, which was renovated as a student residence and re-named Eva Lett House. The Students' Union building was completed on time, provided with a Club license, and named for Dean Wilkinson a former Vice-Chairman of the Governors. Numbers held steady in 1968 and 1969 at just below 600 with the men's total guardedly increased to 40. There were only two BEd candidates in 1968 though, as at York, plans were maturing for a degree course for serving teachers. Like St John's the college had reviewed its structures for students/staff co-operation and the governors applied for variations in the 1967 Instrument, to enable student representation on the Governing Body and Academic Board.

In 1969 a Parliamentary Select Committee was established to enquire into Teacher Education. St John's York was selected as one of the colleges to be visited, and was invited to submit a detailed memorandum in preparation for the discussions. This provided a summary of achievement, aspirations and attitudes in January 1970.[31] It recorded that the college, having accepted a notional student allocation of 950, was still negotiating with DES for increased accommodation; that of just over £1,000,000 spent on capital development at the college since 1945 the Church Board of Finance and the college itself had together contributed £296,000; that the recurrent budget for the previous year had been £554,000; that St John's was now a designated 'Wing' college for Science as well as for Physical Education, with an 'especially generous' equipment grant for these departments; and that it was also an experimental centre for Closed Circuit Television in teacher education. The memorandum admitted a tendency for the new BEd courses to demand a disproportionate share of staff resources in the colleges for 'their best students, the ones who increase their prestige'. The statement on 'Academic Standards' was frank and cautionary:

> The College of Education still finds it hard to shake off some traces of its lowly origin. Students are rarely brilliant; many of them had no great success at school and are not academically ambitious; each generation hands on to its successor an expectation of mediocrity which, in a way is hard to define, acts as a brake on improvement. In recent years our tendency has been to replace lectures by guided reading and pieces of individual study, and examination by continuous assessment. But a system of study such as ours has its own organic life, like a tree. It cannot be scrapped and changed overnight like a piece of machinery . . .

> We should like the Select Committee to take away the impression of this college as a place of higher education able now to hold its own without further violent alteration for a few years while it consolidates its many recent improvements. We have improved facilities, a better notion of our job and a more adult

and self-reliant set of students, and we live in a more open and exhilarating atmosphere than once we did.

The paragraph in the memorandum on 'The Place of religion' made modest enough claims, but provoked one of the most vigorous discussions during the committee's visit:

> The College would wish to be judged as a professional rather than an ecclesiastical institution but the existence in its midst of a ceremonious building and the maintenance within this of even a thinly supported daily practice of ceremonious behaviour under the sign of the crucifix, seems not without its significance as an integral part of the life of a community concerned with forming better human beings and a better society.

The conversations between representatives of the committee and a group of college staff and students ranged over the effects of expansion, optimum size, university relationships, inter-collegiate co-operation, attitudes to 'pastoral care', future scope in the liberal arts and in other professional trainings, the distinctive nature of concurrent teacher education courses, representative structures and opportunities, special problems of training science teachers, and the balance of student intakes. But the central issue, to which the discussion kept returning, seems to have been whether being a Church College made any difference. Lamb was confident that it did; student opinion was divided and there was some resentment of the notion that a college necessarily owed its caring ethos or sense of service to Christian influence. Asked by the chairman, F. Willey, MP, 'What do you think it is that distinguishes you from the other colleges of Education?' Vice-Principal Chapman replied

> Very largely Tradition and I think very largely a link up between the pattern of belief and you might call it the ideology of the student who approaches the college, when he comes here knowing it is a religious foundation in the very modern sense of the word 'religious'. Teaching in itself is a religious activity and is an act of giving. Although in these days we are seeing a loosening, a weakening, and a less rigid atmosphere . . . this is a place where the informing spirit of our activities has that bond of religion as the basis of our understanding of our purpose; we have a kind of framework within which we try to solve our problems.

One student view was that many more students now applied to St John's because they 'regard it as a good college academically' and Lamb agreed that most students confronted with the question 'Are you a Christian' would either say 'No' or indicate that they are, as they ought to be, bewildered by the question.

He told the committee that he did not think chapel-going or doctrinal allegiance were vital, but that the college tried to offer a distinctive experience to students

At any rate, whatever else they will get, they will feel that they are in an ongoing attempt to deal with the mysteries of our human existence and to make some sense of human beings in society.

One of the most forceful statements of what the college was – and was not – trying to do, came from James Fairbairn, Director of the three-year course, a former Johnsman and experienced primary school head teacher:

Surely it is no part of our business to make them Christians in any specific sense. We are a vocationally orientated place and this is bound to rub off . . . I am quite sure that many come to this college because they did not get into university; very many come to us without any vocation, and some leave without it. But the thing that impresses me, as someone who came in eight years ago from school, is how many of them catch it; this is a very impressive thing. One gets a very fair impression of the young people in St John's today, not only of their concern but their sense of belief about something, although one does not like to define this in a mere creed.

Students and staff emerge with credit from this 'Examination of Witnesses' which revealed that even if the college was not always certain of its aims and methods it was continually thinking and arguing about them. The mint condition of the single copy of this parliamentary evidence in the college archive suggests that it was not much referred to afterwards; the full report was published in book form in 1971,[32] but by then incontrovertible evidence of a quite different kind was being weighed by government.

Lamb was to retire in August 1971 and might reasonably have looked forward to a serene last year. But in June 1970 he represented the college at a conference of all college Principals convened, in York, by the DES. A full report of the conference was circulated nationally at the beginning of the new academic year.[33] The opening address had been given by Under-Secretary H. A. Harding, a recent recruit to DES from the Treasury. He sounded a number of warning notes: the national birth-rate had dropped startlingly over the past few years, and since a decline took only five years to affect school populations, no further expansion of teacher education could now be presumed, in spite of the giant forecasts of the Robbins

194

Committee and the now defunct National Advisory Council. The long-awaited expansion of in-service training would now be difficult to finance and colleges would have to transfer resources from initial to in-service training. Harding cautioned that the recent ATCDE policy statement *Higher Education and Preparation for Teaching: A Policy for Colleges of Education* was unlikely to find favour with government. It argued for a proportionate share for the colleges in the expansion of higher education and proposed that they should be grouped in federated units related to universities and should offer degree courses in the Arts, Sciences and Social Sciences, as well as in Teacher Education.

Occupied throughout the 1960s with their own expansion the colleges had not taken much notice of the rapid rise of the polytechnics since Crosland's Woolwich manifesto. Harding now posed some unwelcome questions:

> If monotechnics are bad are polytechnics good? . . . Would development of liberal arts colleges weaken professional education and the standing of education departments? Is there a case for some colleges withdrawing from teacher education entirely and others specialising in professional work alone?

In summing up the York conference, Stanley Hewett, General Secretary of the ATCDE, implied that the Association would continue to press its policy statement, and appeared to shrug off the thinly veiled DES warning that the colleges stood on the verge of serious recession:

> As the conference progressed the feeling grew in strength that the status quo could not be preserved; the colleges must expand and develop . . . It was not only the students in training but also the institutions which trained them, which felt trapped, and this might well help to explain the insecurity and apprehension which the colleges and their staffs felt. It seemed to the Principals . . . that the expansion of higher education of the next decade provided the best and probably the last opportunity to remove the restrictions of development which had inhibited the colleges throughout their history.[34]

The confidence of the college principals was dented, not only by the revelations at York but by the flow of adverse criticism submitted to the Select Committee, to a DES enquiry into the Area Training Organisations, and to the national press. Lukes's subsequent research study confirmed that the colleges had cause for alarm:

> Opinion went through two stages and the first, in the evidence to the 1970 Select Committee, was negative; relentlessly critical of the colleges, which suffered in the limelight. Indeed some university and poly discussions appeared to take place over their

dead bodies (eg poly takeover bids) both sides 'using' them in the binary controversies.[35]

The ATCDE now demanded the full enquiry into teacher education which had been spasmodically urged since 1966 when the DES suspended the National Advisory Council. Government responded promptly. In December 1970 Secretary of State Margaret Thatcher announced the appointment of a committee of seven, to be chaired by Lord James, Vice-Chancellor of the University of York. It was asked to consider the evidence of the Select Committee and the ATO Enquiry; to review present arrangements for the education, training and probation of teachers and to make recommendations, within 12 months, on a range of issues. These included the content and structure of teacher education programmes, the roles of colleges, polytechnics and universities in teacher education, and whether a larger proportion of intending students should be educated alongside entrants to other professions.

There was immediate criticism of the choice of chairman, the smallness of the committee, the limited time-scale, the restricted brief, and the appointment of the committee by the Ministry to which it was to report. Many had hoped for a Royal Commission which would have taken at least two years. In fact the James Committee began its work in January 1971, received a spate of evidence and began drafting its report in April.

Three months earlier, in October 1970, Lamb had written to Lord James suggesting that the discussion between university and college begun in 1967 should be re-opened and a small working party set up

> to explore the possibility of the college becoming an affiliated college of the university, transferring its allegiance from Leeds to York.

His timing was astute; the Vice-Chancellor's reply was encouraging but non-committal.

In his valedictory letter to *The White Rose*, Lamb wrote that the year had been an odd one

> a kind of hiatus between . . . the post-McNair and the post-James regimes.

a succinct summary – to those who recalled the impact of McNair – of how far the college had developed under his leadership. The York and Ripon colleges have between them had six Principals who served the college more than 20 years; none with more energy, care and vision than Philip Lamb.

CHAPTER IX

Through Demolition to Reunion 1971-1980

THE NEW PRINCIPAL AT ST JOHN'S was John V. Barnett, who had been
Principal of Culham College, Abingdon, for 10 years. A scholar of
Pembroke College, Oxford, in 1939, he began his degree in classics, but
after five years of military service, completed it in English. After teaching
at the Royal Grammar School, Lancaster, and at Emanuel School in
London, he was headmaster of Cirencester Grammar School for seven
years before joining Culham. Marjorie Gage had been appointed to
Ripon in the same year so they had already been colleagues for 10 years
on the Council of Church College Principals. Both colleges seemed well
placed in the national teacher education system as they awaited the James
Report. St John's, with 950 students and several specialist courses, was
one of the largest colleges in England, and among the Church Colleges
was second in size to St Luke's, Exeter. Ripon had 580 students including
95 men and Miss Gage wrote optimistically in the Association magazine:

> Applications for next session are already up on this time last year
> so this is encouraging. Our status as a mixed college is now taken
> for granted though many of us find it hard to come to terms with
> the indisputable fact that men students are neither as quiet nor as
> tidy as some women students!. . . This period of waiting for the
> official report is not an easy time for colleges of education,
> particularly as the inspired leaks do not lead one to suppose that
> the future will be necessarily straightford . . . we are just going
> ahead, convinced of our role in teacher training but prepared for
> experiment and change.

Examination results at Ripon were among the best of the Leeds
Institute colleges but there was a notable difference in applications for the
fourth year. At St John's numbers were already almost 100; at Ripon
there were only 10 BEd graduates in 1971 and Miss Gage commented

> Ten is the largest number of successes we have had at Ripon in
> any one year so far. This present year we have only five

candidates. It seems that women students are less interested than their men colleagues in obtaining a degree qualification. Perhaps in 1972-3 the first year in which a 'mixed year' will become a fourth year, the numbers will rise dramatically.

In fact they rose very slowly – nine in 1972 and 16 in 1973 – in spite of a high level of success maintained in the three-year certificate.

As the Local Education Authorities continued to promote the ambitions of their polytechnics and colleges and, in most cases, to resource them generously, the Voluntary Colleges recognised the need for a group identity. In March 1971 the Council of the Church of England College Principals invited the Principals and Officers of the Roman Catholic and other Voluntary Colleges to join them at their annual residential conference. Frank but friendly debate set a precedent; the annual conference has been ecumenical ever since. As the largest group, the 27 Anglican Colleges tried to give a lead and at their Standing Conference, in May, their secretary Canon James Robertson, himself a former college tutor and principal, acknowledged the criticisms levelled against Church Colleges. Secular opinion pronounced them irrelevant in the 20th century, assuming that they could not be open to the full range of truth perceived by a modern enlightened society. Some church voices objected that in curriculum, secular pre-occupations and ethos they were hardly distinguishable from local authority colleges and that it would therefore be honest as well as thrifty for the Church finally to surrender responsibility for teacher education entirely to the State:

> In the face of this pincer movement the colleges are bound to agonise . . . We rightly draw attention to the caring and concerned communities which the colleges truly are. We speak properly of worship; of the ministry of chaplains, staff and students; of participation; of social concerns like immigrant communities, service to developing countries and educational priority areas; of innovatory work in special education; and of meeting the need to raise up young people with a faith to live by. All this is highly important and to be proclaimed, but perhaps *what we need to recapture is something of our instrumental character for contemporary society, expressed in fresher terms*[1] [my italics].

He believed that this 'instrumental character' was expressed in two purposes: to build up human society, for which the church had always had a care, and to build up the church itself.

Principals and governors left the conference aware that, as the colleges confronted recession, 'autonomy' might become a painful experience. There would be support but no prescription from the

13. *Revd James Welch. He was Principal for only four years, 1935-1939, but had a remarkable influence on the College.*

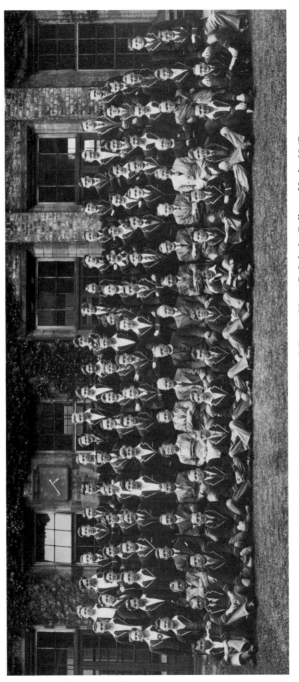

14.   *Principal Lamb with the Staff and Senior Year, St John's College, York, 1947.*

15 & 16. *Contrasts – (above) a small scale Rag, York 1949 and (below) large scale
gymnastics, Ripon Sports Day 1949.*

17. *Sir Charles Morris opens the new Library (now Students Union) at St John's, 1953.*

18. *Ripon College, opening of the new buildings, May 1954. (Left to right) the Mayor of Ripon, Archbishop Garbutt, the Minister of Education Miss Florence Horsbrugh, the Bishop of Ripon and the Principal Miss Valentine Hall.*

19 & 20. *(Above) Cricket at Hull Road, 1956. The rustic scene has changed –
since the early 1960's the skyline has been occupied by the University of York.
(Below) St John's first XV, 1957. The Captain is John Maw, later Senior Resident
Tutor and President, Past Students' Association. He still holds the Club record of
seven tries scored in a single match.*

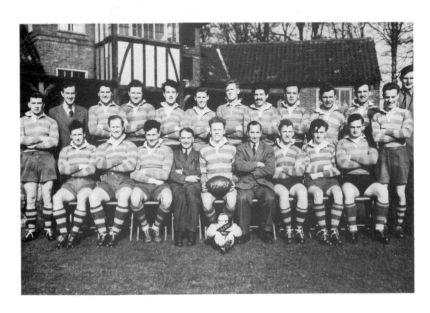

21 & 22. *College Drama – (above) Anouilh* The Lark, *1957, directed by Helen Lamb and (below)* Love in a Village, *an open air production in Gray's Court garden, York Festival 1984, directed by Harold Robinson.*

23. *Lost in wondering admiration. Two youngsters from an educational priority area relax in the main quadrangle, St John's 1971.*

24. *Peter Squires goes for the line. England against France at Twickenham, 1975.*

25. *The Chapel at Lord Mayor's Walk, 1966. Designed by George Pace. Catherine Nutkins' stained glass window (front cover) is the Central Window of the South Transept, left of picture.*

26. *Marjorie Gage, Principal, Ripon College, 1961-1975.*

27. *Celebrating Occupational Therapy: The opening of the Phoenix Block, 1984, (left to right) Paula Juffs (Head of Department), Archbishop John Habgood (Chairman of Governors), John Barnett (former Principal) and Gordon McGregor.*

28. *Christmas Carols in King's Square, York, 1986, for children's charities. This has become an annual event for the combined 'choirs' of the Chapel and the Rugby Club and has raised several hundred pounds each year.*

29 & 30. *(Above) College first XI Soccer, 1986. Most of this side played together for four years, 1982-86, winning five trophies including the British Colleges competition. They are seen here at York City ground with the York & District Senior League Cup. The Captain is Graham Smith, coach Peter Mulligan in back row, right. (Below) Cup winning women's first IV training on the Ouse at York below the College Boathouse, 1990.*

31. *First York Minster Degree Ceremony, 1989.*

32.   The Ripon Campus from the air. Many visitors are suprised at the scale of this 52 acre campus. The Chapel and Assembly Hall are in the centre with the original 1862 building and 1899 Chapel top right. Highfield House is top left.

Council. Each college must work out for itself, according to its location and strengths, its own answers to the perennial questions which Robertson had pondered: What were the distinctive qualities of a Church College? Could they be preserved and developed in the reorganisation of higher education that seemed imminent?

The James Report *Teacher Education and Training* was published in January 1972. Its main proposals were for three 'Cycles' of education and training for teachers: Personal education, Pre-service training and induction, and In-service training which the committee insisted must be greatly expanded as 'a matter of the highest priority'. Colleges and polytechnics should offer three-year degree courses and a new two-year Diploma in Higher Education. It recommended that Teacher Education should be administered through a National Council empowered to award degrees in education and with supporting Regional Councils. As had been suspected while the committee was at work, it was divided about the role of the universities. In the report, five members recommended that the Area Training Organisations based on the University Schools of Education should be abolished and most of their functions assumed by the proposed Regional Councils; two members argued strongly, in a 'Note of Extension' which was effectively a minority report, for the retention of strong working relationships between colleges and universities.

There were startling omissions from a report which had aroused more speculation in the press and the profession than anything since Robbins. There was no statistical justification for the proposals and hardly any argument. There were no forecasts of numbers of students in training, no estimates of numbers or types of institutions to remain involved in teacher education and no reference to finance – even for the proposed massive expansion of in-service education. It was probably the supportive 'Third Cycle' proposals which somewhat muted initial criticisms of the report. But as estimates of the enormous costs emerged in the weeks following publication, scepticism turned to incredulity, and opposition to the entire report hardened. Some college Principals – including the writer – regarded it as a perfunctory and slipshod exercise on behalf of a Ministry which had already made up its mind. But the colleges needed to respond swiftly before government acted.

The ATCDE Principals Panel and the Church Colleges Council were united in opposing the main recommendations. They stood firm for the retention of university links urged in the Note of Extension, rejected the proposal for a new BA(Ed) degree and warned that the Dip HE would not be widely accepted unless it was offered by universities and polytechnics as well as the colleges. In May 1972 the Church of England Board of Education published its response to the James Report. It pressed for the Church Colleges to be recognised as a distinctive group of higher education institutions.

> Our contention is . . . that it would be a diminution of the existing diversity of options open to young people in higher education and advanced further education if it were decided for the sake of administrative neatness to press for the absorption of the colleges into either the present university or polytechnic mould.[2]

It also stressed that the colleges were keen to widen their present commitments

> to include work in general higher education which would derive its ethos and structure from the conviction that this advance is for the health of teacher education as a whole. A wider student community context is essential for teacher training, and the contemporary places problem simply provides the opportunity for a development which is inherently sound in itself.

Recruitment remained buoyant at York and Ripon so, as at most of the colleges, the summer term and vacation passed in a mood of quiet optimism. It soon became apparent however that the period of 'consultation' on the James Report was to be brief; a government White Paper was promised before the end of the year. In spite of DES disclaimers, there was strong suspicion that major policy decisions on the colleges had been determined before the James Report and that there had been little genuine research or planning. Four years later there was authoritative evidence.

The White Paper, *Education: A Framework for Expansion* was published in December 1972. It was relatively short, succinct, and only occasionally ambiguous. The sections on *The Colleges of Education* and *The Organisation of Higher Education*, were bad news for the colleges. The government proposed by 1981 to employ 510,000 teachers in maintained schools. This implied a reduction in teacher education places from the Robbins prediction of 145,000 to a figure between 60,000 and 70,000. The 1972 total was already 114,000; expansion was over. There were reassuring passages about developing in-service education and a section on nursery education which appears even more incongruous 19 years later because almost nothing has been done about it. But the death knells were unmistakable:

> Some colleges must face the possibility that in due course they will have to be converted to new purposes; some may need to close . . . The last few paragraphs can leave no doubt that if, as most of them earnestly wish, the colleges of education are to find a fuller and firmer place in the higher education family, their

staffs must face major changes. The government will be initiating consultations about the fairest ways of protecting the legitimate interests of teaching staff who might be adversely affected.[3]

With mounting animosity between some universities, polytechnics, local authorities and colleges, the notion of a 'higher education family' raised wry smiles in many a staff common room and principal's study – and perhaps still does.

The White Paper made much of the opportunities for colleges to be involved in the promised expansion of higher education, particularly in the arts and human sciences, for which, it was conceded

> the quality and experience of their staff and the strength of their physical resources admirably equip a number of the colleges.

But the DES incantation 'economies of scale' recurred and the Department's determination to allow 'diversification' only in large institutions was barely concealed by the bland phraseology. The preferred model was obvious.

> The logic of the conclusions recorded in this White Paper is that, leaving aside those colleges which find their eventual home in a university, the substantial broadening of function proposed for the great majority of the colleges of education will involve their much closer assimilation into the rest of the non-university sector of higher and further education. Put another way, a college which expands and diversifies, either alone or by joining forces with a sister college or a further education institution – enlarging the range of its courses and extending its clientele will not be easily distinguishable by function from a polytechnic or other further education college.[4]

Government's rhetorical question at York, 'If monotechnics are bad are polytechnics good?' had been answered – by government – with a resounding affirmative. Among staff in the colleges the White Paper was soon dubbed 'A Frame-Up for Contraction'; and so it proved.

Meanwhile, at York negotiations had been resumed between the university and St John's. Following the publication of his committee's report Lord James had written to Barnett, referring back to his exchange of letters with Lamb late in 1970. Final proposals for local government reorganisation had confirmed that from 1974, the University, St John's College, Ripon College and the North Riding College at Scarborough would all be within the same new county of North Yorkshire. Barnett then circulated to all four institutions a discussion paper, *A Proposal for an Association of Institutions concerned with teacher education in North Yorkshire*. It envisaged a range of courses, different from those presently offered by the university, and designed and validated jointly by the university and the colleges. Teacher education courses and a degree in combined studies would be integrated in a modular structure. The proposal was under discussion in the four institutions when first the White Paper and then Circular 7/73 clarified some issues and obscured others.

With commendable speed, the Church Board, in consultation with the colleges, had published in February 1973 its *First Commentary on Education A Framework for Expansion*, demonstrating that the Church was alert to the damaging impact that local authority planning and financial procedures might now have on its colleges. It assumed for the Church Colleges financial arrangements

> not less conducive than the present direct grant from the DES to enabling our voluntary character and supra-local tradition to continue and evolve.[5]

In March the DES published Circular 7/73 *Development of Higher Education in the Non-University Sector*. This put the Voluntary Colleges at an immediate disadvantage by calling for plans for development of higher education to be submitted through Local Authorities. Direct grant for the Church Colleges had not secured direct negotiation.

It now seemed to many of the protagonists, that a power struggle was in progress in which educational considerations would be vulnerable to administrative convenience. To some DES 'policy' already appeared ill-conceived and furtive. In April college Principals were invited to a conference at Oxford sponsored jointly by the DES and the ATCDE to discuss the implications of the White Paper and Circular 7/73. Few colleges appeared strongly placed to sustain a 'free-standing' future. Even St Luke's and St John's among the Church Colleges would, when the proposed teacher education reductions had taken effect, be well below the minimum size of 1,000 students proposed for an institution of higher education. All small colleges and many large urban ones were at risk ; the Oxford conference offered probably the last chance to challenge the assumptions on which the DES proposals seemed to be based.

Secretary of State Margaret Thatcher opened the proceedings with a brisk but conciliatory summary of the White Paper which, she claimed, met six of the seven main propositions in the ATCDE policy statement. A small group of Principals then pressed DES officers for clarification of two main issues: what was the statistical base for the reduced teacher supply target and what was the evidence for 'economies of scale' on which the government based its preference for large institutions? After some sharp exchanges, DES Permanent Secretary, Sir William Pile intervened to concede that the statistical base was complex, unpublished, and not the sole explanation of the target figures. These resulted from a 'policy decision' made partly because the government had to cut back on teaching to buy other things.[6]

He agreed that institutional size was a vexed and unresolved issue but assured the conference that the main intention of the White Paper was not to dismantle the colleges of education nor did the department have pre-conceived solutions for particular situations. It was difficult for delegates at the time – and still is – not to conclude that, like the Secretary of State in 1965, the Permanent Secretary was seriously misinformed about the designs of his senior officers.

In a concluding address to the conference, ATCDE secretary Stanley Hewett mingled optimism with admonition:

> We have got basically what we wanted, though in ways and on terms we did not altogether expect . . . These tasks will make demands on our intelligence, objectivity, integrity, stamina. I cannot pretend that nobody will get hurt in the process. As a group, principals stand to lose most in the way of position and status when institutions are reorganised . . . I can only stress that the way in which the principals face their problems and the problems of their colleges will determine very largely how the staff will face theirs . . . but I do believe that the colleges collectively are on the right path at last . . . There are rich rewards for those with the courage, resolution and foresight to go out and take them.[7]

The *Times Higher Education Supplement* saw things differently in a front page article headlined 'Colleges Concerned to Save Their Skins' and a leading article on 'The Dissolution of the Colleges'. In the following edition the present writer, then Principal of Bishop Otter College, replied for the colleges, pressing their claim to be regarded as leaders in the nation's teacher education

> It is not their skins they are concerned about. It is first, preserving and improving the quality of teacher education . . . and secondly, ensuring that, as far as possible, decisions about higher education are taken for educational reasons and not for economic ones, powerful though these may be.
>
> In this respect the conference was a step forward. We were told clearly, as perhaps the James Committee should have told us, that the cutback in teacher production was a policy choice. The government had decided that it must buy other things instead. Any sector of the education service is likely to respond constructively to the news that the money has run out, especially if it is also offered a voice in discussions about how limited funds

should be redeployed. What any sector is likely to suspect is economic stricture masquerading as educational desirability.[8]

He had been exasperated by the complaisance of the Principals at Oxford and had corresponded with Hewett who regretted the absence of any 'head of steam' from the colleges. Invited by the *Times Higher Education Supplement* to develop his theme in a lead article he urged colleges and local authorities to insist that the dialogue begun at Oxford must continue and the best that the colleges offered to students be retained in diversified contexts:

> a careful curricular blend of the cognitive and the affective; a community which, balancing freedom with responsibility, fosters personal relationships and values: close working relationships with school teachers and children. Such a professional education has taken time to build and takes time to imbibe.[9]

The articles drew much private support but no public follow-up in the educational press. Principals of local authority colleges were particularly exposed; they could not publicly criticise DES policy without appearing to censure their own authorities, most of whom were co-operating readily. Voluntary College Principals were not compromised in this way and had long claimed 'autonomy'. Yet more than a year elapsed before another of them hazarded a national protest, and then only when the closure of his college was inevitable. Joyce Skinner assessed the situation shrewdly

> I feel that there is a slight groundswell in our favour, but it could be too late. The stereotype is too well established.

Barnett returned from the Oxford conference and, after consultation with Miss Gage, arranged for the proposal for a North Yorkshire Association to be further considered at the University of York. He summarised the colleges' position in an article for the May edition of the *Spread Eagle*. He believed the arguments for and against the government's plans had already been widely aired and saw little point in pursuing them further. The teacher education cutback seemed certain to be about 40% which would leave St John's with only 600 places. The college would need to devise courses which could allow students to defer their firm commitment to teaching, preferably for the first two years; yet the courses must also be rigorously professional in content and approach. The three year qualification seemed likely to become a pass degree, so within five years the college should be producing an all-graduate entry to the teaching profession.

> The government requires virtually every college to show how it can merge with a university or a polytechnic or with other colleges so that the new institution includes some 1000 to 2000

students and can offer a wide range of courses leading to careers including education but not exclusively so. St John's has discussed the possibility of merging with York University, but both institutions agree that this is not in the best interests of either. There is no York Polytechnic and so we are discussing with our sister college at Ripon whether we should not together try to meet the new requirements. We are optimistic that this can be done without losing the identity of each college but with greatly increased opportunities for both colleges.

Government had decided to abolish the university-based Area Training Organisations, so colleges would now be free to negotiate with any existing award-giving body the validation of their degree and diploma courses. For Ripon and York this could entail fresh negotiations with Leeds University or an approach to York University, the Open University, the Council for National Academic Awards or indeed any other university. The college was exploring the options:

> For a number of years, since the establishment in York of a University, St John's has been considering whether a relationship of this kind with our close neighbour would not be a wise change. The fact that Local Government Reorganisation puts ourselves, Ripon, North Riding College Scarborough and the University all in the same North Yorkshire Authority's planning area suggests even stronger arguments for such a change. Discussions are now well advanced . . .

In a study of policy it is worth recording – though nothing came of it – that the confrontation at Oxford made some impression on the thinking at DES. In May 1973 Sir William Pile delivered to the Gulbenkian Conference on *Higher Education in the 1980s* a 'discursive address on the White Paper, with a gloss on some of its ambiguities'. He confessed that there were uncertainties:

> There are several aspects of higher education on which not nearly sufficient thinking has been done. First, the size of institutions. I believe this is one of the pathologies of the present system; size, with all its attendant difficulties. Nothing like sufficient thought has been given to the problem of optimum size of institutions and range of sizes. This is a good subject for some academic to spend some time on, because it has to be solved.[10]

The proceedings of the conference were not published until the end of the year. In its annual report Bishop Otter College promptly offered to take up the challenge of a research project on institutional size. There was no response, as there had been none to the ATCDEs final statement, *A Policy for the Development of Higher Education in the Non-University*

Sector. This called for clear differentiation between institutions of higher and further education, definition of maximum and minimum sizes for all such institutions, a radical review of student numbers in the 'non-polytechnic institutions of the non-university sector', and parity of resourcing for university and non-university institutions. The DES could afford to ignore the document, so sharp had been the decline in the Association's influence after its misguided reactions at Oxford. Even the terminology of the statement was destructive; the colleges urgently needed a more positive style than the self-denigrating 'non-polytechnic institutions of the non-university sector' if they were to assert a distinctive identity and function.

No participant in these negotiations can be trusted to offer an objective account and this chapter may already seem unduly caustic. But Lord Briggs, eminent historian and former Vice-Chancellor of the University of Sussex, subsequently offered a dispassionate view of the 'negotiating' style of the DES:

> Public debate about the 'binary system' has been confused for three reasons. First, it was never made clear whether the system was considered to be an 'ideal' or an acceptance, largely for economic reasons, of historical fact, involving the 'systematisation' of what had hitherto been unsystematic dualism or polycentrism in higher education. Second, the bare economies of the systematisation were never clearly set out – relative costs for example, in universities and polytechnics. Third, the implementation of policy was determined largely by civil servants in discussion with local authorities, and much that was happening was hidden from public view. Although a higher education planning group was set up within the Department of Education to consider the relation between the different parts of the system, its work has been confidential and its statistics have never been published.[11]

Nevertheless the civil servants had the power to propose decisions to the Secretary of State; the colleges needed to work with them, and fast.

At the end of April 1973 representatives of the University of York General Academic Board expressed reservations about the proposed association. These centred round the 'mis-match' of subjects, which would require the university to provide assessment in a number of academic and professional areas in which it had little competence and which would create a heavy extra work-load. Barnett argued that this was a strength; unless the new courses were complimentary to those already offered in the university and could be described in significantly different terms

206

it would be hard to justify them and they could only be second class alternatives to what already exists.

The colleges were confident that, as experience and mutual trust grew, the work commitment for the university would decrease. Moreover, it would have seized an opportunity to widen its own offering to undergraduates, particularly in experimental combinations of other academic disciplines with the study of education. The General Academic Board agreed by a narrow majority to refer the proposals to the university boards of study. A final decision would be taken at the June board meeting.

While they waited Barnett and Miss Gage had further discussion on close association between the two colleges. The North Riding College obtained clarification from them about possibilities within the 'North Yorkshire Association', which enabled it to proceed with its own negotiations with the local authority. The existing authority was keen – as the new North Yorkshire was likely to be – to retain its only college of higher education. But the implication of circular 7/73, which allocated student numbers by regions, was that if North Riding College was to receive viable allocations it would be at the expense of Ripon or St John's. Such tensions did not make negotiations easier.

In June the university board decided by a majority of two votes not to proceed with the association. Lord James, whose own position in the debate had been compromised by his Committee's majority support for the severance of university/college relationships, wrote to Barnett explaining that, in the end, the university had felt unable to

assume a tutelary role over another institution of higher education which was embarking on a process of great innovation.

The turn of phrase is significant in the light of the college's subsequent negotiations in the late 1980s for greater freedom and innovation. The decision was a severe disappointment to the colleges and could have been destructive. There was much regret too at the university, where 18 years later, many staff still regard the rejection as the loss of a fine opportunity.

Circular 7/73 called for interim statements of regional plans by November; the colleges had only five months in which to secure a relationship strong enough to support diversification and to attract validation from either a university or the CNAA. Merger proposals were being discussed all over the country and a number of Church Colleges were already involved. Barnett wrote in May on behalf of both colleges, to Archbishop Coggan, Chairman of St John's governors, proposing the speedy establishment of a negotiating committee drawn from the two colleges. The Archbishop approved and a first meeting was held a week after the York University decision. Membership comprised, from each college, two governors, Principal, Vice-Principal, four members of staff and the Students' Union President; Malcolm Jennings (York) and Denham Illingworth (Ripon) were influential staff members. The Principals had circulated the following joint statement:

Declaration of Intent to Amalgamate

We are of the firm opinion that it is paramountly in the best interests of the two colleges, taking into account the following factors:

a) the tenor of the White Paper and Circular 7/73

b) the severe cutback in numbers of teachers to be trained for teaching through three and four year courses outlined in those papers

c) the views expressed by Mr Harding to the Church Colleges at the Standing Conference in May 1973

d) the extremely favourable geographical location of the two colleges in relation to the new North Yorkshire Authority

e) the complementary nature of the two colleges

f) their shared historical origins and close association within the Leeds University Institute of Education

g) their joint potential to provide a wide range of teacher education courses side by side with courses leading to a Diploma in Higher Education and BA and BSc degrees

h) the ease of communication between the two colleges by road

i) their shared commitment to the involvement of the Church of England in service to the national system of education

that their governing bodies should enter into a declaration of intent to amalgamate the two colleges into a single institution at an agreed date.

The two Principals asked both governing bodies to approve the declaration not later than October, so that a submission could be made to DES by the November deadline. The preferred date for amalgamation would be September 1975, though they recognised that 1976 was more realistic. One advantage in the York/Ripon situation recalled Hewett's warning at Oxford; Miss Gage had made clear her intention to retire within two or three years so there was no risk of rivalry between Principals. The third clause of the declaration referred to DES insistence that the aim of any negotiation for merger should be to achieve a single trust deed, governing body, principal and academic board so that unified policy for the new institution was assured. DES did not favour federal

208

solutions, considering them cumbersome and expensive. In further sections of their draft declaration the Principals reassured colleagues and students that the intention was to retain within a unified institution the identity and independent social facilities of each college and to give staff and students the opportunity to choose attachment to Ripon or York.

The first meeting of the negotiating committee approved the draft declaration and recommended both governing bodies to accept it and approve detailed proposals in the autumn term. The governing bodies agreed, and informed both dioceses and the Church Board of Education of their intentions. In September members of the colleges' negotiating committee met with DES officers in London to seek advice and assurances on two questions: Were DES officers convinced that the proposed upheaval in the colleges of education was still necessary? If so, were the colleges' proposals in line with Department thinking in the White Paper and since? For the DES Harding responded emphatically to the first and equivocally to the second. Radical change remained essential for the colleges since White Paper forecasts for teacher supply had been over-optimistic. Much more diversification would now be required of surviving colleges. The York and Ripon proposals seemed promising, but Harding warned that it was 'crucially important' for the colleges to diversify into areas that would gain the support of the new North Yorkshire authority. If they could do this then the DES 'would on the whole view them favourably'.

So in spite of their alleged Voluntary 'autonomy' the colleges had no option but to consult with the local authority to find out how quickly 'approval' might be gained. Barnett wrote to the newly appointed Chief Education Officer for North Yorkshire Dr E. Owens in September and met with him in October. Barnett pressed the urgency of staff changes and approval for new courses. Miss Gage was to retire in August 1975 and if the new college was to be inaugurated in September 1975 DES approval must be obtained by August 1974. This would require a formal submission in March. Owens thought it unlikely that North Yorkshire would consider the issue before the end of the year. Members might feel that the Voluntary Colleges were trying to pre-empt reorganisation, and the new authority must be free to consider different patterns for higher and further education. In Yorkshire, as elsewhere, the result of the DES tactical coup with circular 7/73, was that a local authority could regard even highly reputed Voluntary Colleges in its area as expendable. The good luck for St John's and Ripon of finding themselves together in the same authority from 1974 was balanced by the disadvantage that it was a newly created county with a Chief Education Officer and Deputy both recruited from outside and unfamiliar with the colleges or their previous good relationships with the old West Riding and the County Borough of York.

Meanwhile the degree and diploma awards at both colleges continued to be validated by the University of Leeds, whose Senate was considering its response to the White Paper and circular 7/73. Three options were put forward: the absorption of some of the colleges of education into the university; complete severance of university/college relationships as proposed by the James Report; and further development of the present validation relationships. A working party of Senate soon recommended the third option, in line with the White Paper expectation of a three-year BEd degree:

> The government think it important that this new degree should be subject to validation by the existing awarding bodies . . . and they hope that universities will be receptive to any request that is put to them by a college of education.

Initially the university intended to continue to validate awards only in teacher education. Barnett argued that if this remained the policy the colleges would be forced to seek validation elsewhere. The DipHE and a BA degree in combined studies other than education were crucial to the colleges' diversification and survival. The university responded cautiously, requesting details of academic staff experience and qualifications, establishing a working party to examine libraries and learning resources and discussing how the titles of awards in the colleges might differentiate them from degrees taught at the university. With conservative attitudes prevailing in Senate, the personal diplomacy of Lord Boyle, the Vice-Chancellor became a key influence.

The colleges submitted in October 1973 an outline of a modular degree structure in which units available towards a number of degree programmes would be offered not by discrete college departments but by larger 'areas of study'. While discussions proceeded the college also approached the CNAA which expressed interest in considering proposals for validation. Aware of this, Lord Boyle asked the Leeds Senate to set up a Special Committee, of which Barnett and Miss Gage were members along with the six other Principals of Leeds Institute colleges and representatives of the university faculties. Lord Boyle's chairmanship was decisive. He had brought to university affairs the statesmanship, integrity and foresight he had shown at the Ministry and he now put to the committee the case for closer association between university and colleges. His support was based on more than respect for the traditions of the colleges and a wish to help them through difficulties not of their making. He was convinced that the relationship was important to Leeds because any university which did not foster good relationships across the 'binary line' would create difficulties for itself by the 1980s. University members of the committee were not easily convinced; some doubted the readiness and quality of the colleges and others saw the two year DipHE as a government strategem to divert students from three year university degree courses. They accepted the Vice-Chancellor's advice however and recommended that Senate should agree in principle to the extension of validation arrangements for the colleges. Senate approved the recommendation in December and the Registrar wrote to Barnett inviting the colleges to make specific proposals. Six months after the York rejection prospects for university validation were again bright.

At their October meetings, the two college governing bodies approved the plan for amalgamation and agreed to establish an interim governing body for the new college with an interim academic committee to advise it. A summary of the project was released to the press and the interim governing body gave thought to initial senior appointments. They could not confirm these until the North Yorkshire authority had accepted the project and the DES formally approved it. Yet planning had to proceed and the interim governing body appointed Barnett as 'Senior Co-ordinator', on secondment from St John's, to act as 'principal spokesman and representative of the new college on all negotiating bodies'. By December four academic co-ordinators had also been seconded from the colleges to plan the new institution's courses and structures.

Early in the new year the North Yorkshire authority considered the scheme and in March 1974 Dr Owens wrote to the permanent secretary at DES assuring him that the new Voluntary College was welcomed and that the authority looked forward to helping to develop the potential of the voluntary and maintained colleges in the county. DES officers had asserted such control over the national reorganisation of teacher education, that Harding was able to rule – after a frustrating meeting of college and DES representatives – that the LEA's response, though useful, was not strong enough to warrant the Secretary of State's approval. The North Yorkshire representatives regretted that a more specific response could not be provided until November, when new committees would have considered the plan.

It appears that the Church Board and its officers had under-estimated the potential threat of circular 7/73 and the determination with which the DES would enact it. In other negotiations Church Colleges were already exposed. At Derby, Bishop Lonsdale College was being drawn into a merger with a large LEA College of Technology; at Birmingham, St Peter's College, and at Bristol, St Matthias' seemed likely to find places in their LEA's plans only as merged branches of polytechnics. Small colleges such as St Gabriel's London and Hockerill Bishop's Stortford, were already assumed to be indefensible, and at Exeter discussions were proceeding towards the merger of St Luke's, the largest Church College, with the university. Amalgamations of many LEA colleges with polytechnics and further education colleges were well advanced.

In January 1974 the Church Board published a policy paper, GS 194, *The Future of the Church Colleges of Education*, presenting a summary of each county negotiation involving a Church College, and commenting on the emerging pattern. It emphasised the Church's readiness to co-operate in acceptable strategies based on the White Paper but observed, in the summary on Derbyshire,

> The theoretical willingness of the Church to embark upon this kind of exploration is not always balanced by that of the local authority.[12]

Bishop Otter College though reported on optimistically in paper GS 194, was already embroiled in difficult negotiations with West Sussex LEA. Its Principal had cautioned that the 'theoretical readiness of the Church' might prove excessive. If negotiations proceeded swiftly at Derby they could prejudice the position of other Church Colleges located reasonably near LEA colleges of any kind. DES officers would presume that what had been done at Derby could not be objected to elsewhere; with a few exceptions, the Church Colleges would 'find themselves picked off one by one for merger or closure'. The Board paper now asserted

> If a college in which the church has been encouraged to invest large capital sums can demonstrate that it has a continuing function in the locality in which it is placed, such a proposal could not reasonably be turned down solely because it called for some variation in one of the criteria to be found in the White Paper or Circular 7/73.

It did not address the possibility that 'such a proposal' might be *unreasonably* turned down. Many were.

On the balance between central guidance and local decision, the paper offered a hostage to fortune. It emphasised that the 27 Anglican Colleges formed

> a confederation of autonomous institutions linked by common purposes, common help, common advice and servicing. They are not branches of a centrally directed enterprise.[13]

It is arguable that if they had been more 'centrally directed' they might have been better able to withstand the assault on a teacher education system of which they were the founder members. As it was, DES officers now had an assurance that the Church's central councils were only advisory; government could divide and conquer. The colleges' position

212

was further undermined at this point by the departure of Canon Robertson from their Council to become Secretary of the United Society for the Propagation of the Gospel. His new responsibility was important to the wider Church, but his loss to the colleges could not have been worse timed. For seven years he had been a calm and adroit negotiator, with whom DES officers took no liberties.

None of the Church Colleges was in an easy negotiating position, but Ripon and York were two of the most favoured and they exploited their advantages with energy and skill. Barnett suggested that the North Yorkshire authority should apply for additional teacher education places to protect both the North Riding College and the new Church College, for which the interim governing body had chosen the title 'College of Ripon and York St John'. In June 1974 the DES allocations were announced for the 1975 entry – 105 places for North Riding and 410 for Ripon and York. The reduction was about 25% and would be more severe the following year. North Yorkshire was now convinced that the new college offered the best opportunity for the development of higher education in the country and in September the Education Committee notified DES of its full formal approval. On 22 November 1974, the Secretary of State approved the amalgamation.

The college had 10 months in which to complete the preparation of its new degree programme and begin to attract sufficient new students to make good the reductions in teacher education places over the next three years. Governors and staff were proud of what had been achieved, against the odds, but apprehensive about student recruitment and staff redundancy. Some Ripon staff feared that they might be not amalgamated with St John's but submerged by it. It was known that the DES preference was for mergers within the same city, and suspected that the Department had approved a few distant liaisons assuming that retrenchment would soon compel the new institutions to concentrate on a single major campus.

There was also much spirited optimism at Ripon, however, and the college exploited the White Paper's tentative acknowledgement of a need for more nursery teachers. Miss Gage announced DES approval for a one-term conversion course for nursery teachers at the college in 1974, and the building, on the campus, of a purpose-designed nursery school for 40 pupils. The school was to be owned by the college, but furnished and supported by recurrent funding from the county. Government had promised expansion of In-service education for teachers, and in planning the new college, Barnett and Miss Gage shrewdly offered the North Yorkshire Authority premises on the York and Ripon campuses for Teachers' Centres. The college also joined with the Church's National

Society to establish a Northern Resource and Curriculum Development Centre for Religious Education on the York Campus. All three centres quickly flourished and have greatly strengthened the college's working links with schools and teachers throughout the North East.

The sensitive task of merging two college staffs, with the inevitable redundancies, disappointments, premature retirements, and creation of new academic and administrative structures was achieved in the spring and summer of 1975. Barnett was appointed Principal, Miss Valentine Vice-Principal at York and Revd Herbert Batey, formerly Senior Tutor of Culham College, Vice-Principal at Ripon. The college Bursar was to be Ralph Wilkinson who had joined St John's as Bursar in 1972 after seven years at the University of York; the Academic Registrar was James Shields, shortly to be succeeded by Denham Illingworth. Notable retirements included the two Vice-Principals, Christopher Chapman who had served 27 years at York and Kathleen Teasdale, 28 years at Ripon.

The forecast allocations for teacher education places had again been reduced and the new college was to have only 800 places when the final cuts had taken effect. So the challenge was to recruit heavily to other degree courses if the original combined total of almost 1,600 students was eventually to be restored. Barnett wrote cheerfully to old Johnsmen in *The Spreadeagle* for June 1975

> How we shall fill the balance of 800 places remains to be seen but we are off to a flying start with approvals for the college to offer the new two year Diploma in Higher Education, and three years BA and BSc degrees in Combined Studies . . . it is possible some students may be embarking on them in September 1975 . . . A new prospectus for the College is being designed . . . Our reunification with Ripon adds to the complications but I am happy to report that all concerned have shown such concern and regard for each other that ways round all the problems have so far been found. We are in the heart of the task of dismissing all the staff and of reappointing them to the new college, of devising a new academic structure and of working out how we can minimise the problems of working on two campuses 25 miles apart. The general principle is that students stay put and staff commute . . .

In the same month Miss Gage wrote her farewell letter to the Ripon Association magazine. She reported strong recruitment and good examination results for the last year of the independent college. There had been 585 students, and numbers achieving the BEd degree after a fourth year had risen to 32. Government's reduced targets did not seem to her entirely misguided, since employment prospects had already worsened for teachers and 'a considerable number' of those who had just completed the certificate course at Ripon had not yet obtained posts. Miss Gage stressed one of the advantages of the new combined college:

> Students will be offered a very wide range of courses, of which teacher education will only be one. This is an important step as it will mean that it will no longer be necessary for a student to leave college if a decision to teach proves to be a wrong one – it should be possible to change direction and decide on a different course leading to some new career . . . Both Ripon and St John's have distinguished records and this further planning for them looks promising.

She had herself made a fine contribution to the planning and led Ripon into the amalgamation with enthusiasm and sensitivity, recognising it as the only realistic option. During her 15 years Ripon developed from a strong but relatively isolated women's college of 230 students just embarked on a building programme, into a co-educational college of almost 600 students with splendid buildings, equipment and grounds, and teaching to degree level – a worthy partner in the new enterprise. Hers was one of the least troubled of Ripon's Principalships and one of the most successful.

The College of Ripon and York St John admitted its first students in September 1975; all eligible students of the two former colleges proceeded to the second, third or fourth years. They found a new academic structure, offering a wide range of modular courses frequently enabling students from the BA, BEd and BSc programmes to be taught together. To ensure that students chose combinations of courses which the college could provide and timetable conveniently, two long-serving staff members were appointed to oversee the main programmes. James Fairbairn, former Head of Education at St John's became Director of Teacher Training Programmes, and Malcolm Jennings, former Head of Geography at St John's was designated 'Director of Other Programmes' – there being no certainty about which new programmes would succeed! Anxiety was soon dissipated by a remarkable response to late national advertisements which followed approval by Regional Council and validation by the University, in May. The new BA and BSc programmes began with 80 students; 165 were recruited in 1976 and 193 in 1977. This rapid success was achieved against a further reduction of teacher education forecasts which made it likely that teacher education would constitute only one third of the college's future commitment. There can be little doubt that the flexible and innovative 'modular' degree structure which the college had adventurously adopted was a great attraction to applicants. Over the past 16 years it has been much imitated by other institutions.

This initial success was also despite some discouraging limitations by the University of Leeds. Senate insisted that college students' awards were to be distinguished from those of students attending the university, by the designation *Collegiate* in brackets after the title of the degree and that the duration of an honours degree for the BA or BSc awards must be four years, an Ordinary degree being available for students leaving after three years. Elsewhere three-year honours degrees were already in process of approval by the University of Sussex for Bishop Otter College, and similar approvals were later given to colleges affiliated to the Universities of Lancaster, Liverpool and Surrey. Although the cost of the extra year may have deterred some potential applicants from Ripon and York it did not prevent the college from filling its places.

Staff recruitment was also encouraging though the retirements of such experienced colleagues as Stanley Barnes, Head of Physical Education after 30 years service and Dunstan Adams, Head of Biology after 28, were keenly felt. Each new post attracted a strong field of young, well qualified applicants. Buoyant student recruitment allowed some expansion of staff; new directions also demanded some painful compulsory redundancies. The combined effect was that within four years 45 members of an academic staff of 150 had joined the college since the merger.

Capital development was promising too. In 1976 work began on the conversion of Brook Street School into a new Design and Technology centre under the imaginative direction of Head of Section Edwin Gaster. The vacated Lowther Street building was converted into a second community centre to complement the college's first venture, Hoyland Hall, Barnsley, already well-reputed. The redevelopment of the Holgate building provided more staff studies and better central administrative offices. Another welcome development was the amalgamation of the two Associations of former students. *The White Rose* announced itself for 1977 in a new format 'incorporating the Ripon College Association Magazine and the Spread Eagle'. Annual reunions have been held alternatively at Ripon and York ever since with enthusiastic attendances of between 300 and 400 and college continuing to offer residential accommodation for the weekend. The two Students' Unions had merged in September 1975 and have continued to set an example of co-operative integration to college staff. The York Campus Union premises were now in the former St John's College Library building, the Library having been relocated in the Holgate building.

By April 1975, when the new college had received its necessary approvals, many other Church Colleges were in serious difficulties. From the DES point of view the 'Post-White Paper Reorganisation of Teacher Training' was proceeding very satisfactorily. Plans for more than 100 of the 162 Local Authority and Voluntary Colleges of Education had been provisionally approved, the large majority being mergers with polytechnics, further education colleges or other colleges of education. Defeat for the ATCDE policy had become debacle, touched with tragedy when on 1 May, at the last of numerous meetings at which he had argued the colleges' case, General Secretary Stanley Hewett collapsed and died. He had done all he could to salvage a tolerable settlement from the wreckage of the James Report; the few surviving colleges owe much to his perception and tenacity. Within their membership of ATCDE, however the Church College Principals had individually to advise their governing bodies on separate negotiations for their colleges' futures.

They had agreed to meet in York in April 1975 under the chairmanship of the Archbishop, Dr Stuart Blanch, who as Bishop of Liverpool had led negotiations for St Katherine's College and was now chairman of governors of Ripon and York St John. The conference agreed – too late – that a central strategy was essential. Barnett, currently chairman of the Council of Church College Principals, offered a lead by tabling a proposal for the retention of 18 'free-standing' Church Colleges, with the remaining nine either to close or merge, with some inevitable loss of identity. The mergers of Church Colleges at Exeter, Bangor and Derby had already been agreed in spite of the DES's sudden reversal of its earlier decision that where Church Colleges merged with universities, the teacher education places would *not* be counted against the Church Colleges future 'allocations'. Reluctant negotiations were also in train between the two Durham colleges, St Hild's and Bede, and between King Alfred's Winchester and Sarum St Michael at Salisbury. Barnett had advised a colleges working party

> to look again at possible mergers, rather than closures. A merger has the advantage that the opportunity for rebirth and separation in happier times will be possible. It retains the plant until the test of time can be properly applied to the present predictions. It ensures that even if the future turns out to be as black as it is painted, the full investment of the church in higher education remains employable for that purpose.

There were some vigorous rejoinders from Principals of colleges excluded from the 18. Charles Buckmaster claimed that the closure of St Peter's, Saltley would signal the Church's abandonment of its educational mission in difficult urban areas, the more so as the loss of three London colleges now seemed likely. Bishop Otter was also omitted from the 18 in spite of strong support from the Church Board in paper GS 194. The Principal advised the York conference that he would be willing to back the recommendation that the college should close or merge, provided he could assure the college governors that this would eventually *strengthen the quality* of the Church's involvement in higher education. This could be so only if the conference based its recommendations on the relative strengths of the colleges rather than on such accidental features as geographical location, 'historic share of places' – a concept much favoured by the DES – or obtuseness of particular LEAs. Comparison of strengths might be disagreeable but acceptable criteria should include quality and quantity of student recruitment, strength of validation support from a university or the CNAA, and the energy and initiative to raise capital funds for diversification. There was some support for his suggestions and a tense conference agreed at its final session to request a Board of Education Working Party to review the evidence, propose a central strategy, and specifically recommend the continuation, merger or closure of individual colleges.

Reflection on the York conference led some delegates to conclude that the Church might still have influence on national decisions on education but had no power – even over the future of its 'own' colleges. A sharp instance was provided in Sussex, where Bishop Otter College, well supported by the University, had become the first Voluntary College in the country to obtain validation for three-year honours BA and BSc degrees. The DES, through the regional machinery, was then able to withhold permission for the college to start them, until it capitulated to the government's 'preferred solution' for its future, which was merger with the nearby LEA college to form a new Institute. College Principals could recall ruefully the 1961 report which had claimed for them 'relative freedom from stereotype controls'. Fourteen years later they had exchanged two masters for six. In any significant initiative they now had to obtain the support of the DES, the LEA, the Church Board, a university or the CNAA, the regional HMI, and the Regional Advisory Council for Further Education. The bureaucracy was stultifying and the ultimate exasperation of 'the numbers game' was that, whenever he chose, the DES referee in Elizabeth House, could blow the whistle, change the rules, and order a few more players off the field. There was hardly a spectator left with the energy to protest, or a linesman from any of the other five participating bodies, prepared to wave an anti-bureaucratic flag.

Moveover, within a year, those who had asserted that government policy had been carelessly conceived and furtively implemented, were vindicated by a government enquiry. The Tenth Report from the Expenditure Committee 1976, condemned the DES for 'excessive secrecy' and for a short-sighted approach to long-term policy. It emerged that the Parliamentary Select Committee had itself been denied access to 'planning papers' at the DES. The report described the Department's failure to convene the Central Advisory Council since 1967 as 'a plain default of duty' and was severely critical of its planning organisation, set up in 1971. It deprecated the Permanent Secretary's claim that the planning organisation was 'simply the officials of the department with their thinking caps on' and insisted that planning could not be effectively undertaken as a part-time activity 'after a day's work at the counter'. Particularly galling to dismantled colleges was the exposure of the cavalier attitude of the Department's officers towards research as a basis for policy:

> Nor was the Committee particularly impressed by Sir William's attitude towards research as part indifferent and part nonsense. It says the Department spends substantial sums of money on research but distributes them passively on the basis of research worker's proposals. It finds the criticism that the department lacks research expertise partly justified and recommends a more positive stance towards research. It calls for a much more positive role from the Secretary of State.[14]

The report may have had some impact. Within a year there had been many changes of DES personnel and a new Secretary of State was giving a positive lead in more open discussion of educational policy. It all came too late for the colleges. In spite of the undoubted advantages of the 'diversified context' which accrued from the reorganisation, much of the damage to successful institutions in a potentially good teacher education system was irreparable.

In his 1978 study *Colleges in Crisis*, David Hencke, higher education correspondent for the *Guardian* and the *Times Higher Education Supplement* sympathised with the few who had publicly opposed the demolition of the colleges:

> Those outside the central web of government can only protest either politely in delegations, or more raucously at their national conferences. But they have no guarantee that those at the top will listen. They are left like truculent schoolchildren at the back of the class, shouting at the teacher. At best, if they behave themselves they might become prefects, half identifying themselves with those at the top. At worst, they can be expelled from school altogether or, if they are a college, they can, in Hugh Harding's words, be 'left to wither on the vine' . . .
>
> Even after five years of upheaval the confusion which has dogged teacher education since its birth in 1798 has not been removed . . . Since 1972 the government has had a golden opportunity to reform the system. That it has failed is appalling enough. But to fail and disrupt an entire academic system is unforgivable.[15]

Having, by Hencke's standard, 'behaved itself', the College of Ripon and York St John forged ahead. When the dust settled on DES decisions it was eventually to become one of only seven out of 27 Church of England Colleges to remain 'freestanding' i.e. entirely responsible for its own governance and for the admission and teaching of its students.

In April 1977 the college incorporated the York School of Occupational Therapy which had been attached to the York City Hospital, and soon enrolled large numbers of occupational therapy students on a three-year course in the attractive ambience of a college of higher education. With Teachers Centres, BA, BSc, and BEd programmes, Postgraduate Diploma courses and two Community Centres all flourishing, the diversification of the college seemed established and the wisdom of the merger was widely acknowledged. Few other colleges enjoyed such an attractive prospect.

In 1977 work also began on a scheme for American undergraduates to study courses at the college, for one or two semesters, as accredited parts of their degree programmes. The first 20 students arrived in 1978, and plans were made for exchange links with particular American colleges. The college also received in 1978 an EEC grant to explore the possibility of an academic exchange link with the University of Grenoble. In the summer term the graduation of the first entry to the new college was celebrated with a re-styled 'Going Down' Ball, Chapel Service and Lunch, which have become 'traditional' highlights of the college year.

By 1978 however the assumptions of the 1972 White Paper about the expansion of higher education were under question in Parliament and in LEA council chambers as the national and European economies wilted. After the initial acceptance of new diversified institutes and colleges rumblings were heard that the universities and expanding polytechnics could provide all the higher education the country was likely to need – or afford – through the 1980s. Barnett was a member of the Oakes Committee, set up by the Secretary of State to report on the management, control and finance of higher education in 'the maintained sector'. The Universities Grants Committee was still influential enough to frustrate government attempts to intervene in the management of the universities, though there was growing recognition that the divisions within higher and further education were wasteful and that an overview was desirable. The Oakes Committee Report of 1979 made recommendations which might have strengthened the colleges and institutes. Within a few months of its publication, however, the Labour Government of James Callaghan was replaced by that of Conservative former Secretary of State for Education Margaret Thatcher. The report was shelved and higher education institutions awaited the evolution of new policies.

In the meantime, Barnett acted on his growing apprehension that unless they made their own case the new colleges and institutes would rapidly be considered expendable. He wrote in *The White Rose*

> The national economic situation with the severe restraint on public expenditure could not have created a climate less favourable for the initiation of a new educational experiment and when the general public is anxious and discouraged, it is difficult to communicate new ideas and thinking.

The Church Colleges of all denominations had already joined, with two non-denominational colleges, in an Association of Voluntary Colleges (AVC) ably serviced by the Anglican Colleges Officer, Colin Alves who was its first Secretary.

With a small group of senior principals and directors Barnett now initiated a Standing Conference of Principals and Directors of Colleges and Institutes of Higher Education – now known by its shortened acronym 'SCOP'. Its aim was to draw together all the local authority and voluntary institutions to publicise and develop a conscious 'Third Force' in higher education, complementing the work of the universities and polytechnics. He was himself elected the first chairman, and the Standing Conference rapidly began to make its voice heard and to become an effective unifying body for the colleges.

In the 1978 edition of *The White Rose*, Ralph Wilkinson reflected on *The College as the Bursar Sees It*, acquainting former students with the size and complexity of the new organisation. The college now operated on seven sites in York, on the 52 acre site in Ripon and at Hoyland Hall. It had restored student numbers to almost 1,500 which in a largely residential college demanded a large staff, many of them part-time and shift workers:

> With over 500 employees on the college payroll – more than the number of students in either of the constituent colleges not many years ago – and the complexity of current employment legislation, much administration time is taken up with personnel matters and negotiations with a variety of trades unions . . . The college now rents and manages 130 houses and flats in the city of York, housing 420 students. This accommodation service is thought to be unique in this country . . .

> As the College has to contribute 15% of the cost of all capital expenditure from its private funds, it is necessary to use its plant and residential facilities as intensively as possible throughout the year. In 1977 the college acted as host to over 60 conferences which have produced a gross income of over £70,000. Ancillary

staff are thus kept employed for the whole year, and for many of them vacation time is even more hectic than term time.

The conference programme, which has become a major factor in the college's success, was developed by Wilkinson and has been greatly expanded since 1978.

A central problem for the college was that of enthusing not only DES and HMI but its own students about the innovative modular degree programme. There was increasing interest from government in degree courses directly relevant to employment. The college wished to respond to this – though the University of Leeds showed little interest – and yet to maintain the fundamental value of higher education in developing the intellectual, creative and imaginative potential of each student. By the validation agreement with the University, the first two years of the programme were assessed within the college; only years three and four were assessed by the University. Many students, supported by the Students' Union asserted that the additional 'career-orientated' courses and 'work experience' should be optional.

In 1978 Barnett circulated a long discussion document *Where Are We Going?* It was concerned with problems of assessment, with 'pre-requisites' which if allowed to proliferate would negate the advantages of choice and change offered by the modular structure, and, most of all, with student responsibility for choosing and completing courses:

> We have set ourselves firmly against the view that it is only those things which appear in the taught elements of courses that are really important, or its converse, that if the college suggests that something could be tackled by personal study . . . through off-campus or other forms of practical experience or through non-assessed study in workshop sessions . . . the college considers it to be of less importance.

The paper was much discussed and there was some positive response from students but progress towards full participation in the new programme was slow and uneven. Barnett and his colleagues were confronting the long aftermath of the student protests of the late 1960s and of the sudden reduction, in 1970, of the 'age of majority' from 21 years to 18. For 130 years the two separate colleges of Ripon and York had stood – like all universities and colleges – *in loco parentis* for students under 21. The College of Ripon and York St John could not. It was in many ways a freer and more enabling institution; it was also a more contentious one. The impact of the 1970 legislation on institutions of higher education is hard to exaggerate.

A wider range of courses and professional trainings, more students and more staff made for a lively community. Expanding opportunities in

Music, Art, Drama, Film and Television fostered a variety of student performances, and the Students' Union sponsored cultural, sporting and recreational clubs. The college maintained its reputation for high sporting standards and took pride in the achievements of Peter Squires (1969-72) undoubtedly its outstanding sportsman in 150 years. He played cricket for Yorkshire and from 1973-79 gained a record 29 England Rugby caps as a wing three-quarter. The college staff could also boast three Olympic athletes in Peter Kendrew, swimming coach and pool superintendent, Stanley Wild, British gymnastics champion, senior lecturer in Human Movement Studies, and Nick Whitehead who had captained the British Team at the Rome Games of 1960. Membership of the National Union of Students facilitated student visits to and from other universities, colleges and polytechnics. From 1977 to 1979 20 more new staff were recruited, though the college sustained sad losses in successive years through the deaths of Jim Shields, Associate Vice-Principal at York, Derek Wheeler, innovative Head of the Rural Science Department, and Harold Liversidge who had pioneered Film and Television as under-graduate studies.

In the 1979 *White Rose*, Barnett reported that the arrangements for the Grenoble exchange link were progressing; the first students from Grenoble came into residence at Ripon in 1980. He also noted that the September student entry would be the first in the history of the college all of whom would be reading for degrees or postgraduate qualifications. The last of the three-year certificate students had left in June and the teaching profession was on course for 'all-graduate' status. He also announced he would retire in 1980. A formidable task occupied much of his last year. In February 1979, the Regional Staff Inspector had approved further intakes to the college programmes for 1979 and 1980 only, and requested a review of all courses. This was to be submitted early in 1980 and to include proposals for three-year honours BA and BSc degrees. A 20 page submission was approved by the Academic Board. It argued that the college's record since 1975 justified continued approval of the existing programmes, and referred in support to the preliminary findings of a DES-sponsored research project investigating student development at Ripon and York St John, Bulmershe College and Chester College – *A Study of Student Choice in the context of Educational Change*. It pointed out that, as agreed with the university in 1974, a quinquennial review of the whole college programme had been virtually completed by the spring term of 1979 when the inspectors request had been received. Governors and Academic Board resisted further alterations:

> The review has resulted in major structural changes outlined in this paper and has required the college to make major adjustments in staffing, staff training and resources. It is not

practicable, nor would the validating authority be willing to set aside the vast amount of work involved in the review and embark on a third revision. Furthermore the effect on staff morale, which has undergone intolerable strain throughout the decade would be disastrous.

Barnett was aware that the University of Leeds was still not prepared to validate three-year honours BA and BSc degrees for the college. If the DES through the Regional Staff Inspector were to insist at this point, on three years, the colleges diversified programme would be in jeopardy. Early in 1980 approval came from the RSI for a further entry in 1981; the crisis was postponed.

In July 1980 Barnett retired. He had served 11 years at Culham College, which in spite of his innovations had been closed, and nine years at York and Ripon, which now flourished. His award of CBE in the Birthday Honours List gave pleasure throughout the Church Colleges and the Standing Conference; it was fitting recognition of distinguished leadership.

CHAPTER X

Towards a University College 1980-1991

FOR A SECOND TIME the governors appointed a Principal who was already leading another Church College. Dr Gordon McGregor had been Principal of Bishop Otter College, Chichester for 10 years and was currently chairman of the Council of Church College Principals. After graduating in English from Bristol University he had taught as an education officer in the RAF, an assistant master at Worcester College for the Blind and at King's College, Budo, Uganda and as a lecturer in English Language Teaching at Makerere University College. He had then been a founder member, and subsequently Professor of Education at the new University of Zambia, Lusaka, the first Commonwealth university to be inaugurated independent of the University of London and award its own degrees. Here, as at Makerere, he had taught many British, Commonwealth and American graduates, preparing to teach in East and Central Africa.

In the light of this experience he had been impressed, during his first years at Chichester by academic standards in the colleges and by the readiness of the University of Sussex to respond to creative ideas from its colleges and amend its regulations where necessary to accommodate them. During the run-up to the James Report he had regretted the diffidence of the Church Colleges and, in his first Annual Report in 1971 had suggested that they needed to form a more assertive association

> because few colleges enjoy our sort of university relationship and many are most unequally yoked. The more radical notion of an Independent, Christian, Professionally Orientated, University College appeals to me even more . . . but someone would have to come up with a neater title than mine.[1]

In the summer of 1972, between the James Report and the White Paper, he had represented the University of Sussex, as a Danforth Foundation Fellow in Colorado, USA, studying the transformation of

225

many of the State Colleges of America from teacher colleges to liberal arts colleges. In an article in the winter 1972 *Universities Quarterly* entitled *Towards Confidence in Teacher Education: thoughts after Danforth,* he urged the English colleges to campaign for a more independent future convinced that American experience had much to teach Britain, particularly about autonomous degree-awarding colleges. The article questioned the DES assumption that colleges could prosper only in dependent relationships with established universities or the CNAA.

> British educators have overvalued and exaggerated the parity of esteem accorded to British university degrees. The hegemony of Oxbridge may be over but some degrees are still more equal than others and there is little evidence that greater discrimination or confusion would result from establishing a large number of new institutions rather than expanding the present ones. In Britain we have fewer than 300 institutions teaching degree courses and fewer than 60 of these are dignified by the title 'university' and able to award their own degrees. The USA with roughly four times our population has over 3,000. Evidence from Danforth as well as from many years experience with American colleagues and postgraduate students suggests no great difficulty in distinguishing the excellent from the indifferent. Britain could support 500 independent degree-awarding institutions without creating academic chaos.[2]

It offered a brief description of a prototype diversified college of about 1,200 students, and suggested that some 80 to 100 such colleges could be created out of the current confusion and run at costs much lower than those current in universities. The new colleges would learn from experiments in America with 'work experience' as part of higher education; each would be:

> an independent, professionally orientated, degree awarding institution of higher education, developed by the late 1970s from an existing college of education. Some might haggle over titles. I have no doubt that the right one is 'university' . . .
>
> This new 'University' aims to give its students both a rigorous liberal education and a range of optional work experience. It . . . accepts that part of its proper function is to offer its students, as part of their degree courses, opportunities to prepare, and qualify fully, for their work in the world.

The article drew interest from universities and the DES, but little from the colleges. Stanley Hewett of the ATCDE, enthusiastic for the proposals, doubted whether college principals or governors would fight for them.

Seven years later, the article may have persuaded governors at Ripon and York St John that their new Principal was joining a congenial college moving in a direction to which he was committed. At the September meeting of the college Academic Council he congratulated colleagues on the college's achievements since 1975 and proposed some 'specific priorities'. These included consolidation of the degree structure with firm commitment to career-orientation and work experience; stronger recruitment, especially to the Ripon campus which with only 440 students was vulnerable; expansion of the Conference programme, at Ripon as well as York; further development of libraries, learning resources and computer facilities – staffing ratios being likely to deteriorate; better planned use of teaching accommodation, because most space problems were disguised timetable problems and capital funds were scarce; the setting up of two new Academic Board Committees – a Finance Committee to support the Bursar and keep staff in touch with financial realities, and a Research Committee to promote research activities, grants and Masters Degree programmes so that the college might claim, in Lord Boyle's phrase, to 'teach in an atmosphere of research'; and the strengthening of the college chaplaincies. The present chaplaincies were half-time appointments filled by hard-pressed academics; they should, he believed, now become full-time pastoral appointments supported by student/staff teams:

> In only six years we have seen twenty-seven freestanding Church of England colleges reduced to twelve, with no doubt more casualties to come. The survivors can deserve to continue as Church Colleges only through visible academic excellence, through our care for each other within each college and our support of worshipping communities at the heart of each college. There is no need for a bolder Christian witness to be divisive – far from it. All that is asked is that members of college, of all Faiths or none, should intelligently and sometimes publicly, stand for their truth.

In promoting open debate he assured members that all college issues and procedures were open for discussion. Whenever better ways of doing things were proposed they would be readily adopted.

> You are the experts in your particular subjects and departments: my job is to help you run the college more effectively. We need a two way flow of information and I can promise – short of the personal affairs of staff and students – a policy of full disclosure. Responsibility for decisions will not be ducked but the balance between consultation and decisiveness is always elusive and never pleases everyone. Effective committee work is essential,

but only when individual colleagues cannot reach fully informed decisions.

The Academic Council meetings had not often been well supported, with senior administrators usually absent. The Principal hoped that they could become well-attended termly meetings of academic and administrative staff, and offered to circulate before each meeting a written report on the main issues confronting the college, and to attend to discuss it. The aim was to ensure that before Governing Body or Academic Board made important decisions each would receive the views of Academic Council. This procedure has worked tolerably well for 10 years, with lively discussion at well attended meetings. The 32 reports published since September 1980 summarise the main problems, achievements and shortcomings of the college and provide most of the factual material for this chapter.

At the governors meeting in October, the Principal was surprised to be asked whether it was not now time to abandon the complicated operation on two major sites 25 miles apart and consolidate the college's success on the York location. He replied that the best thing the governors could do if they wanted to collaborate with an imminent government attempt to contract higher education, was to discuss the proposal seriously. If the Ripon campus was surrendered, the college would have its student numbers reduced to about 1,200, and the base for diversification would be undermined. For this reason – apart from the outstanding quality of the Ripon campus and its importance to the city – the governors should regularly discuss the campus but only in terms of expansion and improvement. The governors accepted this advice and have stuck to it, with impressive results. They also accepted the Principal's suggestion that papers for governors' meetings should be available to college staff for information.

In November the college received welcome news that the DES would shortly approve the four-year degree programme, without a time limit; the Principal advised muted rejoicing:

> DES will not, in view of the national financial position and overall higher education recruitment, be permitting any more four year programmes in institutions which do not already offer them. But because of our strong recruitment we are to be among a small number of colleges given approval for the foreseeable future.
>
> This is a tribute to the achievements of the past five years and I congratulate colleagues on it . . . Given the state of the economy however, it would not be remarkable if staff/student ratios were arbitrarily worsened by DES during this year, since a further cut in grant seems likely.

Spirits rose for the remaining weeks of the term and the college was fortunate in the quality of leadership of the Students' Union, which enabled key issues to be frankly debated. Tim Bristow, 1980-81, the first Union President to be elected to serve a second year, was a strong influence towards reasoned attitudes and against 'strikes' and demonstrations which remained current elsewhere. He was well succeeded by Jan Mellor 1981-82, who understood the frustrations imposed by DES vagaries, and kept Union members well briefed. Dr Rhodes Boyson, Minister for Higher Education addressed the Association of Voluntary Colleges in November and was forthright if not illuminating. The Principal reported to the Academic Council

> He stressed his personal commitment to the notion and reality of voluntary colleges. Higher Education, he said, is for the preservation and enhancement of academic learning and intellectual values. It is not primarily about increasing industrial production but must play its part in that . . . There was some scope for the Voluntary Colleges in Adult and Continuing Education and they should use it. He closed with a realistic promise:

> 'When we know where we are going in Higher Education and what resources we have, we shall be able to give you a greater sense of permanence'

> And you can't say more – or less – than that.

The term ended well with the inauguration of a staff Christmas Dinner, soon an established 'tradition'. The Principal looked forward confidently to the New Year. He should have known better.

In Barnett's last year the DES had informed the college that the number of senior academic staff allowed for 'academic administration' outside the teaching ratio must be reduced at once by five. In January 1981 the Principal was invited to join a small group of DES officers and principals to discuss an abrupt change in higher education financing. It was a day of almost unrelieved gloom with one bright spot – a microcosm of government misadventure. Refreshment, when provided at Elizabeth House, was normally frugal and brief but on this occasion as lunch-time approached, an impressively loaded trolley was wheeled in. One of the younger and more perceptive DES officers encouraged the prompt dispatch of the contents. By the time an error had been discovered elsewhere it was therefore too late. There had been a similarly timed meeting taking place in the Secretary of State's office. The Minister's policies were soon to prove highly indigestible but his lunch had been excellent.

The Principal felt obliged to report the more enduring effects of the day's discussion to *The White Rose*

The financial position is tough . . . We have just been told that this year for the first time we shall be 'finance limited' not 'student number limited'. Put starkly this means that success will no longer be its own reward – because the government wants to contract the system – and that even if we, or a successful university can attract more students, government will not pay for more staff! Next year's budget is simply to be this years with some allowance for inflation. So we have to be very prudent in any attempt to go on growing, but if we show any sign of contracting, ie failing to recruit, government will undoubtedly cut both staff and resources . . .

Crisis seems to be normality in education so we might as well accept and negotiate it cheerfully. I'm heartened to find my new colleagues and students at Ripon and York just as ready to do that as were those at Chichester, where we also lived dangerously through the seventies and survived.

The college's recruitment for 1980-81 had been good, with total numbers of 1,620. There had been shortfalls however in some teacher education courses, totalling 48 places – the result of caution rather than shortage of qualified applicants. Staff accepted that in future all allocated places must be filled, even at risk of over-recruitment; in stringent times more must be safer than less. As the spring term progressed government intentions became clearer through the Public Expenditure White Paper. Financial cuts of between 11% and 15% seemed probable for the college over the three years 1981 to 1984. A DES letter of April predicted the general effect:

The government accepts that these reductions in expenditure are likely first to oblige institutions to revise the range and nature of their contributions to higher education and, second, to lead to some reduction in the number of students admitted to higher education with increased competition for places. On the second point institutions are expected to admit as many students as they can consistent with their academic judgement. The plans assume a significant tightening of staffing standards.

Academic Boards all over the country were understandably slower to read the omens than Principals who were in continual touch with national officials and committees, and had to accept responsibility for balancing the budget. In the spring term the Principal put to the college board two proposals for immediate economy. The first was for a shortening of the college academic year by two weeks – a strategem in which DES had

230

expressed interest; the second was for the concentration of courses in Drama, Film and TV at York, and their withdrawal from the Ripon campus. The board rejected both.

The Students' Union took a more realistic view. Responding to the Principal's prediction that little money would be available for capital projects and that the college might as well forget about its submission to DES for a new hall complex at York, it accepted that the present hall would no longer be available every Friday and Saturday for Student Discos. These had often been unruly occasions because it was difficult for the Union to control outside access; damage to college property had been frequent. With tight supervision of bookings it would be worth renovating the hall as a lecture room for college and conference use, as well as a social venue. The Union also, reluctantly, accepted the introduction of 'caution money' to be paid by all students against damage to college property. The contributions were invested each year and the interest paid to the Students' Union after the cost of any unattributed damage had been met; the less the damage the more the Students' Union benefited. The Union welcomed the establishment of Residence Committees on each campus, comprised of staff and students representative of all aspects of the college community, with direct access to the Principal. These have worked well with the guidance of Senior Resident Tutors John Maw and Maureen Nolan. Only once in 10 years has the Principal queried a Residence Committee recommendation. On a range of college issues from car parking and bar hours to building design and action on Aids, the committees have made sensitive and practical proposals which have much improved the quality and confidence of community life. Unaware that Welch had done it better 50 years before, the Principal offered the new committees brief guidance:

> Resident tutors, from their seniority and experience, offer the residential community example and leadership, but not in a paternalistic sense. Both the legal adulthood and the reasonable freedom of all members of the community must be respected. So must our rather more complex right, as residents, to reasonable freedom from each other's freedom.

The Students' Union also reacted positively to the view of the Principal and some members of the Academic Board, that academic standards in the college were uneven and could be greatly improved. Like many academic institutions it tended to be good at making an extraordinary effort, but not so good at making ordinary efforts. The debate over the career orientated courses was resolved by a ruling that any student failing to reach satisfactory standards in them, would come before the Standards Review Committee of the Academic Board just as for unsatisfactory progress in any other part of the programme. In an April memorandum, the Principal warned that, with reduction of places imminent the college would have to be more selective in admitting to the fourth year as well as to the first, if recruitment continued strong. He also reported the effect of the new approach

> Following the end of semester examinations in February, more students than on any previous occasion were referred to the Standards Review Committee and as a result a number of students have withdrawn from the college. However, in the light of the same list of results, it has been a pleasure for me to write, as Chairman of the College Examinations Board, notes of congratulation to some 100 students who obtained credit standards in both their courses last semester.

Levels of achievement, in degree classification and employment success have improved steadily through the 1980s.

In the summer term all college departments were asked to prepare budgets for the coming financial year assuming a 12% reduction of funds. Department heads were assured that Academic Board and governors would take necessary action however disagreeable, that the principles governing decisions would be openly debated, and that the college would not simply apply 'cuts across the board' ensuring equal misery for all. The Principal acknowledged that democratic participation in unpleasant decisions was usually not welcomed, but agreed with Lord Boyle, Vice-Chancellor of the University of Leeds who had advised his Senate

> Involving the departments has the great advantage of encouraging them to concentrate their minds on what they value most and on trying to find ways round the problems.

In the last term of his two year chairmanship of the Council of Church Colleges the Principal circulated to all member colleges of the AVC a discussion paper, *Church Colleges into the 21st Century? What Do the Church Colleges Stand For? Why should Government Continue to Support Them Financially?* Still optimistic about the potential of the surviving colleges, he took a dimmer view of their immediate future than most of his AVC colleagues. Though a strong supporter of the AVC he had regretted at its inauguration that, 21 of its 22 member colleges being Christian foundations, it had not been bold enough to include 'Christian' in its title:

> We were, I suppose, distracted from setting down any clear rationale for our continuation, in the 'sixties by heady expansion and in the 'seventies by traumatic contraction. What I think stares us in the face in the 'eighties is dispassionate extinction at the hands of national and local authorities who are not ill-

disposed to us but are genuinely still asking what is 'distinctive' about us that we should specially deserve to survive. We have traded for too long on our 'Voluntary' status and on our Direct Grant. The first is a somewhat specious designation for institutions whose entire recurrent finance comes from government; the second is about to be swept away. We hardly ever seem to have traded on our 'Churchness'. A study of past documentation, including our own prospectuses, suggests that we have even felt embarrassed by it.

He recalled Archbishop Runcie's charge at the launch of the Church College Trusts, formed from the assets of the closed colleges:

The Archbishop offered us a challenge:

'With the Church itself more able to live with questions and more and more people – not only church people – feeling that materialism is not enough, we have an especially favourable context for Christian Education and Prophecy. Our efforts should be bent to promoting a more believing Church, a more responsible Church and a more prophetic Church.'

What an ironic indictment of us, if the closed college trusts truly do bend themselves to that task, and the surviving colleges don't.

One way of enhancing the quality of the college's work was to improve the working relationship with Leeds University. In July 1981 the Principal put two suggestions to Lord Boyle who, though gravely ill with cancer, willingly gave time to discuss the affairs of the colleges. The first suggestion was to offer the colleges representation on Senate so that they could contribute directly to decisions affecting their development. The second was to remove the added word 'Collegiate' from the description of the degrees awarded to college students. Lord Boyle readily offered to propose Senate membership at the October meeting, and to support the change of degree nomenclature, which he thought would need careful steerage. It was a severe loss to the colleges as to the University when he died in September. Four years were to pass before the two proposals were tested.

Only a month before the college had suffered a direct loss through the tragic death of Neville Brown, Senior Lecturer in English, drowned on a family outing to the Yorkshire Coast. Admired and well-liked by staff and students he had been about to come into college residence, as a resident tutor, with his family. The size and response of the August congregation at the funeral service left a deep impression.

At the September 1981 meeting of Academic Council progress was reported on most of the priorities suggested the year before, particularly on the chaplaincies. In spite of looming financial crisis the governors had accepted full-time chaplaincies and agreed to help fund them to relieve the academic staff budget. A new post of College Chaplain was approved with responsibility for chaplaincy policy throughout the college. From 1981 to 1987 it was filled with distinction by Revd John Young who built up chaplaincy teams, established good relationships with many local parishes and launched the successful 'Chapel Assistant' scheme. Each year, at both the York and Ripon campuses, a graduating student is invited by the chapel congregation to return to college for a further year on a small grant raised by the chapel members – to assist the chaplain and be available to the whole campus community. We have had good support for the scheme from the Church College Trusts, and, since 1988 have been grateful also to the York and Ripon Dioceses which have funded half the stipends of the two full-time chaplains.

On another key issue the Principal's advice proved less congenial. Predicting academic staff cuts of up to 20 posts within two years he proposed as appropriate for a Christian College a voluntary contingency fund to offset the worst effects. If academic staff were prepared to covenant half of the current year's salary increase the college could accrue £160,000 towards the cost of retaining staff who must otherwise be declared redundant; prospects of acceptäble early retirement conditions for older staff looked poor. The plan could be effective only if supported by at least 80% of staff. Debate at the Council meeting was vigorous and the view that government should pay the full costs of higher education prevailed. Only a third of the staff supported the proposal so the Principal withdrew it. If he had timed and presented it more sensitively, it might have succeeded.

Staff and students were however beginning to appreciate the threat to higher education. Prompted by lucid papers from the Vice-Principal Herbert Batey, the Academic Board recognised that not all present areas of college activity could be sustained. A working party had been set up to report on science courses, which were expensive in staff and equipment and suffered from the national shortage of recruits. Some staff recognised the need for broader based science courses and for computer experience for all students. As in the early 70s retrenchment was unpalatable after a period of success. The Principal wrote to the January 1982 Academic Council

> This is an attempt to *support* science studies in the college not to destroy them, but I believe that for the department to continue with precisely its present offering and structure will be to court its own closure.

There was a disagreeable tension for staff and students between the wish to participate in important decisions and unease at the choices, which must involve loss of opportunity for students and loss of jobs for colleagues. There was some interest in a review of the basic aspirations of the college to provide a guideline for decisions, so the Principal circulated a draft statement of the Purpose and Aims of the college which owed much to discussion with colleagues. He also wrote the lead article for a *Church Times* feature on the colleges. It suggested that the distinctiveness of the Church Colleges lay in their vigorous expression of their Christian allegiance through worship, curriculum and style. The attempt at worship was visible in college chapels; Christian curriculum and style were not so easily claimed:

> Each college provides some specifically Christian study opportunities, most obviously in Religious Studies and in Community Work and Studies, but also through the availability of Christian Scholarship and insights in other areas of study and creative activity including science, design, literature, history, art, drama and dance. Small is not inevitably beautiful and the Church colleges vary in size; but they all try to help their members to feel that the college belongs to them and they to the college, and that the college administration is there to support lively ideas and initiatives, to help good things to happen, and to promote the well-being of all members of college with care but without interference.[3]

DES communications during the spring term did not seem much concerned with such lofty aspirations. By March it was obvious that future college 'estimates' would merely be justifications of a pre-determined allocation of funds from DES. The predicted shortfall would require the loss of 21 academic posts within 18 months. DES indicated however that a scheme for premature retirement of senior staff was to be made available. Further analysis by governors and staff showed that not only courses in science but also the college's community centres were at risk. Buoyant overall recruitment was one of the few encouraging features of the year, but Drama numbers at Ripon seemed unlikely to provide viable courses, so with the support of the department the Principal again pressed the withdrawal of Drama from the campus; the Academic Board reluctantly concurred.

Letters were sent to DES protesting against the severity of cuts imposed upon a college which had one of the best national records for cost-effectiveness. But it seemed that the college's successful diversification into BA/BSc programmes, Occupational Therapy, Nursing Studies and large In-Service commitments made it a more tempting target for DES than smaller narrowly-based colleges which might be fatally damaged by severe cuts. In the autumn term of 1982, the Academic

Board declined to vote on a proposal by the Principal for the closure of the Physics Department; the governors postponed a decision on the same proposal, which meant that uneconomic recruitment to Physics continued in 1983.

There was some cheer at the end of the year when the college's Career Orientated BA/BSc degree programme received recognition and a grant from the Royal Society of Arts *Education for Capability* scheme. The positive national publicity was welcome. The college also received a capital loan of £70,000 from the Central Board of Finance – a major contribution to the urgent replacement of the ancient central heating system at Lord Mayor's Walk. Fluctuating interest rates had enabled the Church Board to pay off the huge mortgages on the 1960s expansions earlier than expected but it was a generous gesture to make the windfall immediately available to colleges. The CBF did not expect the 'loan' to be repaid provided the college continued to flourish.

Following a London meeting of the Principal, the Bursar and DES officers, tough argument was reflected in a revised allocation to the college in January 1983, offering some encouragement to Academic Council:

> The college has won its case against a cut of in effect 19% from 1981 to 1986. The average cut was announced as 'about 10%'. We are now being asked to take 11% and will accept that. DES was proposing that we should have by 1986 a student body of 1,580 and 138 academic staff . . . Our actual allocations are to be 1,768 students and 150/152 academic staff. Provided we can carry out our planned programme of early retirements and add two or three more, these allocations are uncomfortable but manageable. The student allocations can be regarded as a vote of confidence in the college. For our part we must ensure that we recruit the allocated numbers in a market that may fall sharply.

It is some tribute to the resourcefulness and resilience of students and staff that the college in fact succeeded in reducing the academic staff by the required 20 posts and over the same period admitted 200 more students. Such economy would of course only be truly 'cost effective' if academic and professional standards were maintained.

Government had already announced the creation of a National Advisory Body (NAB) for Higher Education; its relation to the Voluntary Colleges was unclear. The Principal had previously suggested that DES intended to end the Direct Grant relationship, and he advised the Association of Voluntary Colleges to seek close working relationships with the new NAB. Some Church College governing bodies wished to remain aloof from the National Body, but after keen debate at two AVC conferences the co-operative view prevailed. Government responded by establishing a small Voluntary Sector Consultative Council to work closely with the NAB. It was an advantage to Ripon and York St John that its Principal and Bursar were both appointed to this council, and the Principal also to the Board of the National Advisory Body.

The financial cuts soon had severe effects on the college curriculum. Governors had at last to concede that low recruitment made the costs of maintaining Physics as a degree specialism prohibitive and the department was closed. It was a painful and slow process involving compulsory redundancy of staff; all registered students were permitted to complete their degree programmes so it took three years for the decision to produce significant savings. Hoyland Hall Community Centre, Barnsley was also closed and, since the college was not strictly financed by DES for community work, the future of the Lowther Street Centre in York was also in question. The loss of Hoyland Hall was keenly felt. It had been an example of out-reach by a Church College and, like the work with Educational Priority Areas in the early seventies, owed much to the enthusiasm and energy of Martin Roberts. There were difficult changes too in teacher education. The College had for years specialised in secondary age ranges but was now asked to reduce these severely and expand in primary work where the national need was urgent. This change, accompanying the funding cuts, made the future of Design and Technology uncertain, in spite of recent investment in the workshops.

That problem was compounded by a decision of the University of Leeds. The college believed that a potential source of recruitment to Design and Technology would be mature entrants from industry who would be attracted to a shortened two-year degree course which took account of their experience and skills. Such courses had already been validated in London and Manchester, but Leeds statutes required at least three years residence for any degree award. The Principal regarded a change of statute to facilitate a desirable degree programme as a simple matter. The university did not. The Principal advised the university and the governors that the college should seek validation from either the Open University or the CNAA. At the end of the summer term a small group of senior colleagues held preliminary discussions at the CNAA.

The academic year 1982-83 had been one of the most damaging in the history of the college and had been saddened too by the death of Michael Robshaw, Principal Lecturer in charge of Music at Ripon. A gifted teacher and original composer, Michael had continued to lecture until a few days before he died.

The new year began with some encouragement. The degree results were better than in the two previous years; recruitment remained strong in spite of official predictions of a 'trough' and the college was well reported in the *Sunday Times* magazine's *Good University Guide*. This was a popular review of British Higher Education in all universities, polytechnics and colleges, based on surveys of student opinion and of the quality of resources. A cheering feature of the brief report on the college was that, unlike most of the others, it made no mention of the effect of the cuts. College staff had felt them keenly – and with some anger – but had tried to protect student programmes, facilities and morale as far as possible. It seemed that they had succeeded:

> *College of Ripon and York St John*
>
> Popularity Rating . . . Above Average
>
> Unemployment Rating . . . Below Average *(ie 'good')*
>
> One of the best and most popular of the Colleges of Higher Education particularly for teacher training. Unusually wide range of subjects includes physics and chemistry. Four courses studied from at least three different areas in the first year; only then do students make final commitment to BEd, BSc or BA. All students indicate expected employment in second year and are required to undergo work experience in vacation. No serious library problems. College says proportion getting computer experience will rise to 80%. Students speak warmly of staff. Hall places on site for most; noise only major complaint. Excellent sports facilities. Church of England College. Degrees awarded by Leeds University.[4]

It was one of the most positive reports in the survey, its sole inaccuracy resulting from the research having been completed just before the decision to close physics was taken. The Principal even welcomed the complaint about noise; living on campus himself it gave him an excuse to grumble about it even more than usual.

The survey was widely read and discussed. The influence of the news media was now such that the report probably drew more attention to the college than would have accrued from a great deal of the expensive press advertising that had become fashionable among polytechnics and colleges. HMI inspections continued to commend aspects of the college's work, but the inspectorate too was feeling the effects of cuts and an increasing workload. An inspection of the college's teacher education programmes which covered 10 months in 1983 and 1984 provided good advice, but the written report was not published till 1987, by which time many of the courses inspected had been replaced. This level of inefficiency would not have been tolerated from the college – or within it.

The phased retirement of senior staff robbed the college of much skill and experience. Among those retiring early were the two Deans of

238

campuses, Dr Peter Smith and Marjorie Sills; Director of Design and Publicity, Trevor Jones; Head of Art, Design and Technology, Derek Bolton; Head of Professional Studies, Dorothy Boothman, and Head of Language Studies, Dennis Freeborn, who had pioneered linguistic studies in the undergraduate programme and developed the national 'A' level examination. All had served the college for at least 20 years and none would have wished to leave had circumstances been normal. It is a foolish and wasteful policy which robs students of access to such talents simply for financial economy; it continues into 1991.

For a third successive year the college also suffered the death of a colleague in post. Ivan Lane had for several years skilfully linked the work of the Departments of Art and of Drama, Film and Television on the Ripon campus. He had endured a long spell of ill-health but was still doing fine work as a full-time senior lecturer when he died in October 1983. The cuts in funding from DES forced the college to discontinue the inter-departmental appointment.

Another serious loss – though in more cheerful circumstances – was that of Revd Ned Binks on his appointment as Head of St Katherine's College, Liverpool. After years of popular chaplaincy he had been founder Director of the College's Careers Service and one of the architects of the Career-orientated degree programmes. He was later to move on from St Katherine's to the Principalship of Chester College.

The college was fortunate that large numbers of applicants for admission ensured rising student numbers in spite of government pressure for contraction. During the same period it was therefore able to appoint some younger, well qualified colleagues. The opportunity was taken to redress an imbalance in academic staffing in a college which had two-thirds women students but, in 1980 a large majority of male staff. Of some 60 new academic appointments made since 1980 more than 40 have, on merit, gone to women. The proportion of women holding senior posts has also been significantly, but not yet adequately increased. The offer of permanent appointments to part-time staff has helped to equalise opportunity and status.

In 1983, Archbishop Stuart Blanch retired, accepting a Life Peerage as Lord Blanch of Bishopthorpe. He had been a most supportive chairman of governors and the college was fortunate that he was succeeded by Dr John Habgood, who as former Bishop of Durham brought valuable experience of university teaching and of involvement in the negotiations for the Durham colleges in the 1970s. Ripon and York St John continues to be grateful for his incisive chairmanship and wise advice.

The academic years 1983-85 provided some turning points. Student enrolment was up again to 1,760 in 1984 and 1,820 in 1985. Conference activities were successfully expanded. In 1980 the Principal had suggested that a profit of £100,000 a year could be achieved within five years; in 1983, thanks to the enterprise of Ralph Wilkinson and the conference team the profit was £145,000, the college had won many new friends by its good service and there were many bookings two and three years ahead. In spite of the absurdity that the college, though 144 years old, had no reserve funds of any kind, the governors readily accepted the advice of Principal and Bursar to provide the required 15% of every capital project offered by DES even if this meant running into debt. So a sequence of major building projects was undertaken and completed throughout the decade. By 1985 morale had been lifted by these visible improvements including the new Occupational Therapy 'Phoenix' Block, major renovations of residential accommodation at both York and Ripon, the extension and refurbishing of the Dining Room, Temple Hall and Lecture Theatre at York and the conversion of Owen House at Ripon into a centre for European Students and Language Studies.

The college even wrung some advantage from the premature retirements of senior staff. In 1982 the Principal had acted on shrewd advice from Tom Corser, retiring Head of the Department of Dance, Drama, Film, Television, Human Movement and Music, to invite the individual subject areas within the department to consider the advantages of operating as discrete but co-operating sections. This was tried successfully for a year, and the governors then approved the establishment of three departments – Drama, Film and Television; Human Movement, Dance and Recreation Studies; and Music. This was soon followed by the separation of Departments of Art, Design and Technology, French, English, Linguistics and Language Studies, and Nursing Studies. The new structure seems to have encouraged rather than diminished inter-disciplinary collaboration in the creation of new courses. It has also provided more opportunities for staff leadership and student membership of department boards.

The creation of new departments encouraged a review of the structure of Academic Board. The Principal had suggested that the Board's current composition inhibited decision-making on contentious issues. The 48 members included the Head and at least two members from each department. He proposed a smaller, wholly elected Board, with no ex-officio Head of Department members. Discussion by Academic Council, Board and Governors resulted in a restructured Board of 25 elected members including four elected Heads of Department and four students. This worked with increasing effectiveness, but in 1989-90 had to be modified to include more Heads of Department as required by the Education Act.

In 1984 the Governors and Academic Board accepted the Principal's advice that the college should formally apply to the CNAA for recognition as an institution offering the Council's awards, and for specific approval of a two-year BEd degree in Design and Technology. At a time of diminishing staff and increasing work-loads this was not a popular decision but it was to prove a crucial one and was loyally supported. Vice-Principal Herbert Batey, and Director of Academic Planning Allan Pattie gathered information from all academic and administrative departments and prepared detailed submissions to the Council on the curriculum and working style of the college. Staff and students had to think through together exactly how things worked so that they could write down how they worked. They learned a lot in the process, removed a few anomolies and spurious 'traditions' and were reassured to discover that most members of the college knew what they were up to most of the time. It was a salutary exercise, not much enjoyed at the time, but culminating in a successful 'general visitation' by Council Officers. This was followed by intensive preparation of the degree submission by a team of Design and Technology and Professional Studies staff chaired by Edwin Gaster, Head of Design and Technology who had led the department through remarkable developments in curriculum and resources over 10 years but was now undergoing treatment for cancer. In June 1985 the degree was approved for a September start. Edwin Gaster retired for health reasons, but took obvious pleasure in the early achievements of his successor, Barry Clay, and in the generous funding that was made available to the department through the Manpower Services Commission after the college had refused to take additional students unless resources and staffing were improved. He died in April 1986, much mourned in college and well remembered, not least through the continuing success of the department.

In his report to Academic Council for January 1985 the Principal recalled the objectives proposed in 1980, most of which had been achieved. In an outline development plan he proposed new targets including the expansion of Nursing Studies, Design and Technology, Drama Film and Televison, Information Technology, Science in Education, and Teacher Education. Cuts in the preceding two years had suggested that the college's efforts in Teacher Education were not much appreciated by the DES and with a strong direction towards primary training now evident, the college had cause to be grateful to its Director of Teacher Education, James Fairbairn, who was to retire at the end of the year. He had served on the Bullock Committee which had produced the report on teaching English, *A Language for Life* and had consistently advised the College against over-concentration on the secondary work in which St John's York had largely made its reputation. A significant range of primary courses had therefore been retained and students and staff were well pleased when, following the long inspection of 1983-84 the NAB requested the college in May 1985 to plan an expansion of more than 200 places in primary teacher education over the next five years. Fairbairn was succeeded by John Lee who combined the directorate of Initial and In-service Teacher Education, having led the In-service work for the 10 years of the new college. Under his guidance new courses have been introduced, recruitment has remained high in quality and quantity in spite of the bruising treatment meted out to the teaching profession, and the college looks confidently to further expansion of teacher education as the present phase nears completion.

The original intention of NAB was that in diversified colleges the expansion of teacher education would be at the expense of recruitment to BA programmes. The Secretary of State, Sir Keith Joseph, assumed little overall expansion and a reduction of commitments in the humanities. The growing reputation of the college's Career Orientated BA/BSc programmes, commended by HMI and recruiting heavily, enabled it to evade this trap and retain reasonable breadth of course choice for students. This was crucial to the health of the integrated modular structure which allowed deferred choice of likely career and which students identified as one of the most attractive features of the college programme.

Student/staff relations continued friendly, but not without contention. As the national student grant system became less supportive year by year the charges for residence and catering became a focus for protracted negotiation with the Students' Union. Each new entry needed to be convinced that the proceeds of all college activities were paid back into the college to improve student facilities and services and that in no way could the college 'make a profit' out of student residence. Governors regulated charges carefully each year on the advice of the Bursar and in comparing charges in other universities and colleges students needed to assess the quality of provision. In the summer of 1985 student patience ran out – with a good deal of sympathy from the college administration. A campaign of 'action against rents' was announced. It is some testimony to relationships that, having decided to launch a 'Rent Strike' the Students' Union was prepared to take the advice of the Principal and Bursar on the most effective and least damaging way of conducting it. In the end a £30 rent rebate was agreed, honour was satisfied on both 'sides' little harm done, but a lot of time and energy misdirected. The episode was to have a valuable sequel.

Throughout these annual negotiations it had become almost a ritual for the Students' Union to assert that, at the rents proposed there would be a short-fall of students willing to come into residence. Principal and Bursar would predictably respond that this would present no problem because the college would readily convert surplus residential accommodation for academic, administrative or all-the-year-round conference use. As the 1986 negotiation reached its climax the student executive was adamant that there would be at least 30 vacant rooms at Ripon, at the proposed charges. The Principal therefore announced that the elegant Highfield House at Ripon, which accommodated 22 students and a college tutor, would be redeployed for one experimental year, as a college Short Course and Conference Centre. The centre proved so successful and lucrative that, at the end of the year even student governors accepted that the benefit to the college would be greater if Highfield remained a permanent Short Course Centre. Four years on it is a nationally reputed feature of the Ripon Campus and a key resource for the college's new Department of Continuing Education.

The National Advisory Body was now exercising a strong influence over the planning of higher education outside the universities; within this 'public sector' the polytechnics were dominant. The Voluntary Sector Consultative Council was vigilant for the interests of the Church Colleges but could do little to alter the relative scale of their operation. In a sector for which government in 1986 intended minimal expansion the 21 Voluntary Colleges had 22,000 students while the 29 polytechics had 185,000. As in 1971 there were administrators who speculated that the work of all the surviving colleges of higher education – Church and LEA – could easily be subsumed within the polytechnics – with perhaps one or two new polys designated. It was argued that a smaller group of more powerful institutions would provide a better service. In November 1985 the *Times Higher Education Supplement* carried a provocative but fair leading article, drawing attention to some anomalies and limitations of the Voluntary Colleges, hinting that they could be 'reorganised' out of existence, and hoping that their case would be argued 'with concern and passion'. In the edition of 22 November the Principal responded.

He acknowledged that joint support from government and the Church laid upon the Church Colleges

> a special obligation and opportunity. This is to provide a good quality higher education in a context in which the possibility of belief in God, and the study and practice of the Christian Faith are taken seriously. The colleges should be attempting this openly and unaggressively, with absolutely no pressures, explicit or subtle, on freely recruited students and staff, in three ways:
>
> First by encouraging within the college an open but supported worshipping community – it is honest enquiry and

243

commitment that matter, not building 'monumental chapels'. Second through the truthful and considerate treatment of all college members by one another, regardless of status or belief. Third, by providing opportunities – never requirements – for college members to consider Christian insights and contributions to the intellectual, creative and professional disciplines offered in the college and to ethical, moral, political and social issues. . . .

Some of us who argued strongly that the church colleges should offer to come under the aegis of the National Advisory Body three years ago did so because we wanted publicly to remove any false impression that the church colleges either got or wanted any more favourable treatment from government than local authority colleges, or polytechnics. But having seen 30 out of 51 church colleges of all denominations closed or merged within the last 10 years we have learnt that neither their buildings nor their staff can be redeployed for educational or community purposes anything like as easily as those of local authorities. So I for one want to say clearly to government and any interested members of the electorate : 'Don't withdraw support from any more such colleges unless you are sure you understand what they are trying to do and have concluded either that they aren't doing it or that you don't want it done.'

There remained the difficulty – which Bishop Bell had negotiated in the 1940s – of asserting distinctiveness without unction or implied criticism of other types of institution. In an article invited by the *Catholic Herald* the following month the Principal developed a theme of the THES article :

These are taxing ideals among a people largely indifferent to religion and most of us fall short of them most weeks. If we were found not even seriously attempting them, then I believe we would deserve to be closed or handed over to local authorities. But we Christians also need to recognise that our efforts and witness, such as they are, can be nothing but enhanced by the commitment of any polytechnic, university or authority college which also suceeds in offering higher education in a Christian context even though, unlike the Church's colleges, it has no moral obligation to do so. We offer any such institution our warm support and co-operation.

As part of its witness to the Christian Faith, the college was trying to foster international opportunities for students and good relationships between different racial groups, particularly in support of ethnic minorities in Britain. In York and Ripon, cities which in spite of their attraction for tourists, have two of the lowest proportions of ethnic minority residents in the country, these aims were not easily achieved, but in 1986 and subsequent years the college made progress. Academic Board and governors approved for publication a policy statement on multicultural education:

> As a Christian Foundation the College of Ripon and York St John welcomes the development of the United Kingdom as a multicultural society. The college commits itself to foster good relationships between all ethnic groups, and to eliminate racial discrimination and disadvantage. The college recognises that this will necessitate periodic review of its practices in the employment of staff and the provision of educational services . . .
>
> The college undertakes . . . to encourage student and staff applications from members of ethnic minority groups and to assure them of equal opportunity with all other applicants.

The college promised to continue its support of local ethnic minority groups and to involve them in the planning of educational activities which concerned them. Progress in student recruitment from ethnic minorities is perceptible, but slow, partly because Leeds and Bradford can offer excellent home-based higher education opportunities to the nearest large ethnic minority communities for many of whose members our residential tradition may be unattractive. This remains a major challenge in the new decade and the next century.

In 1986 the college urged students to take greater advantage of its international study and exchange programmes in Europe and the United States. These had started well in 1980 but by 1985 there was a disturbing imbalance – many more American and European students coming than Ripon and York students going. A team of colleagues set about redressing the balance and persuaded the Principal – which took about 30 seconds – to visit the University of Grenoble, the Free University of Amsterdam, Keene State College, New Hampshire, Union College Schenectady and finally Ripon College, Wisconsin where, at the Commencement he was honoured with the degree of Doctor of Letters for services to international education. The warmth of the American and European friendship, and publicity within the college had good effect; relationships with all these institutions have strengthened and exchanges equalised. College has added to the programme – which also features strong direct recruitment from the United States – exchange and study links with the University of Oslo, University of South Florida, Potsdam College New York, Colleges in Zwolle, Netherlands, and Lüdwigsberg, Germany, and the International Christian University in Tokyo.

Meanwhile the college has not neglected its local communities. In spite of stiffer DES regulations on the loan or hire of premises the York and Ripon campuses are heavily used by local organisations and by the Open University. The Access courses run jointly with the York College of Arts and Technology and with Harrogate and Northallerton Colleges provide opportunities for large numbers of local mature students to gain places in higher education. Many are attracted to the part-time degree programmes for BA, BSc, MA and MEd. When the long established York Settlement was forced to close because of the withdrawal of county and city grants the college offered to take over many of its Continuing Education courses, in co-operation with the University of Hull and assisted by a small grant from the Rowntree Trust. Close relationships with local schools continue through Teacher Education programmes, while Nursing and Occupational Therapy students and staff work with many local hospitals and health centres.

Any quest for diversity could become too diffuse if clear aims were not established. Through much of 1986 the Academic Council, Academic Board and Governors considered a redraft of the earlier Statement of the Purpose and Aims of the college. In October they approved a version which has been reproduced in four successive college prospectuses of which a total of 120,000 copies have been sent all over the world. College cannot claim to achieve it all yet, but does claim to get nearer every year to a declaration of intent which is reviewed every year and has not yet needed alteration.

The Purpose and Aims of this Church of England College

The College was founded by the Church of England in 1841 to extend the Church's service to the nation. Its original purpose was to educate teachers for the Church's 'National' Schools, many years before government began directly to provide schools and colleges. The College has greatly extended the scope of its service to society since 1841 and is now directly financed by government. But its fundamental purpose remains to provide excellent higher education in a Christian context.

The College aims to create the Christian Context through:

Support for worshipping Christian communities and chaplaincies at Ripon and York in a college open to staff and student members of all faiths or none.

Opportunities for all members of College to encounter, without coercion, Christian insights and experience in the moral, ethical, social, political, religious and philosophical issues which arise within higher education programmes, and to explore these alongside a variety of other insights.

The College aims to maintain:

An open, participatory style of College management in which all members are encouraged to contribute to discussion and decisions.

An open recruitment policy concerned to provide equal opportunity for women and men, for members of ethnic minorities, for disadvantaged applicants and for the physically handicapped.

High quality residential, cultural and recreational provision, shared, respected and well cared for by all members of the College community.

Opportunities for these facilities of the College to be shared with the local communities of Ripon and York.

The College is committed to offering:

Initial and in-service education and training for four specific professions: Teaching, Occupational Therapy, Nursing and the Ministry of the Church.

A wide range of subject studies within the Humanities, the Sciences, the Creative and Expressive Arts, and Design and Technology.

BA and BSc programmes with a strong emphasis on developing student skills.

Advanced Diploma and Masters Degree courses for post-graduate students.

Part-time study opportunities, at diploma, degree and post-graduate level, especially for mature students.

Programmes of Continuing Education for a wide range of groups.

Active sponsorship and support for staff research and further study.

The College aims to provide opportunities for students to:

Choose combinations of course units to build programmes suited to individual talents, enthusiasms and developing career intentions.

Postpone and change, within necessary limits, their choice of subjects and career intentions in the light of their developing experience and personal inclinations.

Experience co-operative learning fostered by excellent teaching and resources, and gradually to accept full responsibility for their learning.

Study parts of their degree programmes in Universities and Colleges overseas and to study alongside overseas students taking accredited courses at Ripon and York.

Benefit from stimulating and enjoyable experiences – intellectual, creative, aesthetic, social, recreational and spiritual – which will encourage life-long self-education, and creative responses to change.

Develop informed concern for our own multi-cultural and multi-faith society and for those of the Third World and to act upon this concern.

Serve the local communities of Ripon and York, particularly the disadvantaged and handicapped.

In the academic years 1986 to 1988 the college made progress in spite of continuing cuts which had diminished the budget, in real terms, in every year since 1981. There were more improvements to buildings; the DES had come to rely upon the college being willing to accept, every March in the last few weeks of the financial year, a capital grant from unspent funds which was conditional on the college being able to start the project before the end of the financial year – which was the end of the month! It was a strange way to deploy tax-payers funds, but thanks to the resourcefulness of the Bursar and his team and the willingness of the governors to come forward with their 15% – usually borrowed – a major project has been completed every year from 1981 to 1991. The Temple Hall foyer, cloak-rooms and coffee bar provided a welcome reception area in 1987 and 1988 saw the start of the final, £500,000 phase of one of the best Design and Technology Centres in the country. The Department of Drama, Film and Television which had been ably expanded by David Powley and his colleagues, redesigned its Studio Theatre in the former college chapel and also received a complete renovation and extension of its Film and TV centre. Good student care for facilities had by now become a feature of college life and the growth of conference bookings reflected appreciation by many national organisations of the amenities and hospitality of the college, of the quality of its catering, and of the beauty of its well-tended gardens and grounds.

In 1986-87 numbers were up again, to 1,860 and, for the first time – contrary to doleful prophecies of 1980 – there were more than 600 students on the Ripon campus. The college's increased allocation of teacher education students seemed justified by heavier recruitment to both the BEd and Postgraduate programmes. This was against a national downturn of 11% probably precipitated by disenchantment with government policies and attitudes towards the teaching profession. As at most colleges, students and staff had been resilient to the cuts and remained cheerful, partly by assuming that cuts represented yet another crisis in education which would in due course be surmounted and followed by a return to 'normal' funding. But the sociologist, A. H. Halsey, speaking at a conference of the Higher Education Foundation, took a different view, which the Principal commended to Academic Council:

> 'People have spoken, tacitly assuming that we were in abnormal times, that we have some sort of unprecedented crisis on our hands, of the universities, of higher education and of our cultural life in general. I think that is totally wrong. What in fact has happened is that *we have returned to something like normality*. The age ranges at this conference represent the last two or three generations to live through a particular and quite bizarre episode in the history of the higher learning. An episode lasting about thirty years, in which next year's income is bigger than this year's and this year's bigger than last year's. That situation is most extraordinary. It has never happened before and it may never happen again. We have been living through abnormality and peculiarity, and what is shocking us – or in the metaphysical language we have been using 'putting pressure' on us – is the reversion to normality.'[5]

This analysis is probably correct, but in any case the attitude recommended makes good sense as reductions in staffing and maintenance funds continue into the 1990s.

In 1987-88 government funding remained niggardly but at least there were signs of a changing attitude towards the case for expanding higher education to produce more highly trained men and women. The Principal reported to the Yorkshire press:

> Colleagues and students have united to face severe economies rather than yield to government demands to reduce student intake. We welcome the recent change of policy by a government which now seems to share our view that there are strong economic reasons as well as strong moral and social ones for increasing access to higher education.
>
> The college has been asked by the Department of Health to expand its highly reputed department of Occupational Therapy, which has the largest student application in the country, from 140 places to 180. With an expert Careers Service supporting the careers courses and work experiences required in all its BA and

BSc programmes, the college offers students excellent employment prospects. Job success from Teacher Education and Occupational Therapy is virtually 100% and from the BA and BSc courses 88%. There are very few universities, polytechnics or colleges in the country that can match these figures. Students also benefit from international communities at Ripon and York with more than 100 students a year from USA and Europe following accredited degree courses, and with flourishing Exchange programmes giving our college students a term or a full year overseas.

Through 1986 and early 1987 the Principal had been a member of a Working Party of the NAB under the chairmanship of (Sir) Christopher Ball, charged to report to the Secretary of State on ways of improving the management of higher education in the 'public sector'. Its report, *Management for a Purpose*, published in March 1987 reflected on evidence from polytechnics, colleges, the DES, industry, commerce, and management consultants. The college benefited from scrutiny by three firms of management consultants commissioned by the NAB. They reported favourably on its organisation and management, providing about £20,000 worth of 'free' advice.

In February 1987 the Governors and Academic Board approved a Development Plan for the college, drafted by the Principal, for the three years to 1990. It set an optimistic target of 2,030 fte students but proposed further economies through the closure of under-subscribed courses and the concentration of more subjects at either York or Ripon. It assumed a staff/student ratio of 1:13 but the Principal warned governors that Academic Board and Council did not yet share his conviction that

> even further academic staff cuts would have to be made if we were to make additional funds available to create the learning resources essential for our students to be taught in the larger groups and less frequent meetings which I believe are unavoidable.

The financial position was getting worse. On the advice of DES officers the college had gone into debt on its 1985 current account by over £200,000. Further cuts had increased the deficit. The governors own capital fund had been over-stretched each year by building projects and was also more than £200,000 overdrawn. From 1981 to 1983 they had bought several houses in York, useful for student and staff accommodation but primarily intended as insurance against a rainy day. Governors now accepted advice from the Principal and Bursar that it was raining hard; property prices had risen, so several house sales cleared the capital debt by 1988, though each year brought fresh building projects which would renew the deficit.

The college also launched an Opportunity Fund, inviting former students and staff and friends of college to covenant or subscribe towards what it hopes will become the first substantial endowment fund the governors have ever had, to celebrate the 150th Anniversary in 1991. The purpose of the fund is to support students' cultural, sporting, professional and recreational activities which were once reasonably well provided for by government grant but no longer are. As in 1981 there is still a strong conviction among students, staff – and Principal – that government *ought* to provide fully. Ten years later that view is probably unrealistic and certainly unhelpful to the college. A supportive Past Students Association whose members were prepared to give generously to their college would be a great strength in the difficult decade which lies ahead. The recent Presidency of John Maw, Senior Resident Tutor of the college, has already done much to persuade the Association in that direction, and to encourage more recent graduates to join.

At the end of the academic year in 1987 Vice-Principal Herbert Batey, now a Canon of Ripon Cathedral, retired from the college, much honoured by students and colleagues. For 12 years he had presided over the Ripon campus, given wise and sensitive advice to students and staff at both Ripon and York, and injected realism – and a number of astringent papers – into college planning and decision-making. The governors appointed to succeed him, Dr John Axon a Cambridge man, from Fitzwilliam College, who had been senior lecturer in English at the Ripon College from 1967 to 1972 and had then gained administrative experience as Head of English at Northampton College, at Nene College and finally as Head of English and Drama at Homerton College, Cambridge.

In the long vacation 1987 the college suffered another severe loss when Dr Roy Hallam, Head of Professional Studies, died suddenly on holiday in France. He had succeeded Dorothy Boothman in this key post after several years as deputy and in his scholarly and persuasive style was working towards a reorganisation of the Department. Once again a large congregation of students and staff assembled in the chapel at the height of the August holiday, to mourn our loss and the family's, but to give thanks too for a fine contribution to college life.

By academic year 1987-88 the college's relationship with the CNAA was well established and the first students had graduated from the two-year BEd degree programme. The Principal now asked Governors and Academic Board to give thought to their preferred choice of validation for college awards in the future. He had written to the Vice-Chancellor at Leeds suggesting four areas of change and development for the university's relationship with the college. After a long inter-regnum Lord Boyle had been succeeded by Sir Edward Parkes, a former chairman of the UGC and an informed supporter of the Voluntary Colleges. During the 1980s universities had themselves become more vulnerable to the cuts which had afflicted the colleges so there was a keener awareness of mutual difficulties. Some Senate members however still had reservations about according parity of esteem and description to college degrees, not least because it might expose the university to criticism of the disparities in the funding of institutions and degree programmes. But there was a positive response to the Principal's proposals, as he reported to Academic Council in January 1988:

> There was some unease last term about the forcefulness of the letter I had written to Sir Edward Parkes on the future of college validation. In the event the response was as I had hoped and more than I expected. The college has put itself in a strong position by making the effort to achieve 'dual validation' and approval as a CNAA institution; it makes sense to use that strength. By the end of the term Senate had agreed to remove the term 'collegiate' from the description of our awards, the location of our college degree ceremony at York Minster had been agreed in principle, discussions were in train for further relaxation of mature student entry requirements and for membership for college staff of the university subject boards. Right at the end of term came an invitation to recruit all our students through UCCA, the Universities agency. We are examining the implications of this last offer promptly, but with care.

Staff and students took confidence from a sense that the quality of their work was better appreciated by university colleagues. There was talk of a new status for the college to strengthen the 'affiliation' of the past 67 years. All this owed much to the unobtrusive influence of the college's University of Leeds governors, notably Dr John Brindley and Dr Sheila Gosden. The University Colleges Board was stirred to swift action by its new chairman Professor Brian Hogan.

1988 brought other good developments. Student recruitment from USA and Europe expanded and Dr Robert Griffiths, Director of the European Study and Exchange Centre at Ripon was honoured for his contributions to French scholarship and Anglo-French university co-operation, by the award of the Order of Chevalier de Palmes Academiques. He pioneered the college's relationship with the University of Grenoble and for the academic year 1990-91 is Visiting Professor there. The college's European connection was now so well reputed that when the EEC announced the start of its ERASMUS project for the encouragement of university exchange and study abroad, Ripon and York St John was awarded three of the first dozen British contracts. HMI approval and strong support among employers of graduates for the college's career oriented degree programmes was reflected in its selection as an early starter in the generously funded *Enterprise in Higher Education* project sponsored by the Training Agency. David McAndrew, former Head of the Department of Language and Literature directs the college project, which should receive about £500,000 over five years to enhance the vocational elements of college programmes and the skills and opportunities of all students. 'Enterprise' may have become an abused word but there is no necessary tension between the values of this project and those of the Christian Faith. Since its foundation the college has stood for the conviction that those privileged to enjoy higher education should repay that privilege through trained, skilled work for society. Rightly directed our Enterprise Project will promote no more, and no less, than that.

The 1988 Education Act introduced reforms and opportunities for higher education. The National Advisory Body was to be wound up and a Polytechnics and Colleges Funding Council (PCFC) established, to work parallel to a Universities Funding Council which was to replace the University Grants Committee. The college was left with an undeserved liability from the NAB and the DES Direct Grant, in the form of a large recurrent funding deficit resulting from the incorrect classification and consequent underfunding of its two-subject honours degree programmes over a three year period. After long argument with NAB, DES and PCFC the justice of the college's case was admitted but the debt was not written off. Through skilful management an underpayment of £1m has left, by 1990 a recurrent deficit of £300,000 which the PCFC has allowed the college three years to clear. It is an unfair handicap, but the college will surmount it.

Less acceptable provisions of the Education Act reflected DES insistence that new Articles of Government for polytechnics and colleges must prescribe smaller Governing Bodies and Academic Boards with reduced representation for staff and students. The college has carefully considered these requirements, believes them to be ill-informed, and is determined – whatever formal structures may be required – to maintain the close consultation with students and staff which have served it well. For many members the 'open participatory style' aspired to in our Statement of Purpose and Aims, is central to our Christian witness. The Principal reported to Academic Council in September 1989:

> The new Instruments of Government give principals even more power and the tight national deadlines we now work to make it tempting to act without consultation. We need the checks and balances of a fully involved staff. What Niebuhr said of the world is true of a college: 'Man's capacity for good makes Democracy possible; Man's capacity for Evil makes Democracy essential'.

In September 1988 the college for the first time had more than 2,000 actual students and seemed on course for the 1990 target. It was the biggest, best qualified and probably most active student body in 147 years. Contributions to college academic, professional and community deliberations from the Students' Union, from student members of college committees and from clubs and societies were excellent and the range of cultural and recreational activities wide. High standards were maintained in sport, particularly by women students in hockey, athletics, rowing and korfball, and by men in soccer and cricket. The Principal should be forgiven – but probably won't be – for suggesting that the outstanding achievement of the decade was again in Rugby Football; the club, having celebrated its centenary in 1983, has taken pride in the achievements of Geoff Cooke, St John's RFC 1959-62, as Manager of the successful English National XV.

In April 1989 the PCFC institutions were formally incorporated and polytechnics and colleges which had formerly been owned and administered by Local Authorities became independent of them. With some of them becoming registered charities – as the Church Colleges are – and the rest incorporated companies, the term 'Voluntary College' lost much of its usefulness in distinguishing older foundations set up by public subscription. In November 1988 the Association of Voluntary Colleges had reconstituted itself as a Council of Church and Associated Colleges. The PCFC, of which the Bishop of London, former chairman of the Church Board of Education, is a member, established as one of its few committees a 12 member *Committee for Church and Associated Colleges*, to which the Principal of Ripon and York St John was appointed. For the first time in their long history the Church Colleges are formally represented within the government's planning and funding structures. The first year of working within the PCFC proved agreeable and efficient, in spite of disruptive preoccupations with what are alleged to be industrial and commercial styles of management and financing. Competitive 'bidding' has limited value and may have limited life, but there are signs that the Council will support colleges and polytechnics that can plan adventurously and manage efficiently.

Each PCFC institution was requested to submit to the Council by June 1989 a strategic plan for the three years to 1992. There was much alarm and protest from some member institutions at the requirement to reveal their brilliantly original designs on success. The college takes the view that it is when other institutions *stop* copying its ideas that it will get worried. It benefited from the planning it had already done for 1987-1990 and predicted a student body of 2,300 by 1992, further worsening of staffing ratios to 1:15, more single campus subject concentrations, a new programme of undergraduate initial Nurse Training as part of the national *Project 2000*, and the reduction of the four-year BA and BSc programmes to three years. The last decision was taken reluctantly, since recruitment to these programmes has been carefully monitored throughout the decade and has improved from good to excellent. But the student grant and support system has declined drastically and it is apparent that a majority of students now experience real financial difficulties, so – with strong student support – the college decided that it could now offer to its increasingly able, well qualified and confident students, a high quality honours degree programme in three years and had a moral obligation to do so.

The strategic plan also announced the college's determination to protect its high quality residential higher education – for which the government has made clear it has no intention of paying – and disposing of some of its saleable assets at both York and Ripon. These may pay for new residential buildings and – when they became essential – for new academic and professional premises too. College has no family silver to sell but does have quite a lot of family grass. Before it took important decisions on what to sell and who to sell it to it was important to rationalise subject locations as economically as possible for the next decade. A working party chaired by Vice-Principal John Axon conducted this delicate exercise in public and energetically, enabling governors and Academic Board to take some harsh decisions. From 1991 the entire BA and BSc programme will be concentrated at York. Chemistry and Rural Science have been permanently withdrawn from the programme, and Music, French and Religious Studies withdrawn for the present but with their offerings strengthened in the Teacher Education programme. The retitling of the BEd degree as a BA with QTS (Qualified Teacher Status) may enable subjects whose recruitment has been uneven to re-establish themselves in the non-professional BA programme if costs permit. At Ripon the loss of BA places will be made good by the introduction of Initial Nurse Training and by the expansion of Teacher Education and Continuing Education programmes.

Throughout the 1980s the college seemed to have carried a heavy load of tragic loss. It was to continue to the end. News came through in January 1989, that American student Kate Hollister, flying home at the end of her first term in York, had been on board the Pan American plane destroyed by sabotage over Lockerbie. It emerged that Kate had been shy and nervous in the early days of the programme but had become enthusiastic and successful by mid-term and full of plans for the rest of the year. She is commemorated in the annual award of the Kate Hollister prize for a student who makes outstanding progress and contributions in the American programme. The summer vacation was yet again marred by the loss of a senior colleague when John Hill, Principal Lecturer in

Primary Education died suddenly, early in September. He had been an outstanding tutor and classroom teacher for 21 years and a touchline devotee of the college soccer and rugby clubs. Cancer forced the premature resignation of Keith Martin, Principal Lecturer in charge of Art at Ripon who had served the college with unflagging cheery competence for 21 years and died after only a brief retirement.

The new academic year opened with the college degree ceremony in York Minster – the first in the 700 years of that great church. The graduating year – which included the first 14 Masters graduands – had achieved the best results in the history of the college – the third successive year to do so. The college orchestra, choir and organists provided memorable music and after the ceremony some 800 graduates and guests lunched on the Ripon and York campuses. Those present knew that a new 'tradition' had been established and were grateful to colleagues in the university administration for their meticulous arrangement of the occasion and for agreeing that the CNAA graduates should receive their degree parchments from the Archbishop as chairman of governors. Through the autumn and spring terms discussions proceeded briskly on the conditions under which the university might accord to the college the title 'A College of the University' and the style of 'University College'. It was agreed that there was to be no infringement of the status of the college as a Church Foundation, nor of the governors' responsibilities for organisation, employment of staff and selection and discipline of students. The college would remain a PCFC institution – with the expectation that PCFC and UFC will co-operate closely in future. The college had decided to accept the invitation to recruit its students through UCCA from 1990 and there was strong conviction in college and university that, after 69 years of affiliation, the new title would be a true indication of the nature and working style of the college. Though retaining its proper autonomy it would function for academic purposes as if it were a very large faculty of the university, at Ripon and York. In the summer term 1990 the negotiations were completed and the Senate and Council of the University approved the status and title 'A College of the University'.

The academic achievements of staff and students merit the new status. The degree results of graduands presented at the second Minster ceremony in September 1990 were for a fourth successive year the college's best and well up to British university norms. The drop-out rate was the lowest in the country and more than 90% of the graduates took good honours degrees – 10 firsts, 123 upper seconds and 140 lower seconds. Masters programmes are now well established and the college looks towards its first doctoral supervisions. Though it remains primarily an undergraduate teaching institution, a research culture has been steadily established and the Research Committee publishes an impressive register of publications, research in progress and consultancies undertaken. The research profile of the staff has been transformed by a concerted programme of staff development. In 1980 fewer than one quarter of the staff held research qualifications – 14 doctorates and 27 masters degrees between 172 staff. In 1991 the proportion is three quarters – 38 doctorates and 79 masters degrees held by 152 staff.

It seems likely that this has had its effect on student recruitment as well as attainment. Academic Registrar James Sellwood and his colleagues have coped with dramatically increased applications over the past four years, but the first year with UCCA broke all records. In December 1988, when most subjects had closed applications, college had received nearly 5,000; in December 1989 the figure was almost 8,000 – which might well have doubled had it remained 'open' as many colleges do. From these applicants departments chose a highly qualified entry of 700 – 200 more than the target – which has given the college in October 1990 a total student body of 2,410 – 2,228 fte. The Strategic Plan target for 1992 seems certain to be exceeded. Students are coming to subject departments and programmes many of which have been highly commended by HMI and by external examiners. HMI have encouraged claims for 'excellence' in bids to the PCFC for students in Health Studies, Teacher Education, Design and Technology and Drama Film and TV. Thirty years ago Philip Lamb predicted that the advent of women would raise academic standards. It is notable that in 1991 six of the areas most praised by HMI, validating bodies and students are led by women: Occupational Therapy by Paula Juffs; Nursing Studies by Gwen Vardigans; Library and Learning Resources by Frances Walder; English and Related Literature by Anne Price; the Careers Service by Sheila Cross and the Postgraduate Certificate in Education programme by Philippa Scott.

The student body showed impressive maturity in the early weeks of the autumn term when the college was having great difficulty accommodating the huge over-recruitment. It is not only in their degree programmes that they accept greatly increased responsibilty. Under the guidance of Dr Mary Connor, Principal Lecturer in Counselling, a Student/Staff Counselling Network of trained volunteers has developed as an effective and unobtrusive support to students and staff. The college is also unusual in having maintained a highly supportive team of Resident Tutors living on, or very near, the campuses at York and Ripon. Backed by excellent Health Centres and college doctors, the value of these support services to the tax-payer is seen in the college's very low 'drop-out' rate; their value to the college as a community is incalculable.

Progress is good yet financial cuts and staff losses continue. In the academic year 1989-90 Romano Zavaroni, inventor and director of the Recreational Management programme retired early on health grounds. So did Brian Sourbut, Head of English, who as Emeritus Senior Research Fellow of the college, bravely continues his translations of Ibsen's poems, which the college looks forward to publishing. Over the next two years, other premature retirements will include John Lee, Director of Teacher Education, Malcolm Jennings who was promoted in 1975 to be Director of Other Programmes with no students and within 10 years was Director of BA/BSc Programmes with 1,000 students; John Maw, Senior Resident Tutor and Deputy Head of Professional Studies; David Powley, Head of Drama, Film and TV; and George Charlson, Head of Human Movement Studies. All have served the college(s) for at least 20 years, are well below normal retirement age and would not have wished to leave had the college been adequately financed – nor would the college have considered inviting them to do so. Not all their posts will be filled because staffing costs must be reduced by £130,000; some of their responsibilities will be allocated to other colleagues, but some services to students will simply be withdrawn. The college deserves better, as it enters its 150th year.

From one student in 1841 on a one-year course, to 2,400 in 1991 on a range of Masters and Bachelors degrees is a progression to celebrate and of which, for a few months to be quietly – perhaps noisily – proud. Then off again to the next developments, and two or three strategic plans to take the college into the new century. At the 150th Anniversary Commemoration of the first Church College foundations, at Westminster Abbey, in May 1989, Archbishop Runcie found inspiring words, taking his text from 1 Corinthians, 2:

> Your Christian tradition provides the surest way to preserve a care for students which is personal, not sentimental, and a conviction that community matters because everyone matters to God . . .

> In so doing, your colleges will make a witness from within – within Higher Education *and* within a Church which must never let you down . . .

> Herbert Butterfield once said that Christianity kept open 'a Spring ever generative of new things'. Often the new things sail off under other auspices. Our task is to keep alive that fresh spring. From that spring came the life of your colleges. From that spring may all of you, whatever your beliefs, find inspiration, refreshment and vision for all that lies ahead.

'We do impart wisdom, although it is not a wisdom of this passing age . . . we impart a secret and hidden wisdom of God.'[6]

'From within Higher Education and within the Church'. Perhaps, for Ripon and York St John, 'Independent, Professionally Orientated, Christian University College' may not be a bad description after all.

Epilogue

A Church College for the Twenty-first Century?

IN 1974 THERE WERE 27 COLLEGES of the Church of England and the Church of Wales, all of them freestanding, that is, entirely responsible for the admission and teaching of their students. By 1989 only 12 survived, eight of them freestanding. So the title of this book – and of this epilogue – is not rhetorical. There will be continuing pressures against the survival of relatively small institutions of higher education. Unless we make strenuous and successful efforts there may be no Church Colleges in the new century. The foregoing chapters have attempted objective assessment of the progress of the college and offered some dispassionate indications of how it might earn healthy survival. What follows is neither dispassionate nor objective, but purely personal opinion resulting from one man's limited experience.

I believe that this college – like the other surviving Anglican colleges – can earn the continued support of the Church, the government and the public, if it will go on working towards its stated Purpose and Aims and come closer to achieving them. I am not alone in this view. In 1981 the Council of Church College Principals commissioned and helped to fund a research study by the Culham Institute which had been established from the closed Culham College. The study[1] was of the influence and effectiveness of the Church Colleges. It addressed the question 'What justification can validly be put forward for the retention of the Anglican Colleges in the 1980s and beyond?' We committed our Council to the widespread publication of the research findings even if they proved entirely negative.

In fact they offered some encouragement. Of 7,500 people consulted from a range of professions and standpoints, a large majority considered that the colleges of the 1980s were effective and should be supported. They were judged to be providing sound higher education and professional training in multi-disciplinary institutions well suited to preparation for teaching, nursing, occupational therapy, youth and community work and various forms of Christian ministry. They were also considered to be, at least to some extent, centres of Christian study and scholarship. Like all research studies this one has its limitations but the Church Colleges are the first group of British higher education institutions to submit themselves to such scrutiny. They have learned from it.

In November 1988, in association with the Roman Catholic, Methodist and Free Church college foundations, they formed the Council of Church and Associated Colleges out of the former Association of Voluntary Colleges and published a Mission Statement. It was drafted from the Ripon and York St John Statement of Purpose and Aims and asserts on behalf of all the colleges

> Their purpose remains to provide high quality education in a context in which the practice and study of the Christian Faith are taken seriously.[2]

I believe we can fairly claim that the recent degree results, employment success and personal development of our students at Ripon and York St John indicate that some high quality education is being offered here and that students are being challenged to achieve excellence. I think we can also show that through our college chapels and our degree programmes in Religious Studies, the practice and study of the Christian Faith are taken seriously. But we have much more to do – as our own Statement declares – to establish convincing claims to distinctiveness as an open Christian College. First, we have to substantiate our claim to offer significant 'Christian opportunities and insights' in the college curriculum. The Culham study revealed much scepticism on this issue among the staffs of the colleges and in a subsequent paper the project director, Dr John Gay, commented

> Among a substantial number of college staff there was a grave suspicion of any theological attempts to influence the curriculum and nearly a third of them felt that there was no place for the application of Christian insights in the curriculum . . . Whatever the reasons for the reluctance of staff to acknowledge the possibility that Christian insights might have relevance outside the conventional religious domain, the fact that the reluctance exists is a major constraint on the ability of the colleges to develop a distinctive contribution based on their Christian foundations . . .[3]

This reluctant response may well have resulted from a proper concern among staff that academic freedom and scholarly integrity must be as carefully nurtured in the Church colleges as in any other university or polytechnic institutions. In a wide ranging enquiry the questions in this sensitive area were probably too few and too simple. We have made some progress in this college through specific discussions at departmental and academic board level which indicated strong majority assent to the *notion* that the curriculum of a Church College should provide components and opportunities that might well not be available in a secular foundation. But I doubt whether a neutral observer would detect such assent in our current prospectus – which is designed to present to intending students a summary of the most important opportunities we offer. In a college which admits – not just willingly but enthusiastically – students and staff with many different beliefs and philosophies this is bound to be a contentious matter. Indeed the contention itself is important and should be continual. The point is well made in a valuable contribution to the debate, *Christian Perspectives for Education* edited by two Church college lecturers, Leslie Francis and Adrian Thatcher:

> . . . what is at issue in the identity crisis of the colleges is a cognitive matter. The Christian faith makes genuine knowledge claims about what there is to be known and what responses are appropriate to that knowledge. These claims are certain to be contentious in the present day, but that provides an additional reason for articulating them as clearly and publicly as possible and not (as so often happens) maintaining a silence about them in case they provoke a mild incredulity from the surrounding secular milieu . . .

> The Christian tradition . . . offers a point of view that is not tied to any political party, pressure group or programme. Critical, value-laden analysis has always been part of the Judaeo-Christian tradition. It began with the biblical prophets who cried out for justice for the poor . . .[4]

The challenge is clear and, in my view, inescapable. That is why I put it first in the concluding chapter of our celebratory symposium *150 Years: The Church Colleges of Higher Education*[5] in which I suggested a ten-point programme of action for the surviving Church Colleges. Here in our own college, the Governors, Academic Council, Academic Board and Students Union need to sustain the debate and action we have initiated until we have clear decisions and statements from all departments, advertising in the prospectus the special curriculum opportunities students can expect to find here. We shall be in no danger of indoctrinating or of infringing academic freedom if we keep in mind Moberly's rebuke to the British universities of the 1940s. The challenge for us remains to equip our students to

> disentangle and examine critically the assumptions and emotional attitudes underlying the particular studies they pursue, the

professions for which they are preparing, the ethical judgements they are accustomed to make, and the political or religious convictions they hold.[6]

The curriculum is the biggest task that confronts us in our quest for a distinctive Christian ethos but there are many other aspirations in our Statement we have to work at. Our claim to be open to student and staff applicants with disadvantages and disabilities is reflected in modest advances we have made in widening access to the college. By resisting pressure – often from women students – to ensure a social balance of the sexes in the student intake, we have maintained opportunities for women, who – on merit – comprise two thirds of our student body. Our part-time degree programme has given special opportunities to locally resident mature students, most of them women and many of them parents. We must extend those opportunities and overcome the serious difficulties of finance and planning permission which we have encountered in our efforts to provide childcare facilities. At the same time we need to mount a planned campaign for the recruitment of ethnic minority students and staff and for those with physical disabilities. Discussion within college committees has convinced most members that ethnic minority recruitment to York and Ripon which are two of the 'whitest' cities in Britain, will continue to be difficult in spite of our declared interest, and that the conversion of our facilities to make them convenient for the physically disabled will cost a lot of money that we do not have and are unlikely to be given. But having acknowledged our shortcomings and set an energetic Equal Opportunities Committee to the job of finding solutions, I believe we can make great progress in the next nine years. We need to remember that the college was founded to bring education to the poor and the disadvantaged and that, as our former chairman William Temple insisted, the Church which founded it is itself an unusual institution because it exists entirely *for the benefit of non-members.* We have become a very popular college and – with plenty of other problems created for us by government policies – it might be tempting to evade this responsibility and recruit entirely from the very able well-qualified school leavers who apply to us from families which are already privileged and successful. I hope we will resist that temptation – to which I believe too many of our most 'successful' Church schools have succumbed – and use a careful measure of discrimination to achieve a just and balanced student intake.

Our progress towards wider access should be matched by progress towards more open government in college. We are not bad at this and we work at it; but we are not yet good at it. There are several reasons why open processes are important but above all should be the Christian conviction – shared by some other religious and political creeds but by no means all – that all men and women have talents, skills and opinions to contribute to the common good. The college will also serve the interests of all its members by employing their judgements towards college decisions; training in decision-making is an important part of the preparation which higher education offers towards mature, participatory citizenship. But all that lays an obligation on the college administration to ensure that our consultative processes and committee work are well organised, so that college members who give their time will consider it well spent, find the procedures interesting and rewarding even when the decisions are disagreeable, and therefore stay involved.

Our convictions about open government should extend beyond the college. It is an essential safeguard of the freedom of all its members that the college should have no firm political alignment but that does not absolve it from expressing views on educational and other political issues on which members achieve either consensus or a clear majority verdict. We need, I believe, more internal argument about national policies and should be ready to offer public support for good government decisions and reasoned public criticism of destructive ones. We have a fair record on this in recent years but are too easily seduced by specious interpretations of 'academic freedom' into regarding almost all government interventions in higher education as 'interference'. One theme of this study has been 'autonomy' and the Church colleges delusions about it. Government has, throughout the life of this college, been heavily and properly involved in higher education, spending the tax-payers money on it. The many national reports quoted above illustrate this, and the emollient advice of the Bryce committee of 1895 remains incontrovertible

> On the whole then, it is well, in face of what is now actual fact, to recognise that political control goes necessarily with the bestowment of public money.[7]

I believe that under present legislation the Church Colleges are offered a generous measure of academic and organisational freedom. If, as Christian educators, we want total independence we must be prepared to foot the total bill – and should remember that our Founders were not.

A college that is working for equal opportunities and open decision-making should be prepared to address the vexed question of pay. Again, we have made a small start by examining differentials, rejecting the excesses of the 'industrial models' held up to us by some government departments and questioning, for example, whether the principal needs to be paid more than any other member of college. Many higher education staff deplore the government's removal of fixed, mandatory, national scales, but we could turn an unworthy policy to advantage. I believe the teaching profession made a well-intentioned but pernicious error, in establishing 'responsibility allowances' as an integral feature of post-war salary scales. The *most responsible* thing anyone can do in a school or college is to work with students at the teaching/learning process; yet we have consistently paid administrators more than teachers, thereby devaluing the very work the college exists for. We should now take our chance to re-examine rates of remuneration and ease away some of the worst disparities between what we pay, for example, senior academics and the secretarial and support staff who share some of their most important responsibilities. As a college with a talented staff for whom there will be limited scope for promotion, we need to shed the current assumption that leadership is burdensome and stressful and must therefore always be paid for. We should try again – after one unsuccessful attempt – to devise acceptable ways of sharing responsibility perhaps for limited periods of office, with little or no extra salary offered. There is great untapped initiative and leadership potential in our staff common rooms and we have the example of hundreds of voluntary organisations in which thousands of men and women willingly exercise high levels of responsibility without remuneration, *because they believe in the cause and because leadership is exhilerating.* We should not exploit this human virtue, but we should give it scope. I write as a convinced believer in Trades Unions, but an even more convinced believer in the parable of the Labourers in the Vineyard.

In the previous chapter I hinted that we should be wary of the misuse of the word 'enterprise', and of the worst excesses of the 'enterprise culture' and the 'vocational thrust' in higher education. But we should use to the full the opportunities they offer, and should secure for our students a proper balance between education for full living and training for effective work. In this ambition, as in so many others, the students and tutors of other countries and continents have a lot to teach us. Extending and deepening the college's international relationships is, I believe, one of our central Christian obligations to God's multi-racial world.

None of these aims is self-authenticating; they are all contributions to the one central purpose of the college – the provision of excellent higher education for all our students. With intellectual and professional demands on students and staff increasing, and the resources we need to meet them being reduced year after year, these are tough targets to set ourselves. The next decade would be difficult enough without them. Nothing new in that. If you have read this far you will know that every decade of the college's life has been difficult. But in the 1850s, while Hodgkinson fended off unjust accusations of heresy, and Miss Cruse struggled with poor health and deplorable facilities, Browning wrote

> Ah but a man's reach should exceed his grasp or what's a heaven for?[8]

And now we have a 150th Anniversary to celebrate.

Notes and References

Chapter I
(pages 1-20)

Monkgate 1841-1846

1   See for example: Rich, R. W., *The Training of Teachers in England and Wales during the Nineteenth Century,* CUP 1933 and Sandiford, P., *The Training of Teachers in England and Wales,* New York, Teachers College, Columbia, 1910.
2   Rich, *op. cit.,* p. 22.
3   Sidney Smith to Lady Holland, 7 July 1812, quoted in C. N. Smith, Letters of Sydney Smith, London 1953, Vol. 1, p. 219.
4   See McClure, J. Stuart, *Educational Documents, England and Wales, 1816-1963,* Methuen 1967, p. 3 and passim.
5   Murphy, J., *Church, State and Schools in Britain, 1800-1970,* Routledge, 1971, p. xiv.
6   Burgess, H. J., *Enterprise in Education,* SPCK, 1958, p. 64.
7   Report of the Parliamentary Committee on the State of Education 1834, quoted in McClure, *op. cit.,* pp. 39-40.
8   Purcell, E. S., *Life of Cardinal Manning,* MacMillan, 1896, Vol. 1, p. 149.
9   Smith, F., *The Life and Work of Sir James Kay-Shuttleworth,* Murray, 1923, pp. 61-62.
10 Letter to the Duke of Bedford, 1839, quoted in Smith F., *op. cit.,* p. 86.
11 Burgess, *op. cit.,* p. 79.
12 *White Rose* (The Magazine of the Old Students' Association), Vol. 11, No. 6, 1893.
13 Minutes of Committee of Council on Education 1847-48, Vol II, p. 440.

Chapter II
(pages 21-37)

Lord Mayor's Walk and the College for Mistresses 1843-1854

1   McGregor G. P., *Bishop Otter College and Policy for Teacher Education, 1839-1980.* London, Pembridge Press, 1981, p. 46.
2   Newsome, D., *The Parting of Friends,* London, Murray, 1966.
3   Chadwick, O., *The Victorian Church,* London, Black, 1966, p. 219.

[4] Etherington, W. (unpublished thesis), *St John's College, York, 1841-1914,* York, 1969 (MEd University of Leicester), pp. 93-103.
[5] Copy in Archives at York Campus, College of Ripon and York St John.

Chapter III

(pages 38-54)

Expansion – and Migration 1854-1863

[1] See Smith, F., *The Life and Works of Sir James Kay-Shuttleworth,* London, Murray, 1923, p. 147.
[2] Burgess, H. J., *Enterprise in Education,* London, SPCK, 1958, p. 147.
[3] Purcell, *op. cit.,* Vol. I, p. 419.
[4] Newsome, D., *The Parting of Friends,* London, Murray, 1966, p. 222.
[5] Purcell, *op. cit.,* pp. 421-23.
[6] Ibid., p. 427. Also Burgess, *op cit.,* pp. 155-157.
[7] Ibid., p. 428.
[8] Ibid., p. 432.
[9] Schools Inquiry Commission 1868 (Taunton) Report, Vol. IV, p. 603.
[10] Newcastle Commission Report 1861, pp. 643-645.
[11] Hansard 3rd series, Vol. 166, c. 180-181.
[12] Newcastle Report, Vol. IV, pp. 394-408.
[13] Ibid., pp. 168-169.
[14] Taunton Report, Vol. IV.

Chapter IV

(pages 55-72)

Separate Colleges 1863-1880

[1] Hansard Third Series, Vol. 165, c. 229.
[2] Newcastle Report, p. 169.
[3] General Report, 1867, p. 121.
[4] Gent, G. W., *Memorials of St. Marks College,* London, White 1891, p. 13-14 and 67-69.
[5] Ibid.
[6] Pritchard, F. C., *The Story of Westminster College,* 1851-1951, London, Epworth, 1951, p. 48.
[7] Bradbury, J. L., *Chester College and the Training of Teachers,* Chester, 1975, p. 123.
[8] Bartle, G. F., *A History of Borough Road College,* London, 1976, p. 33.
[9] Naylor, L., *Culham Church of England Training College for Teachers,* 1863-1953, Abingdon, Abbey Press, 1953, p. 49.
[10] McGregor, G. P., *Bishop Otter College and Policy for Teacher Education,* 1839-1980, London, Pembridge Press, 1981, pp. 79 sq.
[11] Hurt, J., *Education in Evolution,* Hart Davis, 1971, p. 202.
[12] Adams, F., *History of the Elementary School Contest in England,* Chapman and Hall, 1882, p. 177.

13 Rich, R. W., *op. cit.,* p. 179.
14 McGregor, *op. cit.,* p. 81.
15 Ibid., Ch. 3, *passim.*
16 Taunton Report, Vol. 1, p. 619.
17 Ibid.
18 Ibid., pp. 656-659.
19 Etherington, W., MEd Thesis, Leicester Univ., 1969, *passim* (College Archive).
20 Hansard, February 17th, 1870.
21 Burgess, *op. cit.,* p. 201.
22 Cruickshank, M., *Church and State in English Education,* MacMillan, 1964, p. 35-6.
23 Morley, J., *Life of Gladstone,* MacMillan, 1905, Vol. II, p. 308.

Chapter V   *(pages 73-104)*
The Dual System Extended
1880-1908

1 Wilkinson, A. M., Ripon College 1862-1962: *The First Hundred Years.* Ripon College, 1963, p. 27.
2 Fuller, F. W. T., *The Churches Train Teachers,* unpublished PhD Thesis, University of Exeter, 1973, pp. 130-135.
3 Rich, R. W., *op. cit.,* pp. 194-203.
4 Minutes of Evidence before the Royal Commission on Education, 23 June, 1886, pp. 495-505.
5 Report of Cross Commission, pp. 242. Quoted in McLure, *op. cit.,* p. 138.
6 Sir Rhodes Boyson in *The Observer,* 25 February, 1990.
7 Report of the Royal Commission on Secondary Education, 1895; quoted in McLure, *op. cit.,* p. 145.
8 Sutherland, Gillian, *Policy Making in Elementary Education,* 1870-1895, OUP, 1973, pp. 331-337.
9 Simon, Brian. *Education and the Labour Movement,* 1870-1920, Lawrence and Wishart, 1965, pp. 186-191; quotation p. 187.
10 Hansard, Fourth Series, Vol. 105, Quoted in Van der Eyken, *Education, the Child and Society,* Penguin, 1973, p. 79.
11 Fitzroy, A. W., *Memoirs,* quoted in Murphy, J., *op. cit.,* p. 94.
12 Letter, 11 August 1959 to E. Taylor (college archives). Quoted in Etherington, p. 210.
13 Rich, R. W., *op. cit.,* p. 209.
14 Etherington, *op. cit.,* pp. 249-253.
15 Ibid, p. 254.
16 Committee of Council Report for 1895-96, p. 170. Quoted in Etherington, *op.cit.,* p. 256.
17 Memorandum of 18 October 1905, in the Public Record Office, Ed/21/19311. Quoted in Etherington, *op. cit.,* pp. 259-260.

[18] Etherington, *op. cit.*, p. 264.
[19] Scott Coward. Report on Elementary Schools and Training Colleges, 1902, p. 178. Quoted in Etherington, p. 267.
[20] Welpton, W. P., *Primary Artisan Education,* Longmans 1913. Quoted in Etherington, *op. cit.,* p. 270.
[21] Board of Education Report 1904-5, p. 40.
[22] National Society Annual Report, 1907, p. 23.
[23] G. Wigglesworth (1882-4), in *White Rose,* December 1912.
[24] Binns F. G. (1901-03), in *White Rose,* Vol. 41, No. 1, 1935.

Chapter VI *(pages 105-124)*

A Long Survival; War and Recession 1908-1930

[1] National Society Annual Report 1912, p. 177.
[2] Holmes, Edmund, *What is and What Might Be,* London, Constable 1911, p. 148.
[3] Ibid., p. 7.
[4] Board of Education Report for 1920-21.
[5] Times Educational Supplement, 4 July and 18 July 1918.
[6] Andrews, L., *The Education Act 1918,* London, Routledge, 1976, p. 79.
[7] Foster, H., in *The Spreadeagle,* 1973, p. 15.
[8] Burnham Report, 1925, p. 107.
[9] Gosden, S. and P. J., *The Institute of Education and the Affiliated Colleges,* University of Leeds Journal, 1988, p. 63.
[10] Tawney, R. H., *Secondary Education for All: A Policy for Labour,* 1912, p. 67.
[11] Hadow Report, *The Education of the Adolescent,* 1926, Chapter III, p. 70.
[12] Ibid., Chapter II, p. 175.

Chapter VII *(pages 125-152)*

Through Depression and War
to Butler and McNair 1930-1945

[1] Report of the Consultative Committee on Primary Education, 1931, Introduction, p. 18.
[2] *The Times*, 30 January, 1933.
[3] Zebedee, D., *Lincoln Training College*, 1862-1962, Lincoln 1962, p. 109.
[4] *Scrutiny*, Vol. 1, No. 3, December 1932, p. 247.
[5] Zebedee, D., *op. cit.,* pp. 142-3.
[6] Full Inspection Reports on Training Colleges, No. 30: York Training College, p. 9.
[7] Quoted in Ripon College Magazine, 1934.

[8] See for example, Musgrave, P. W., *Society and Education in England since 1800*, Methuen, 1968, p. 95.

[9] Spens Report, 1938, Summary of Recommendations, pp. 376-381.

[10] Howard, Anthony, *RAB: The Life of RA Butler*, MacMillan, 1987, pp. 110-139.

[11] Ibid. and Iremonger, F. A., *William Temple*, OUP, 1948, pp. 569-578.

[12] Temple, W., *Our Trust and Our Task*, National Society, 1942, p. 8.

[13] Council of the Church Training Colleges, Report, 1 July 1943.

[14] Norwood, C., *The English Educational System*, Murray, 1928, pp. 9-10.

[15] Report of a Committee appointed by the President of the Board of Education to consider the Supply, Recruitment and Training of Teachers and Youth Leaders, 1944, Introduction.

Chapter VIII   *(pages 153-196)*
Expansion Towards Maturity 1945-1971

[1] Bishop Otter College Magazine, June 1946, p. 7. See McGregor, *op. cit.*, p. 178.

[2] CAF Paper 208, *Church Training Colleges*, London, SPCK, 1947, p. 3.

[3] Ripon Association Magazine, 1954, p. 10.

[4] Ibid., p. 13.

[5] *The Completion of the Reconstruction of the Church Training Colleges*, London, Church Information Board, 1955, p. 5.

[6] Ibid., p. 17.

[7] Morris, P. R., in *Towards a Policy for the Education of Teachers*, ed., Taylor, W., Butterworths, 1969, p. 118.

[8] *Education in 1960*, Ministry of Education, 1961, p. 72.

[9] *The Supply of Teachers in the 1960s*, London, HMSO, 1958, p. 8.

[10] Ibid., p. 9.

[11] Murphy, *op. cit.*, p. 120.

[12] Report of the Ministry of Education's Central Advisory Council entitled '15 to 18', London, 1959, p. 131.

[13] CA 1277, *The Expansion of the Church Training Colleges for Teachers*, January 1959, p. 1.

[14] Ibid., p. 5.

[15] CA 1359, Report by the Board of Education, 1961, pp. 6-7.

[16] Kogan, M., ed. *The Politics of Education*, Penguin, 1971, p. 82.

[17] Church Board of Education, *Evidence to the Committee on Higher Education*, Church Army Press, July 1961.

[18] Report of the Ministry of Education's Central Advisory Council entitled 'Half Our Future', London, HMSO, 1963, p. 105.

[19] Ibid.

[20] *Higher Education*. Report of the Committee on Higher Education, London, HMSO, 1963, p. 270.

[21] Report of Conditions of Service in Colleges of Education, ATCDE, Autumn 1968, p. 8.

22 Lowndes, G. A. N., *The Silent Social Revolution*, 2nd edition, London, OUP, 1969, pp. 314-316.
23 Van der Eyken, W., *Education, the Child and Society*, London, Penguin, 1973, p. 468.
24 Kogan, *op. cit.*, p. 193-4.
25 Ibid.
26 Ibid., p. 170.
27 Murphy, *op. cit.*, pp. 122-3.
28 Report of the Working Party on the Communication of the Christian Faith, London, Council of Church Colleges, January, 1966, p. 8.
29 Taylor, W., *Society and the Education of Teachers*, London, Faber, 1969, p. 12.
30 Bantock, G. in Taylor, W., ed., *Towards a Policy for the Training of Teachers*, Butterworths, 1969, pp. 122-3.
31 Select Committee on Education and Science. *Teacher Training*, Minutes of Evidence, 29 January 1970, London HMSO, February 1970.
32 Willey, F. and Maddison, R. E., *An Enquiry into Teacher Training*, London, ULP, 1971.
33 DES Report: Conference of Principals of Colleges of Education, York, 1970.
34 ATCDE *Higher Education and Preparation for Teaching*, A Policy for Colleges of Education, London, 1970, p. 10.
35 Lukes, J. R., *Power and Policy at the DES: A Case Study* in *Universities Quarterly*, Spring 1975, p. 145.

Chapter IX (pages 197-224)

Through Demolition to Reunion 1971-1980

1 Robertson, James, *In a Glass Darkly*, London, Council of Church Colleges, 1971, p. 4.
2 A Submission by the Board of Education . . . on the James Report, GS Misc. 16, 1972.
3 *Education: A Framework for Expansion*, CMND 5174, HMSO, December 1972, pp. 44-45.
4 Ibid., p. 46.
5 A First Commentary by the Board of Education on 'Education a Framework for Expansion', GS Misc. 21, 1973, pp. 7-8.
6 Quoted in ATCDE Communique, Series 3, No. 8, April 1973, p. 2.
7 Report of DES/ATCDE Conference of Principals, April 3-6, 1973, pp. 1 and 5.
8 THES, 13 April 1973.
9 THES, 20 April 1973.
10 Fulton, O., ed., *Higher Education in the Eighties* in *Universities Quarterly*, Winter 1973, p. 24.
11 Briggs, Asa, *Development of Higher Education in the United Kingdom, Nineteenth and Twentieth Centuries* in Niblett, W. R., ed., *Higher Education; Demand and Response*, London, Tavistock 1969, p. 106.

[12] The Future of the Church Colleges of Education, GS 194, January 1974, p. 7.
[13] Ibid., p. 5.
[14] *The Times*, 23 September 1976 and see Tenth Report from Expenditure Committee, HMSO, September 1976.
[15] Hencke, D., *Colleges in Crisis,* Penguin, 1978, pp. 122-123.

Chapter X   *(pages 225-259)*
Towards a University College 1980-1991

[1] Bishop Otter College, Annual Report, 1971.
[2] *Universities Quarterly*, Winter 1972, pp. 17-30.
[3] *Church Times Supplement*, The Church Colleges of Higher Education, February 1982.
[4] *Sunday Times Magazine*, 25 September 1983.
[5] Halsey, A. H., The Chairman's Summing Up, in *Higher Education Newsletter*, No. 11, Higher Education Foundation, June 1986.
[6] *150 Years: The Church Colleges of Higher Education*, ed., Brighton, T., WSIHE, 1989, pp. 194-5.

Epilogue   *(pages 260-265)*

[1] Gay, J. D., *et al. The Future of the Anglican Colleges*, Abingdon, Culham Institute, 1986.
[2] Council of Church and Associated Colleges: Mission Statement, November 1988. Quoted in *150 Years: The Church Colleges of Higher Education, op. cit.,* p. 174.
[3] Gay, J. D., *The Churches and the Training of Teachers in England and Wales* in McClelland, V. A., ed. *Christian Education in a Pluralist Society.* Ch. 11.
[4] Francis L. and Thatcher A., eds., *Christian Perspectives for Education,* Gracewing, 1990, pp. 171-2.
[5] McGregor, G. P., *Church Colleges for the Twenty-first Century?* in *150 Years, op. cit.,* pp. 172-189.
[6] Moberly, Sir W., *The Crisis in the University,* London, SCM Press, 1949.
[7] Report of the Royal Commission on Secondary Education 1895, quoted in Bevan, J. *From Whisky Money to the Switch: Higher Education and the State.* Higher Education Newsletter No. 13, June 1987, p. 16.
[8] Browning, R. *Andrea Del Sarto* in *Men and Women,* 1855.

Archbishops of York and Chairmen of College Governors, St John's York

Edward Vernon Harcourt	1841-1847
Thomas Musgrave	1847-1860
Charles Thomas Longley	1860-1862
William Thomson	1863-1890
William Magee	1891
William Maclagan	1891-1908
Cosmo Gordon Lang	1909-1928
William Temple	1928-1942
Cyril Garbett	1942-1955
Michael Ramsey	1956-1961
Donald Coggan	1961-1974

Bishops of Ripon and Chairmen of Ripon College Governors

Robert Bickersteth	1871-1884
William Carpenter	1884-1911
Thomas Drury	1911-1920
Thomas Strong	1920-1925
Edward Burroughs	1925-1934
Geoffrey Lunt	1935-1946
George Chase	1946-1959
John Moorman	1959-1975

Archbishops of York and Chairmen of Governors College of Ripon and York St John

Stuart Blanch	1975-1983
John Habgood	1983-

College Principal's, York

Revd W. Reed	1841-1848
Miss Winifred Cruse (Women's College)	1846-1862
Revd G. C. Hodgkinson	1848-1854
Revd H. G. Robinson	1854-1963
Revd G. Rowe	1863-1879
Revd S. De Courcey Baldwin	1879-1893
Revd E. E. Nottingham	1893-1908
Revd H. Walker	1908-1935
Revd Dr J. W. Welch	1935-1939
Revd A. A. Cock	1939-1945
Revd Canon P. J. Lamb	1946-1971
J. V. Barnett	1971-1975

College Principal's, Ripon

Revd G. Sheffield	1862
Revd Canon E. B. Badcock	1863-1890
Revd O. P. Whalley	1891
Revd Canon G. Garrod	1892-1908
Revd Canon I. A. Smith	1908-1930
Miss E. Lett	1930-1945
Miss V. Hall	1946-1960
Miss M. Gage	1960-1975

Principals, College of Ripon and York St John at Ripon and York

J. V. Barnett	1975-1980
Dr G. P. McGregor	1980-

Roll of Honour

The College Memorial Plaques in the Chapel at Lord Mayor's Walk list the following students of St John's College, York, who were killed in the two World Wars.

1914–1918

J. J. Moore	'80–'81	A. Heathcote	'09–'11
H. Leslie	'95–'97	C. E. Dickens	'09–'11
H. Scholefield	'97–'98	A. E. Cannell	'09–'11
C. Branfoot	'97–'99	F. W. A. Stubbs	'09–'11
J. Thompson	'98–'99	M. V. Jude	'09–'11
J. W. Tindle	'98–'00	R. G. Kew	'09–'11
C. C. Wood	'00–'02	N. Webster	'10–'12
D. G. Joy	'00–'02	J. Burrow	'10–'12
R. Perry	'02–'04	R. P. Jones	'10–'12
R. B. Appleby	'03–'05	G. O. Burrell	'10–'12
C. W. Wood	'03–'05	J. Harrison, V.C.	'10–'12
F. Klein	'04–'06	F. Hunsley	'10–'12
F. Welburn	'04–'06	C. E. Savage	'11–'13
H. Marshall	'05–'07	E. Batley	'11–'13
S. Raynor	'05–'07	J. R. Hinchcliffe	'11–'13
T. Sugden	'05–'07	E. Fairless	'11–'13
A. Turner	'05–'07	W. L. Roper	'11–'13
J. P. Garlick	'05–'07	J. Essex	'11–'13
W. H. Hemingway	'06–'08	P. Shaw	'11–'13
C. W. Drury	'06–'08	H. T. Jackson	'11–'13
J. M. Downend	'07–'09	R. Keal	'11–'13
A. Hanley	'07–'09	J. B. Bushby	'11–'13
T. L. Lees	'07–'09	F. J. Nock	'11–'13
E. Raynor	'07–'09	H. Wilkinson	'11–'13
A. G. Smith	'07–'09	M. Fullerton	'12–'14
S. B. Horsman	'07–'09	A. Howell	'12–'14
F. A. Murdock	'08–'10	F. Seed	'12–'14
F. J. Watson	'08–'10	R. W. Myers	'12–'14
G. G. Dixon	'08–'10	C. Barraclough	'12–'14
T. A. B. Kitson	'08–'10	J. C. McIntyre	'12–'14
A. Burnitt	'08–'10	H. Midwood	'12–'14
A. F. Jackson	'09–'11	W. Robinson	'12–'14

A. Thorp	'12–'14	C. Myatt	'13–'15
J. E. Wilson	'12–'14	H. Tindall	'14–'16
H. Day	'13–'15	C. F. Butler	'14–'16
H. A. Earnshaw	'13–'15	N. Bradley	'14–'16
R. Haworth	'13–'15	R. Hadall	'14–'16
P. Lister	'13–'15	A. Harris	'14–'16
R. Oakley	'13–'15	J. H. Procter	'14–'16
D. Ball	'13–'15	W. T. Samuels	'14–'16
C. A. Slack	'13–'15	M. Williamson	'14–'16
A. Street	'13–'15	W. Worthy	"14–'16

1939–1945

L. T. Holmes	'29–'31	K. M. Liddle	'37–'39
G. H. High	'29–'31	W. G. Hill	'37–'39
A. W. Weston	'29–'31	J. Curle	'38–'40
G. W. Armer	'30–'32	W. D. T. Halstead	'38–'40
A. F. Crass	'31–'33	G. Hocking	'38–'40
P. W. Green	'31–'33	R. Jackson	'38–'40
H. A. Harker	'31–'33	E. Lindsey	'38–'40
J. Mason	'31–'33	R. G. Thomlinson	'38–'40
H. Barlow	'32–'34	S. Walker	'38–'40
A. Robe	'32–'34	H. Clegg	'39–'41
H. Gofton	'32–'34	J. Hague	'39–'41
C. Harrison	'32–'34	G. Tate	'39–'41
S. Woodhead	'32–'34	J. Monks	'39–'41
L. W. Calderhead	'33–'35	R. H. Thorne	'39–'41
O. E. Hulme	'33–'35	A. E. Adams	'40–'42
J. H. Newton	'33–'35	H. Barwick	'40–'42
W. H. Hoggard	'33–'35	K. G. Earnshaw	'40–'42
S. A. Errington	'34–'36	R. Harrod	'40–'42
A. Williamson	'34–'36	S. W. Poynts	'40–'42
J. L. Rowe	'35–'37	K. Whalley	'40–'42
A. J. Theasby	'35–'37	J. Wilkinson	'40–'42
G. C. Ankers	'35–'37	B. Wrightson	'40–'42
L. A. Jefferies	'35–'37	A. Greenwood	'42–'44
H. Ward	'36–'38	J. C. Lewis	'42–'44
T. L. Megoran	'36–'38	C. C. Ridgway	'43–'45
J. A. Edgar	'36–'38	T. Holden	'42–'44
J. Leaf	'37–'39	P. Cardwell	'43–'45

Index

277

Chester College, 12, 13, 15, 16, 18, 19, 61, 65, 98, 106, 113, 127, 223, 239

Chichester, 10, 12, 77, 127, 128

China, 90

Christ's College, Cambridge, 4

Christ Church College, Canterbury, 175, 185

Church Assembly, 128, 155, 156, 167, 170, 171, 174, 175

Church Board of Education, 149, 169, 170, 171, 174, 175, 176 and passim

Church Central Board of Finance, 120, 127, 128, 129, 137, 146, 148, 155, 156, 167, 170, 192 and passim

Church College Trusts, 233, 234

Church Colleges Federation 1917, 114

Church Commissioners, 126

Church of England Education Society, 36

Church Times, The, 235

Churchyard, Revd O., 67

Cirencester Grammar School, 197

Civil Service, The, 82

Clarke, (Sir) Fred, 102

Clay, Barry, 241

Clifton, York, 113, 146

Close, Revd F., 68

Cock, Revd A. A., 147, 148-152

Cockin, Canon, 156

Coggan, Archbishop, 187, 207

Coleclough, James, 161, 182

Coleridge, Derwent, 16, 61

College of Preceptors, 99

College of Ripon and York St John, 213 and passim

Committee of Enquiry and Correspondence 1838, 8, 12

Committee of Privy Council for Education 1839, 8, 9, 10, 18, 19, 22, 24, 28, 30, 31 and passim

Committee of York and Ripon College, 10, 11, 17, 18, 19, 21-31 and passim (see also Governing Bodies, York and Ripon)

Coney Street, York, 116

Conference of Directors of Education 1928, 120

Connor, Dr Mary, 257

Convocations of Canterbury and York, 86, 87

Cooke, Geoffrey, 254

Cooke, HMI, 31, 32, 53

Cooper, C. H., 93

Copping, J. R., 145, 149, 151, 160, 162, 182, 187

Copps, A. J., 116

Cordukes, Edward, 1, 13

Corser, Tom, 240

Council for National Academic Awards (CNAA), 183, 205, 207, 210, 218, 226, 237, 241

Council of Church and Associated Colleges (CCAC), 254, 261

Council of Principals of Church Colleges, 118, 127, 146, 156, 167, 175, 197, 198 and passim

County Hospital, York, 12

Cowie, HMI, 47, 52, 66

Crewe College, 106, 163

Crimea, 91

Cromwell, E., 61

Crosland, Anthony, 185, 186, 195

Cross, Sheila, 257

Cross Commission, 75, 76-79, 80, 85, 87, 93, 95

Crosskey, Dr, 78

Crosthwaite, Bishop, 100

Crowther Report, 170

Cruse, Miss Mary, 23, 54

Cruse, Miss Winifred, 22, 23, 29, 31, 32, 33, 34, 36, 37, 52-54, 55, 56, 57, 66, 265

Cuddesdon College, 153

Culham College, 61, 66, 146, 149, 197, 214, 224, 260

Culham Institute, 260, 261

Cull, F. W., 99

Czechoslovakia, 163

Danforth Foundation, 225

Darlington College, 74

Dartford College (Osterberg), 125

North Riding College, 201, 205, 207, 213
North Yorkshire, 201 and passim
Northallerton College of F.E., 246
Northampton College, 251
Norwood Report, 1943, 119, 140
Norwood, Sir Cyril, 140, 186
Notre Dame College, Liverpool, 42
Nottingham, Revd E. E., 98, 99-104, 110, 120
Nottingham University College, 79
Nyasaland, 90

OAKELEY, HMI, 95, 98
Oakes Committee, 220
Occupational Therapy Department, 99, 220, 235, 240, 246, 249, 257
Old Students Calendar, 143
Oleh, Nigeria, 143
Open University, The, 205, 237, 246
Opportunity Fund, 251
Osmondthorpe School, 182
Our Trust and our Task (Temple), 139
Owen, Dean Mansfield, 126
Owen House, Ripon, 240
Owens, Dr E., 209, 211
Oxford College (later Culham), 75
Oxford Conference 1973 (DES/ATCDE), 202-204, 205, 208
Oxford Day Training College, 102
Oxford University, 7, 33, 39, 79, 100, 153

PACE, George, 182
Pakington, Sir John, 49, 68
Palin, Miss E. F., 80, 109
Papal Brief, 1850, 35
Parkes, Sir Edward, 251, 252
Partridge, Canon, 128
Pattie, Allan, 241
Peace Pledge Union, 149
Pearson, Miss, 151
Peel, Barbara, viii
Peel, Sir Robert, 9
Pembroke College, Oxford, 197
Pestalozzi, 7, 8
Peterborough College, 135, 163
Philpotts, Bishop, 34

Pickfords, 188
Pile, Sir William, 202, 205, 219
Pix, Revd J., 33
Plowden Report, 125
Polytechnics and Colleges Funding Council, 253, 254, 256, 257
Poore, Revd Leonard, 151, 188
Powley, David, 248, 258
Practising School, Lord Mayor's Walk, 29, 32, 47, 70, 96, 97, 98, 101
Practising School, Ripon, 55
Preston, 38
Price, Anne, 257
Princess Royal, 164
Pritchard, F. C., 61
Procter, Miss M., 182
Project 2000, 255
Public Expenditure White Paper 1951, 230
Pupil Teachers, 24, 65, 76, 78, 79
Pusey, E. B., 34

QUEEN'S College, London, 62
Queen's College, Oxford, 12
'Queens Hall', 8
Queen's Scholars, 24, 29, 32, 33, 45, 48, 52, 53, 60, 61, 70, 71, 97

RAILTON, William, 18
Ramsey, Archbishop Michael, 172, 179, 180
Reading University (College), 79
Red Cross Society, 109
Reed, Revd William, First Principal, viii, 12, 14, 15, 16, 17-28, 33, 34, 35, 41, 66, 97, 131
Revised Code, 1862, 59, 60, 61, 62, 64, 92, 107
Rich, R. W., 62, 94
Ridgeway, Revd J., 61
Rigg, Revd A., 61
Ripon, Bishop's Palace, 19
Ripon Cathedral, 53, 73, 90, 107, 108, 121, 181, 251
Ripon Cathedral School, 134
Ripon Chapel 1963, 180
Ripon City Library, 135
Ripon College, Wisconsin, 122, 245

St Catherine's College, Cambridge, 98, 100
St David's, Bishop of, 38
St Gabriel's College, 217
St George's Boys Club, 150
St Hild's College, Durham, 125, 217, 239
St John's College, Cambridge, 55, 64
St John's College, York, 110 and passim
St Katherine's College, Liverpool, 127, 217, 239
St Lukes College, Exeter, 149, 170, 197, 202, 212, 217
St Margaret's Lodge, 90, 105, 125, 138, 142
St Margaret of Scotland, 85
St Marks College, Chelsea (later 'St Mark and St John'), 16, 19, 33, 48, 61, 67, 101, 113, 120
St Martin's College, Lancaster, 185
St Mary's Church, Battersea, 55
St Mary's College, Cheltenham, 172, 180
St Maurice's Church, York, 26
St Michael-le-Belfrey Church, York, 26
St Peter's School, York, 43
St Thomas's School, Lowther Street, 173, 189, 216, 237
Stainer, Sir John, 73
Standing Conference of Principals, 221, 224
Stanley, Lord, 9
Stanley, Lyulph, 91, 92
Start, William, 14, 16
Stevens, Roy, 163
Stopford, Bishop Robert, 156, 166
Stow, David, 8
Stratford-on-Avon Grammar School, 105
Stringer, Joseph, 67
Students' Christian Union, 112
Students' Union, 148, 181, 188, 190, 191, 216, 222, 229, 231, 242, 254, 262
Sudan, 163
Sunday Times, 238

Sunderland College, 106
Superannuation Act 1918, 115
Sutton on Derwent, 104
Swansea College, 74
Synge, J. M., 163
Syria, 163

Taunton Commission 1868, 47, 52, 63, 64, 82
Tawney, R. H., 119, 141, 170
Taylor, Miss, 55
Taylor, Professor W., 190, 191
Teasdale, Kathleen, 172, 214
Temple, Archbishop William, 120, 121, 126, 128, 139, 140, 141, 147, 149, 150, 166, 263
Temple, Frederick, HMI (later Archbishop), 47, 75, 83, 85
Tendall, G. F., 100
Thailand, 163
Thatcher, Adrian, 262
Thatcher, Margaret, 196, 202, 220
The Doctrine of the Church not to be Prescribed in the Normal Schools (Hodgkinson), 34
The Education Muddle and the Way Out (Webb), 85
The Tempest, 163
Theatre Royal, York, 188
Thirty-nine Articles, 36
Thornton, HMI, 131
Thurtell, HMI, 19
Times Educational Supplement, 115
Times Higher Education Supplement (THES), 203, 204, 219, 243, 244
Times, The, 92, 127
Tinling, HMI, Canon, 58
Tottenham (All Saints) College, 75
Tractarian Movement, 25, 26, 34-36, 38, 44
Trades Unions, 265
Trent College, 105
Trevor, Canon George, 43, 44, 45
Trevor, Miss Enid, 75, 76-78, 87, 94
Trinder, Miss, 55
Trinity College, Cambridge, 28
Trinity College, Carmarthen, viii, 27
Truro College, 135